Leaks, Hacks, and Scandals

translation
TRANSNATION

SERIES EDITOR **EMILY APTER**

A list of titles
in the series
appears at the
back of the book.

Leaks, Hacks, and Scandals

ARAB CULTURE IN THE DIGITAL AGE

Tarek El-Ariss

PRINCETON UNIVERSITY PRESS
PRINCETON AND OXFORD

Published by Princeton University Press

41 William Street, Princeton, New Jersey 08540

6 Oxford Street, Woodstock, Oxfordshire OX20 1TR

press.princeton.edu

Library of Congress Control Number 2018952194

ISBN 978-0-691-18192-9

ISBN (pbk.) 978-0-691-18193-6

British Library Cataloging-in-Publication Data is available

Editorial: Anne Savarese & Thalia Leaf

Production Editorial: Ali Parrington

Text and Jacket/Cover Design: Leslie Flis

Production: Erin Suydam

Copyeditor: Aimee Anderson

This book has been composed in Minion Pro

Printed on acid-free paper. ∞

Printed in the United States of America

10 9 8 7 6 5 4 3 2 1

In Memory of Barbara Harlow (1948–2017)

In the idea of the roué there is thus an allusion to debauchery and perversity, to the subversive disrespect for principles, norms, and good manners, for the rules and laws that govern the circle of decent, self-respecting people, of respectable, right-thinking society. *Roué* characterizes a leading astray [*dévoiement*] that calls for exclusion or punishment. The roué is thus indeed a sort of voyou, in this sense, but since a whole gang of voyous lies in wait for us a little further down the road, let's put them off a bit longer. The libertine roués of the Regency described by Saint-Simon are the debauched members of a good, decent monarchic society on the road [*voie*] to corruption. They thus announce in their own way the decadence of the monarchic principle and, from afar, by way of a revolution and a beheading, a certain democratization of sovereignty. For democracy, the passage to democracy, *democratization*, will have always been associated with license, with taking too many liberties [*trop-de-liberté*], with the dissoluteness of the libertine, with liberalism, indeed perversion and delinquency, with malfeasance, with failing to live according to the law, with the notion that "everything is allowed," that "anything goes."

—Jacques Derrida, *Rogues: Two Essays on Reason*

To write the scandal of the speaking body, to speak the scandal of seduction, that which grounds, in my view, the literary order, the theoretical order, and the historical order in turn, to do this here will thus mean attempting to articulate something at the crossroads of several disciplines (the point where psychoanalysis, linguistics, philosophy, literature, etc., meet and fail to meet . . .) and at the crossroads of language (where English and French, or theoretical language and literary, rhetorical language, meet and fail to meet); attempting to articulate not so much what is *said* or could be said but what is happening, taking effect, producing acts, what is being *done* or could be done between speaking bodies, between languages, between knowledge and pleasure.

—Shoshana Felman, *The Scandal of the Speaking Body*

CONTENTS

ACKNOWLEDGMENTS

The research for this book started in the late nineties when I became interested in new Arabic writing and the effects of new media and communication technologies on culture and politics in the region. When the Arab uprisings erupted in 2010, I was in the process of completing my first book, *Trials of Arab Modernity*. Once completed, I moved from the affects of modernity to digital affects, from the body of the disoriented Arab traveler in nineteenth-century Europe to Arab bodies making a scene and shaming dictatorial regimes in squares, on streets, and online. This led me to explore exposure, scene making, and leaks, tracing a genealogy in Arabic writing, communication, and critique of power starting in the classical period. While my first book ended with the euphoria we were all experiencing at the start of the uprisings, this book confronts the violent and unsettling state that has engulfed the region since then. Such confrontation made writing this book all the more difficult, if not painful at times, requiring much support and encouragement that I would like to acknowledge here.

I thank *Transnation/Translation* series editor Emily Apter for taking on this project and for believing in its potential after hearing my *mal-élevée* talk, "The Leaking Subject," at the Sorbonne in 2015. Her vision and mentorship over the years showed the way for intellectual risk taking and academic rigor. I'm grateful to Princeton University Press and Anne Savarese, Thalia Leaf, Ali Parrington, Stephanie Roja, Aimee Anderson, and all those at the press for their hard work on this project.

The institutional support I received over the years was key to researching and writing this book. My gratitude goes to *Europe in the Middle East/Middle East in Europe* (EUME) and the *Forum for Transregional Studies* in Berlin for providing me a fellowship in 2012–2013 that allowed me to lay the book's foundations. I'm particularly grateful to Georges Khalil, Friederike Pannewick, Angelika Neuwirth, Barbara Winckler, and Christian Junge. I also thank the *American Council for Learned Societies* (ACLS); the fellowship they awarded me in 2015–2016 allowed me to complete the manuscript. I thank the College of Liberal Arts at the University of Texas at Austin, which made accepting these fellowships possible. I'm also grateful to Dennis Washburn, Associate Dean for International Studies and Interdisciplinary Programs at Dartmouth College for supporting this book's production. I would like to thank the *Journal of Arabic*

Literature (JAL) for publishing an earlier version of chapter 3 as "Fiction of Scandal," and Georges Khalil and Friederike Pannewick for reprinting it in their anthology *Commitment and Beyond: Reflections on/of the Political in Arabic Literature since the 1940s*, and Tarik Sabry and Layal Ftouni for including a subsequent version of this essay in their anthology *Arab Subcultures: Transformations in Theory and Practice.*

In Austin, my deepest gratitude goes to Kristen Brustad and Mahmoud al-Batal: their culture of care and pioneering spirit created an opening that moved students and scholars of Arabic into a new dimension from which there is no turning back. I'm also grateful to have found in Austin the beautiful and brilliant Yoav Di-Capua, my friend and intellectual companion, who will be with me always. Together we thought freely and radically, crossing disciplines, genres, and traditions, and together we were able to foster an intellectual community and train students who are now leaving their mark on the field. I also would like to thank my Austin colleagues Kamran Ali, Benjamin Brower, Tracie Matysik, Judith Coffin, Kathleen Stewart, Ann Cvetkovich, Peter Rehberg, Neville Hoad, Samy Ayoub, Hannah Wojciehowski, Joseph Straubhaar, Elizabeth Richmond-Garza, Mia Carter, Brian Dougherty, and Blake Atwood for their support and engagement.

At Dartmouth, my new home, I'm grateful for the friendship and support of Jonathan Smolin; his vision and determination inspires and moves mountains. I'm also grateful to Susannah Heschel, whose brilliance and energy makes me want to think deeper and do more. I also thank Graziella Paratti, Michelle Warren, Gerd Gemunden, Silvia Spita, Barbara Wil, Bruce Duthu, Elizabeth Smith, Lynn Higgins, Kevin Reinhardt, Chad Elias, yasser alhariri, Jessica Smolin, Michelle Warren, Klaus Milich, Katherine Hornstein, Victor Witowski, Keith Walker, David LaGuardia, Nirvana Tanoukhi, and Eman Morsi for their warm welcome and support.

I thank my interlocutors who read, edited, and provided suggestions at the various stages of the project. I'm eternally grateful to Michael Allan, Yoav Di-Capua, Camille Robcis, Hatim el-Hibri, Zeina Halabi, and Anna Ziajka Stanton, who edited the manuscript. This book couldn't have been completed without their generous engagement. I'm also grateful to my friends and guardian angels, Moneera al-Ghadeer, Muhsin al-Musawi, and John Borneman. I also thank Chafica Omari in Beirut for giving me the space to heal and write when I needed it the most, and Fawz Kabra and Tom Eccles from CCS at Bard College for allowing me to see my work as art. I also would like to thank my dearest friends and family Arwa, Aziz, Ahmad, Sinan, and Rami Shaibani; their encouragement and generous support over the years allowed me to devote the time needed to research and write this book; I'm so lucky to have them in my life. I'm also grateful to my family and friends in Beirut, New York, Hanover, and Berlin.

I would like to thank my esteemed colleagues and dear friends in the field who invited me to give talks at various stages of the book's development. My deepest gratitude goes to Brian Edwards at Northwestern; Orit Bashkin at the University of Chicago; miriam cooke and Ellen McLarney at Duke; Marwan Kraidy at the University of Pennsylvania; Nadia Yaqub, Sahar Amer, and Zeina Halabi at the University of North Carolina at Chapel Hill; Walid Raad at Cooper Union; Milad Doueihi at the Sorbonne; Andrea Khalil at Queens College-CUNY; John Borneman at Princeton; Camille Robcis at Cornell; Nadia Al-Bagdadi and Aziz al-Azmeh at Central European University; Nadia El Cheikh and Bilal Orfali at the American University of Beirut; Muhsin al-Musawi at Columbia; Carole Rizkallah al-Sharabati, Karim Bittar, and Fadia Kiwan at Université Saint-Joseph; Christine Tohme at Ashkal Alwan; Ina Blom, Stephan Guth, Rana Issa, and Teresa Pepe at the University of Oslo; Carol Bardenstein at the University of Michigan-Ann Arbor; Michael Allan and Bish Sen at the University of Oregon at Eugene. I'm also grateful to the invaluable feedback I received at various conferences, talks, and workshops from Tracy McNulty, Timothy Murray, Jonathan Culler, Deborah Starr, Rayya al-Zein, Omar Ghazzi, Abdelkarim al-Amry, Sangita Dasgupta, and all the colleagues and students who engaged my work.

The most painful and heartfelt acknowledgement of all is for my mentor, friend, and Austin colleague, the heroic Barbara Harlow (1948–2017), to whom I dedicate this book. Barbara's passion, generosity, engagement, and curiosity inspired me and pushed me forward. I remember the many evenings when I stopped by her house after leaving my office at night, sat at her kitchen table, and told her about what I had just read or wrote. When she fell ill in the summer of 2015, Barbara was reading and commenting on drafts of chapters from her hospital bed. She was so excited about the book, and she's the one who said, "It's time to send out the manuscript, it's done!" After her recovery and what appeared briefly as a return to normal life, Barbara was readmitted to the hospital in January 2017 and passed away soon after from an unstoppable leakage. Barbara, this book is for you.

NOTE ON TRANSLATION AND TRANSLITERATION

I followed style and transliteration guidelines of the *Chicago Manual of Style* (15th ed.) and the *International Journal of Middle Eastern Studies* (*IJMES*). For Arabic names, I followed the most commonly used transliteration in English. I used published translations of Arabic texts when available. All other translations are mine.

Leaks, Hacks, and Scandals

The image in figure 1 is a screenshot of the hacking of the website of the Lebanese Ministry of Energy and Water responsible for the country's electricity in April 2012 by a group called Raise Your Voice, a self-proclaimed offshoot of the global hackers collective Anonymous.[1] Protesting poor living conditions and inadequate social services, the hackers not only crashed the government agency's site but also substituted one text for another. Reenacting an electric cut, they transformed the cursor into a flashlight that needs to be moved around in order to light up an otherwise dark screen. This act of hacking defaces the ministry website through a textual and technological performance that involves viewers as active participants who need to move the cursor in order to reveal the text. But what is being exposed through this hacking? Is it the text itself, the reading practice directed toward it, or the failing nation-state unable to fulfill its duties vis-à-vis its citizens? What writing genre, aesthetics, and critique of power does the flashlight make legible?

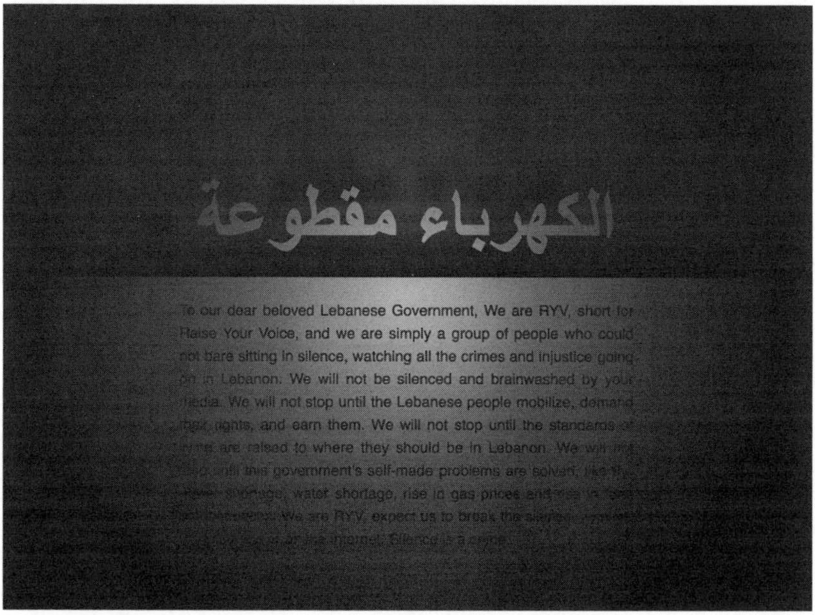

Figure 1. "Electricity is cut off." Ministry of Energy and Water, April 16, 2012, http://www.energyandwater.gov.lb/.

The cursor-turned-flashlight conjures up the Lebanese Civil War (1975–1990). The flashlight was the invariable war fetish, always close by, always at hand to confront the absence of the state, the unpredictability of darkness. Affecting the eyes' sensitivity to light and obscurity, the act of hacking forces the pupils to dilate and contract to access more light, more text, and more memory. The intervention has specific physiological effects that knock down and open up, shut down and light up, revealing multiple experiences and calls for action. Understanding this process requires an engagement with the question of affect, which characterizes these acts of writing and performance. The "affective" hacking exposes and brings to light texts and histories arising from the intersection of the metaphorical and the material; the body and the screen; and the act of contestation both as a writing practice and as a cyberattack that crashes a website and forces the eye to adjust in order to expose a new text, an old one.

Involving acts of infiltration and reading, the digital performance draws in the viewer as a victim of governmental neglect and war violence, and as a compulsive subject who cannot but click and move the cursor. Hacking intervenes not by enlightening citizens or by providing them with hitherto unavailable information that would heighten their political consciousness, but rather by enticing them to shed a light that comes from the present and from the past, and to experience this information as something unacceptable, linked to war trauma and the ongoing withdrawal if not collapse of the state. Shedding light as opposed to enlightening, the flashlight as opposed to electric light, constitutes a visual and affective exposure (*faḍḥ*)[2] that shames, makes a scene, causes a scandal, and reveals in the process new codes of writing. What are these codes and who are their authors?

The code writers or hackers in this example "are simply a group of people who could not bear sitting in silence, watching all the crimes and violations."[3] These people are viewers who transcend their condition of spectatorship in order to hack and write, introducing a new way of seeing, showing, and exposing. As the act of hacking turns off the screen, it puts the light at the fingertips of other viewers or browsers who now discover but also activate the scene of scandal online. This interplay between hackers and browsers constitutes an economy of writing and contestation that requires a set of conceptual tools that account for processes of simultaneity, compulsion, and commitment. Specifically, how do we begin to theorize this inability to remain silent and not to expose, hack, leak, click, and share? Is this a strategy of confrontation or an inability not to confront that goes viral, mobilizing more and more viewers and hackers who cannot but see, show, share, and expose?

The political intervention arises from a digital condition affecting bodies, texts, and models of consciousness wherein "silence is a crime," and breaking the silence is staged through modes of exposure and circulation taking place "whether in the streets or the Internet." It is the "group of people" such as the one discussed above who act both by design and by compulsion, both voluntarily and involuntarily, that the book investigates, examining how their acts, examined collectively against the backdrop of technological development, political upheavals, and cultural tradition, are redefining the meaning of Arab culture. Drawing on literary studies, media studies, and digital humanities, and focusing on the Arab world in a transnational context, *Leaks, Hacks, and Scandals* examines the radical transformations affecting the way stories are told, dissent is expressed, and canons are produced in the new millennium.

WRITING CODES

The Internet unleashed scandal and exposure—mediated by acts of hacking, leaking, and whistleblowing—both in the Arab world and beyond. The Arab practice of *faḍḥ* (exposing, making a scene, shaming, causing a scandal) is an act of last resort, performed in the street by people reduced to using their bodies to fight back, as happened in Egypt's Tahrir Square and elsewhere in the Arab world starting in 2010. While talk shows on satellite TV, starting in the mid-1990s,[4] have showcased this embodied scene of *faḍḥ*, traditionally associated with the vulgar and depicted in works by the great Egyptian author Naguib Mahfouz (1911–2006), the Internet transformed it into a new stage for political confrontation involving acts of hacking and leaking but also violent confrontations on social media, with insults and outbursts violating traditional codes of civility (*adab*). The overlapping of traditional scene-making (*faḍḥ/faḍīḥa*)[5] with what could be referred to as the scandal.com culture (WikiLeaks, YouTube, etc.) characterizing "the digital age" that I refer to in the subtitle has ushered in a new generation of activists and bloggers, and hackers and leakers, who are increasingly occupying the position of the "intellectual speaking truth to power." This book sheds light on the scene of the hacker and leaker's "truth" by examining the toll that its speaking takes on the body. What new models of commitment are emerging from this affective economy? What is the role in this new environment of the traditional intellectuals who produced literature, established the canon, and confronted power at earlier times? What literary and political anxieties are playing out in this new landscape?

With the Arab uprisings starting in 2010, intellectuals (*muthaqqafūn*) who saw it as a part of their commitment (engagement, *iltizām*) to intervene and speak truth to power were disoriented, unable to foresee, engage, or understand who this "group of people who could not bear sitting in silence" were or where they had come from, much less how they were able to mobilize or what affective "truths" they were speaking. While these intellectuals were trying to find their bearings in a precarious environment, Arab bloggers and activists on the ground mounted campaigns to shatter the silence in the face of violations and atrocities, organizing street protests and leaking images and videos of abuse predating if not precipitating the uprisings.[6] Practicing exposure (*faḍḥ*) against authoritarian regimes, this "group of people" also confronted the disorientation and at times complicity of intellectuals with power. Egyptian activist and blogger Rasha Azb denounced and lamented the generation of author Bahaa Taher, which, despite its long history of activism, ended up supporting military rule and defending the "despotic state" in 2013.[7] A new model of contestatory politics and affective writing tied to acts of leaking, hacking, and exposure has put in question the role of intellectuals and of their corresponding media platforms and material culture from newspapers to novels.[8]

For this older cadre of thinkers, the novel was at the center of the production of political consciousness. This interpretation has traditionally drawn on Benedict Anderson's *Imagined Communities*; Taha Hussein's and Tawfiq al-Hakim's notions of *adab* (literature, culture, civility) and *udabāʾ* (authors-intellectuals); and Jean-Paul Sartre's *littérature engagée* or Souheil Idriss's *iltizām* (commitment).[9] The valuation of individual privacy and the narrative of modern subjectivity more generally have been traced to the rise of the novel from the eighteenth century onward. Nancy Armstrong argues that the "self-enclosed and internally coherent identity" of the modern subject is intimately tied to "eighteenth-century epistemology and moral philosophy."[10] Examining the British novel's role in producing this identity, she argues that "the history of the novel and the history of the modern subject are, quite literally, one and the same."[11] In this vein, Anderson famously argues that modern subjects started imagining themselves as members of the same national community that stretches into the past through reading practices and the circulation of novels and newspapers in the nineteenth century. "The novel and the newspaper," writes Anderson, "provided the technical means for 're-presenting' the *kind* of imagined community that is the nation."[12] The reading practices that Anderson identifies give rise to homogenous secular time at the basis of national consciousness. This book examines the constellation of modernity that Anderson and others theorized, explaining what happens to the subject of modernity, and of Arab modernity specifically, in the digital age. How are interconnected concepts such as nation, community, power, intellectual, author, and novel recoded or hacked in the Arab world in the twenty-first century?

The novel as edifice and main framework for interpretation shaping the microcosmos of the public sphere and generating political consciousness is no longer central to the landscape that this book examines. A new consciousness—a digital consciousness—is emerging from coded, fragmented, viral, and hard-to-read texts. *Leaks, Hacks, and Scandals* examines novels that become cropped, marked, and circulated online, often used as incriminating evidence against their authors, warranting jail or death. It investigates the ways in which the notion of online "followers" who leak, hack, and raid transform our understanding of "public" and "readership" and of the effects of reading practices, given the models of circulation that Anderson identified. The viral and fragmented texts and their reading practices online have drastic implications on models of writing and contestation, and literary meaning and canon formation, both in the Arab world and beyond.

In Ahmed Naji's *Using Life* (*Istikhdām al-Ḥayāt*) (2014), it is not only the case that "[t]he city branches out. The city beats, the city bleeds," but also that the author function and the work and its reception proliferate and burst at the seams.[13] The launching of this graphic novel by Egyptian blogger, author, and journalist Ahmed Naji took the shape of a vernissage—a literary and artistic event showcasing books but also T-shirts and mugs featuring the illustrations of Ayman Al Zorkany. Set in a dystopian Cairo following the 2011 uprising, the novel depicts a landscape of street closures and repression and traces the emergence of secret organizations and a new generation engaging in graffiti art and subversion tactics. Less than two years following its publication, a selection from the novel published in the literary journal *Akhbār al-Adab* triggered a lawsuit by a reader, who accused the author of violating public morality. When reading Naji's sexually explicit passages, this reader experienced a "drop in blood pressure." The lawsuit landed the author in jail; it also earned him the Pen Award and international solidarity that started on social-media platforms before moving to the op-ed pages of international newspapers such as the *Guardian* and the *New York Times*.[14] Literary critics who engage Naji's work thus have to contend with new writing genres, art practices, affective collapse, lawsuits, imprisonment, online activism, and global literary systems.[15] This book examines the intertwining of those events and practices that are recoding the literary in the digital age.

While Naji's narrator in *Using Life* is involved with hacker groups seeking to produce something akin to WikiLeaks, Abdo Khal's narrator in *Throwing Sparks* (*Tarmī bi-Sharar*) (2014)[16] leaks gruesome torture and abuse videos. The narrator in this Saudi novel, which won the Abu Dhabi–based International Prize for Arabic Fiction, also known as the Arabic Booker,[17] acts like activists or jailers who leak videos of detainees being beaten and tortured. While the novel points to a mimetic relation between leaks and literature, the author function is further recoded by the hacking of Khal's own Twitter account in 2012, engulfing the author in the fiction that his work embodies. By going online, the author has permanently entered his text, thereby revealing a new entanglement between fiction and reality, literary production and online circulation. This requires an investigation of the fiction of scandals and leaks playing out within the text and conditioning the text's production, circulation, and reception.

With online writing and circulation, and the preponderance of Gulf-based prizes dedicated primarily to the Arabic novel, the novel is being celebrated, yet its "literary" value is being established in completely new ways. *Leaks, Hacks, and Scandals* examines the meaning of Arab culture as it arises from the breakdown in canon formation due to lawsuits by disgruntled readers and due to new prizes, global market trends, and the decentralization of cultural production. How significant is the fact that the most sought-after prizes are situated in the Gulf? Does this geographical and economic shift herald a change in the meaning of Arab culture as the product of the *Nahda* (the Arab Renaissance)—a process that shaped political and ideological models in the region?[18] This book tries to answer that question by focusing on examples from Egypt and the Gulf and by examining the effects of economic, technological, and political developments on new definitions of literature and culture.

Khal and Naji's works reveal new ways of writing and of "being public" that no longer correspond to a literary model of *Nahda bildung* or to a subversive model of *jīl al-sittīnāt* (the 1960s generation).[19] This new novel enters into a global literary system yet remains untranslatable, carrying over a materiality that could not be fully subsumed or fully represented.[20] A new writing emerging from leaking and the fiction of scandal as well as untraceable tweets and data mining, online fights and trolling campaigns, and flickering texts that appear and disappear, can no longer be studied under a microscope or in a lab. It has become impossible to engage these texts and political practices by trying to identify their origin, commonality, structure, and essence, thereby reproducing the old-fashioned encyclopedic study and nomenclature imposed on literature, culture, and politics. Moments of crossing (translation, world literature, readership) are adopting alternative pathways and producing different effects and relations that resist through untranslatability what Emily Apter identifies as a liberal economy of literary circulation that crosses borders yet keeps them intact.[21] Examples such as those of Naji and Khal force us to begin to chart the characteristics not of a *literature 2.0* but of *literary studies 2.0.* It is within this new model of literary studies, shaping and being shaped by technological shifts and political developments that arise from the Arab world yet also occur globally, that this book is situated.

Approaching hacking (*tahkīr, ikhtirāq*), leaking (*tasrīb*), revealing (*ifshā'*), proliferation (*tafashshī*), and exposure and scene-making (*faḍḥ*) as writing and political practices, as well as conceptual tools for understanding Arab culture in the digital age, *Leaks, Hacks, and Scandals: Arab Culture in the Digital Age* explores contemporary writing practices and activism against the backdrop of new media and the Arab uprisings. Moving beyond the "codes" of modern Arabic literature, culture, and politics, it theorizes a new intertwining of aesthetics and politics by exploring affective forms of protest, incivility (*qillat adab* or "lack of *adab*"), digital consciousness, hacking and cyber-raiding, and knowledge and fiction as leaks and scandals. While *adab* has been examined as a comparative practice that could be traced to the nineteenth century,[22] this book contests the association between Arab subjectivity and the project of *adab* (as *bildung*) and *ta'dīb* (disciplining, punishing, rendering civil).[23] To exploit the instability of *adab*—to explore its security holes and identify its leaks—is to disentangle it from *ta'dīb* (disciplining) and from the emphasis on Arab literary and technological borrowing from the West—starting with the rise of the novel and the modern subject to the entrenchment of colonial institutions and the more recent advent of satellite TV and the Internet. In this light, this book examines the intersections between the digital and the subversive in the Arab tradition, tying Twitter to the classical genre of *akhbār* (news, anecdotes, lore), leaking and hacking to practices of exposure (*faḍḥ*), and contemporary leakers and hackers to mystics and jinn. I explore comparatively Arabic registers of leaks and scandals as they shape and are shaped by transnational contexts and the classical tradition. The focus on the Arab world in dialogue with hacking and leaking scandals and the history and theories of leaking and scene-making makes the Arab world not so much a case study but rather a framework to reflect theoretically on new definitions of literature and culture, on their relation to the political and the digital, and on their genres and critiques.

DIGITAL WORLD-MAKING

In "Postscript on the Societies of Control," Gilles Deleuze argues that technology and new media in the age of corporations accelerated models of circulation that made resistance impossible.[24] Deleuze ties in the rise of the corporation with a "soul" and marketing apparatuses to new media's role in forging post-subjects. Deleuze writes: "We no longer find ourselves dealing with the mass/individual pair. Individuals have become '*dividuals*,' and masses, samples, data, markets, or '*banks*.'"[25] These new societies of control have undermined the modern institutions of the family, the army, and the school, theorized by Foucault as the sites for the production of modern subjectivity, and cast doubt on the ability of unions to resist through traditional means. From the *individual* and the Deleuzian *dividual*, we move with the practices of digital, literary, and political *faḍḥ* explored in this book to the *outdividual*, wherein the inside could never be veiled, and the subject's interiority could never be maintained. This "inside" is compulsively shown and must be shown[26] as part of an affective economy of hacking, leaking, and scene-making.

Foucauldian notions of political subjectivity but also of discursivity, power, representation, and surveillance and the primacy of the gaze that informed readings of modern literature and culture, along with postcolonial theory and *Nahda* studies starting with Timothy Mitchell,[27] need to be questioned in the new landscape I identify.[28] Foucault's disciplinary model obscures the new scenes of writing, performance, and acts of contestation and violence leaking out of novels (and making novels leak) and videos analyzed in this book's various chapters. Cyberspace has resuscitated if not amplified the Place de Grève[29] and its spectacle of cruelty, as seen in leaked videos of torture and humiliation, from Khal's depictions in *Throwing Sparks* and the Abu Ghraib pictures during the US invasion of Iraq in 2003 to the gruesome performances of ISIS's head- and limb-severing starting in 2012. This violent staging of the body of the condemned with which Foucault inaugurates *Discipline and Punish*, and which allegedly moved behind closed doors with the march of modernity and the suturing of its coherent subject, has now escaped from—leaked out of—secret prisons and police stations. Likewise, the public festivals controlled and tamed by British colonialism and a complicit bourgeoisie, as Mitchell argues in *Colonizing Egypt*, have returned to center stage as Arab productions on social media and streets and in new writings. This return thus requires a critical attention to the untamed as such, which is unfolding in confrontations online, in literature, on the street, and on TV screens, recoding in the process the meaning of literature and culture.[30] From the demise of the ocularcentric or visual order of modernity and its unified and all-seeing gaze we move in the digital age to flickering screens and dilating pupils.

Political and epistemological notions of modernity as theorized by Foucault and taken up by Mitchell have been too quickly applied to cyberspace and new media in light of recent Arab political developments. The Internet, given its inception as a closed environment for communication experts and enthusiasts, became identified as a Habermassian public sphere,[31] namely a forum for sharing and debating ideas intrinsic to democratizing processes. Assessing the success of political change but also evaluating the "causes" of the so-called Arab Spring led to questions such as: Was democracy achieved or did the revolution fail? Is the absence of a clear political agenda on the part of activists to blame for the failure of the Arab uprisings? These questions and their underlying assumptions and interpretive models moved us away from the nondiscursive, the uncivil, the unruly, the scandalous, the affective, and the leaking and fleeting texts, words, and images. Understanding new texts and practices requires a theorization that would confront both the Orientalist reading of the unruly mob[32] or the irrational oriental Other, as well as the projection of a particular model of the liberal democracy onto contemporary Arab culture and politics in an allegedly post-Orientalist framework. How can we read other spheres and publics that neither grow out of the eighteenth-century salons nor fit Habermas's model of the rational and ethical subject?[33] And could we think of political configurations and dissent that arise from untamed spaces of interaction and affective writing practices without forgoing, altogether, the "subject" as a historical, philosophical, and psychological narrative of the self?

In *Publics and Counterpublics* Michael Warner critiques Habermas and refines his model, specifying that the public sphere is an ideal that was, from the start, fraught with contradictions, and that Habermas himself never tried to recuperate it fully but rather sought to hold contemporary culture to its ideals.[34] These ideals, however, perpetuate a fantasy of social and political change that cast intellectuals as its project makers.

> Publics are conjured into being by characterizing as a social entity (that is as a public) the world in which discourse circulates; but in the language ideology that enables the public sphere, this poetic or creative function of public address disappears from view. Rather than help to constitute scenes of circulation through style, intellectuals are supposed to launch transparently framed ideas into the circulation of an indefinite public. Of course, if intellectuals thought of themselves as involved in world-making projects, it is not clear that intellection would be more effective than, say, corporeally expressive performances. It is not clear that intellectuals would have a naturally leading role in the process at all. And hence it is perhaps not surprising that the professional class of intellectuals should seem reluctant to abandon the conception of public discourse whose inadequacy they continue to discover.[35]

Warner's critique of the intellectual class and of the public-sphere argument as its framework and assumed ideal entertains alternative models of engagement and cultural production involving performance but also models of circulation and simultaneity occurring at the intersection of the street and the Internet, as I argue in this book. More radically, the very notion of the intellectual who operates within a public sphere that has now allegedly moved online is also questioned in Warner's critique, as we will see in chapter 2, with activists in Egypt, and in chapter 4, when established authors go on Twitter to expand their readership.

Warner's notion of counterpublic as "poetic world-making" takes into account the kinds of performances and affective economies explored in this book. Drawing on the binaries of center and periphery, men and women, upper and lower class, queer and hetero, and theorizing spaces of subversion and viscerality that are constitutive of publicness, Warner argues that counterpublics "are defined by their tension with a larger public. Their participants are marked off from persons or citizens in general. Discussion within such a public is understood to contravene the rules obtaining in the world at large, being structured by alternative dispositions or protocols, making different assumptions about what can be said or what goes without saying. This kind of public is, in effect, a counterpublic: it maintains at some level, conscious or not, an awareness of its subordinate status."[36] This model is fundamental to my interpretive framework, up to a certain point. The scenes and sites of exposure I investigate and the fiction of scandal I analyze could not be reduced to the position of the margin that Warner theorizes. In Arab cyberspace the marginal and the mainstream constantly intersect, decentralizing power as one coherent regime of oppression and the activist as its site of resistance. When tweeters gain thousands or millions of followers, marginal groups or a tech-savvy generation have thus gone mainstream, bringing authors and intellectuals as well as the general public into their realm, seeking information, news, and entertainment. The same applies to politicians and media outlets that go on Twitter to make statements, and that get their news from leakers and scene-makers on social media, such as the Saudi tweeter Mujtahidd, the subject of chapter 3.

Risking hacking and humiliation, the intellectual and ruling class experience great anxiety on social-media platforms. Saudi critic and public intellectual Abdallah al-Ghadhdhami aptly captures this anxiety when describing his experience on Twitter. Acknowledging its potential for new communication and political change, al-Ghadhdhami expresses fascination and deep anxiety about this threatening realm of the scandalous, leading him to revert to a recognizable interpretation upholding the coherent subject, the public sphere, and *adab* as the necessary code of civility. In the digital landscape I describe, a new configuration of public, language, communication, power, and subjectivity emerges. I argue that an engagement with the affective, the compulsive, and the sensorial is necessary to theorize the producers and followers of leaks and scandals. This engagement allows us to reconstitute and make legible those narratives and practices integral to a new form of subjectivity that breaks with the models developed by Althusser (interpellation) and Foucault (subjectivation), to name a few. The event of the leak and the scene of exposure, both online and off-, create a new subject through processes of contestation, circulation, and writing.

With the accessibility of the Internet via inexpensive, handheld devices that operate as bodily extensions, and that make conversation and confrontation in colloquial Arabic accessible to all, the idea that the Internet is a product of the West that makes its "users" complicit in Western identities, if not political projects (as traitors or foreign agents), no longer holds. A new relation to technology and language ushers in epistemological frameworks that allow us to gauge the kinds of consciousness, subjectivity, and political contestation emerging from street and online performances of leaking and scene-making in the Arab digital age. In this context scholar Milad Doueihi argues that "the polyphonic dimension of digital identity has the *potential* to embed diverse cultural specificities within digital culture and thus possibly relativize and minimize its universalist tendency."[37] Citing the examples of Iran, China, and Saudi Arabia and the Arab world more generally, Doueihi goes on to reflect on particular uses of technology for specific social and political conditions. Doueihi writes: "Another important aspect of blogs, less visible in the United States and in Europe, is their growing political use against oppressive regimes and the ensuing censorship."[38] Arab or Chinese cyberpractices are not simply acts of translation and adaptation: they recode and remake the function of the digital in relation to specific cultural and political contexts. This recoding then radiates, moves, and informs other systems and uses, as we have seen during the Arab Spring and the Occupy Wall Street movements. When we begin to consider the digital as a condition, or as a landscape, that enables certain connections and intersections, then the engagement with specific examples from the Arab world or elsewhere informs our understanding of digital practices and phenomena in a transnational context.

In a similar vein scholar Brian Edwards moves beyond the "American Century" as a fixed historical and epistemological center of the global and of the transnational to ask: "Should cultural critics who are attentive to the rapid and transnational circulation of images, ideas, and public forms focus on the circulation itself—how it happens, what circulates, and so forth—or on the more local meanings that adhere to or emerge from or are hidden by these forms in motion?"[39] This question identifies a cultural sphere and a critical intervention emerging from specific traditions and locales that are in constant dialogue with—in fact, shaping—a transnational context. Edwards extends this to culture and literature in the Arab world, arguing that "global flow of cultural forms across national literatures—fueled by digital technologies that allow easy and rapid transport of literary texts and of visual and aural material—must be attended to without ignoring or occluding more local (i.e., national) contexts, literary traditions, and meanings."[40] Edwards thus creates a comparative framework that examines global flows in relation to specific literary and cultural traditions. This is precisely the direction I take and develop in this book, without reducing these phenomena to either a networked public or to an Arab exceptionalism.

Edwards's argument that circulation disturbs the unidirectionality (from the West or America to the Middle East) of meaning and power is particularly relevant at a time when critique seems to stop at the identification of the source or center of this power and at listing its misdeeds. In this context Edwards writes:

"I extend Warner and Said to a circumstance that their own considerations of eighteenth- and nineteenth-century texts quite reasonably do not address, the digital age and the digital circulation of texts, which produce a different means of summoning a public—a more complex circumstance for the text—than the means used in the analog age."[41] I, too, push against Warner, not only to liberate the meaning-making potential of object circulation, as Edwards argues, but also to situate this meaning in the media that shapes and is shaped by circulation as such, namely, by the digital as such as a condition of *outdividuality*, scene-making, and leakage. Emerging from the intersection of media studies and Arabic literary studies, the framework I propose opens up new interdisciplinary possibilities that question the forms of textuality and processes of circulation, the nature of publics, canon formation, and political contestation emerging from the scenes and sites of Arab culture in the digital age.[42]

Henry Jenkins argues that new media foster nonhierarchical forms of interaction, leading us to "anticipate that digital democracy will be decentralized, unevenly dispersed, profoundly contradictory, and slow to emerge."[43] In *Spreadable Media: Creating Value and Meaning in a Networked Culture*, Jenkins et al. develop this argument further, coining the term "spreadable media" as the condition for the possibility of staking political claims and effecting change in an environment often deemed closed, top-down, and controlled by corporate interests and machinations. Jenkins presents the circulation that Edwards identified in this way: "As material spreads, it gets remade: either literally, through various forms of sampling and remixing, or figuratively, via its insertion into ongoing conversations and across various platforms."[44] This spreadability, mediated by a participatory logic, "leads to audiences using content in unanticipated ways as they retrofit material to the contours of their particular community. Such activities are difficult for creators to control and even more difficult to quantify."[45] Following a logic of continuity with older media, Jenkins et al. argue that, "rather than looking at platforms such as YouTube and Twitter as 'new,' we consider these sites where multiple existing forms of participatory culture—each with its own historical trajectory, some over a century old—come together, which is part of what makes such platforms so complex to study."[46] According to Jenkins these not-so-new media are used by groups "who seek to build a base to bolster alternative forms of cultural expression; enthusiasts for particular brands that have become signposts for people's identities and lifestyles; bloggers who seek to engage others about the needs of local communities; collectors and retro audiences seeking greater access to residual materials;

members of subcultures seeking to construct alternative identities; and so forth."[47] And finally, distinguishing spreadable media from viral media, these authors write: "Yet the viral metaphor does little to describe situations in which people actively assess a media text, deciding who to share it with and how to pass it along. People make many active decisions when spreading media, whether simply passing content to their social network, making a word-of-mouth recommendation, or posting a mash-up video to YouTube."[48]

Decision making and agency distinguish the communication model upon which Jenkins's work rests. Whereas virality bypasses the subject, according to Jenkins, spreadability affirms the notion of the participating subject within the context of a public sphere transposed online: "We feel that it very much matters who sends the message, who receives it, and, most importantly, what messages get sent."[49] The emphasis on "who" is key; notions of sender, recipient, and message are still invested in models of integrality and wholeness. Beyond the Derridean theorem that the message (the digital letter) does not always reach its destination, the subject I examine in this book makes decisions and has agency yet is also not entirely in control of these decisions and their intended meanings and recipients. The model I present doesn't do away with agency yet could not be reduced to it.

Jenkins's movement from centralization to decentralization in the digital age is reversible, making it all the more difficult to entertain the emergence of a new democratic public sphere, however unstable and contradictory it might be. It is the very idea of democracy and of its fundamental constituents (participation, ethics, equality, intersubjectivity) that needs to be rethought beyond the public-sphere paradigm. Scholar Mohamed Zayani critiques the democratization thesis associated with the perception of the Internet as public sphere. He argues that in the absence of institutions necessary for Habermas's public sphere, it is impossible to reduce all audiences to a public with an identifiable teleology of democratization as the only path to social and political change.[50] Media and communications scholar Marwan Kraidy takes this critique further to examine the artistic practices and performances emerging from the Arab uprisings in *The Naked Blogger of Cairo*, reading the body as a key site of cultural, artistic, and political production.[51] Kraidy tells the story of the Arab uprisings by focusing on creative insurgency, examining the representation of the body as instrument and medium, symbol and counter-icon that could be broken up, reconstituted, mocked, and staged. For Kraidy performance as art practice and as bodily nudity (in reference to Egyptian blogger Aliaa Elmahdy who posted naked pictures of herself online to the shock of the entire Egyptian political spectrum including civil-society activists) becomes key in thinking about processes of dissent and aesthetic and cultural production. Kraidy's analysis makes possible a debate about the digital as a site and a stage, and not only as a sphere. On this stage unfold artistic performances but also, I argue, acts of hacking and raiding that need to be analyzed in order to understand the development of Arab culture in the digital age.

Theorizing new formations of social and political bonds tied to specific media and reading practices beyond the public-sphere model devised by Habermas, in *Affective Publics: Sentiments, Technologies, and Politics*, Zizi Papacharissi engages Massumi, Deleuze, and Protevi to argue: "The construct of affective publics builds on the idea of networked publics to explicate what publics look like when all they render and are rendered out of is the sharing of opinions, facts, sentiment, drama, and performance."[52] These affective publics, suggests Papacharissi, are "networked public formations that are mobilized and connected or disconnected through expressions of sentiment."[53] She claims: "The technologies facilitating affective formations are technologies that facilitate networked circulations of affective flows produced, distributed, and further remixed through mediated communication channels . . . It is fitting that affect resides in the fluidity presented by the convergence of actual and virtual, as it is aided by the confluent weave of reality and fantasy presented as technology suggests what is and what could be made possible."[54] The notion of affective publics operating both online and off- is crucial but, as in my critique of Warner, I do not consider them to be an isolated phenomenon. *Leaks, Hacks, and Scandals* identifies the sites through which Arab culture in the digital age is performed. Far from identifying a specific phenomenon, the book examines those practices, attacks, and hacking and leaking events that make up a new mainstream.

A broad engagement with new models of critique and subjectivity is necessary to understand the erosion of the modern associated with the industrial age, the Enlightenment, and Romanticism, including the Marxist and Freudian systems of meaning and critique to which the latter two gave rise.[55] In this light the book investigates assemblages, rhizomes, digital consciousness, virality, and affective forms of knowledge that jolt the public and prevent it from not knowing. Viewers cannot look away from scandals and leaks: they are drawn to the unfolding narrative of the secret that *must* be revealed, and to the embodied exposure performed in viral videos and acts of hacking. The knowledge production that interests me is precisely the leakers' and hackers' knowledge. This knowledge is the outcome of processes that break in and break down; stretch the limits of the knowable, the law, the body, and the forbidden; and imagine a complicit audience moved by its desire to *know more* and attend, if not take part in, a gruesome and titillating spectacle. The public is not a "closed organism" but rather a porous one, clicking and sharing online. This affective power reengages an apathetic reader and consumer of news, redirecting his/her compulsions to bring about a different kind of awareness and political engagement.

The interpretive framework I offer in this book emerges primarily from the events I examine in the Arab world and beyond. The theory emerges through close readings of these events, taking into account cultural history, political context, technological development, language, media, and genres. My work raises the question of subjectivity online, specifically how hacking and leaking force us to rethink the Arab subject of modernity, or more specifically, the subject of *adab* in the digital age. Through the prism of the subject who communicates, protests, and writes through hacks and leaks, I reflect on Arab culture in the digital age.

From Plato to Descartes to Hegel, the history of the subject has informed and grounded social and political narratives of identity and models of Otherness. The Hegelian subject, upholding its contradictions, has also been read as the European and Eurocentric subject par excellence.[56] Contesting the coherence of the narrative of subjectivity as a Eurocentric and teleological history of consciousness and progress, enlightenment and emancipation, I examine breaches and fissures through which information leaks and connections are made. In this context I critique as well the Lacanian split subject associated with lack, recoding lack and symptom as political and aesthetic affects that unsettle the relation between the subject and the body, lack and gender. Hacks, fragments, and leaks are productive connections mediated through digital and literary networks that resist or need not be veiled and suppressed by the imago at the mirror stage. The political affects I identify unsettle the lacking or Oedipal subject and its structure of desire that encompasses the political and its cultural spheres, from the nation-state and its forms of authority (leader/father) to literary canons (the novel). Specifically, I argue that the collapse of a particular Arab symbolic order associated with *adab* and the project of modernity gives rise to new definitions of the modern subject's realm and constituents (novel, public sphere, etc.) emerging online and on the street from violent rituals including raids, hacks, and leaks. This collapse is tied to political developments, technological transformations, and economic shifts within the Arab world that are precipitating new definitions of culture.

THEORETICAL FRAMEWORK: THE LEAKING SUBJECT

The first Gulf War (1990), which roughly coincided with the collapse of the Soviet Union, marked the advent of neoliberalism in the Middle East,[57] undermined traditional leftist and pan-Arab movements and co-opted large swaths of the Left into new cultural institutions and media platforms, from newspapers to TV channels, funded by Gulf states. The second Gulf War (2003) brought about the material dismantling of the Arab nation-state and its institutions in Iraq, unleashing sectarian tensions into a full-blown explosion ending with ISIS. With the advent of the Internet and the decentralization of literary production, a generation of dissidents and cultural agents filled a critical void, practicing new forms of writing and contestation that played key roles in precipitating the Arab uprisings that started to emerge in the new millennium. Thus, the years 1990, 2003, and 2011 mark the acceleration of foreign intervention and sectarianism at the political level, thereby eroding the already beleaguered modern projects of the nation, and of the subject, that could be traced to the *Nahda*, and that took different shapes and forms, from Nasserism to Baathism. The events I examine in this book result from an alignment of various historical, economic, political, technological, and cultural phenomena that created the necessary conditions for a new way to understand Arab culture in the digital age.

The US invasion of Iraq in 2003 not only toppled a dictator but also put in question the viability of the nation-state as a political and social model emerging from *Nahda* discourses and practices. This material and symbolic collapse of the Arab nation mirrors another symbolic collapse at the heart of the liberal democracy. A new generation of transnational dissidents, who considered this invasion an example of shameless and vindictive imperialism beyond the purview of international law, sought to expose the abuse and violations of this war and its effects on the citizens of the liberal state. Figures such as Julian Assange and Chelsea Manning, and organizations like WikiLeaks and Anonymous, practiced new forms of contestation, seeking to expose a corrupt and excessive political power but also to restore, in some instances, a lost liberal ideal and social contract that could be traced to the eighteenth century.

Emerging from the Middle East, yet shaped by and shaping global transformations, the events I examine in this book take 2006 as a watershed year that marked the advent of a constellation involving political developments, digital activism, and new writing practices both in the Arab world and beyond. This was also the year in which WikiLeaks was founded, partially in response to the 2003 US invasion of Iraq, and the year in which the first torture video in Egypt was leaked and uploaded on YouTube by activist and journalist Wael Abbas. Both of these events inaugurated a new form of activism confronting authoritarian regimes and governments skirting international laws. They were launched by "a group of people who could not bear sitting in silence, watching all the crimes and violations," as I discussed regarding the Lebanese ministry hacking in the opening lines of this introduction. These two events happened independently of each other and involved different actors and practices, scopes, and technologies. Yet they unleashed hacking and leaking practices that embarrass, shame, and expose, and, in doing so, engaged a transnational public with accounts of political abuse and scandal as it unraveled online and in major newspapers. Tied to hacking and scene-making, the leak as forbidden text and as information, as political drama and tell-all fiction, exposes a new relationship between the aesthetic and the political that took on a new meaning and relevance with the Arab uprisings from 2010 onward.

Julian Assange, WikiLeaks' founder, took credit for the events of the Arab uprisings, which culminated in mass demonstrations and regime change across the region, starting in Tunisia in 2010.

> In relation to the Arab Spring, the way I looked at this back in October of 2010 is that the power structures in the Middle East are interdependent, they support each other. If we could release enough information fast enough about many of these powerful individuals and organizations, their ability to support each other would be diminished.... When you shake something up, you have a chance to rebuild. But we're not interested in shaking something up just for the hell of it. I believe that if we look at what makes a civilization civilized, it is people understanding what is really going on. When Gutenberg invented the printing press, the end result was that people who knew something of what was going on could convey that information to others. And as a result of the Internet, we are now living in a time where it's a lot easier to convey what we know about our corner of the world and share it with others.[58]

In this passage Assange situates his intervention in continuity with the Gutenberg project, which produces a civilizing effect on those in other corners of the world. Slavoj Zizek reads this "hacktivist" narrative as part of a global enlightenment project as well, comparing Assange to d'Alembert, WikiLeaks to the "Encyclopédie."[59] However, this enlightening and civilizing process, moving from the Renaissance to the Enlightenment to the digital age, is also put in question—in fact, mined—by the actions and observations of Assange and Zizek themselves.

While Assange frames his leaks as a "release of information" that has the effect of "shaking something up," Zizek claims that the information associated with the leak is always already known: "We didn't really learn from Snowden (or from Manning) anything we didn't already presume to be true—but it is one thing to know it in general, and another to get concrete data."[60] What is the difference between "knowledge" and "concrete data," between "enlightening" and "releasing," between bringing about awareness or consciousness and "shaking something up"? What are the implications of these distinctions on our understanding of the nature and framework of acts of hacking and leaking in a transnational context? Is "concrete data" a reference to a material and affective expression of hacks and leaks that shake systems and viewers by forcing pupils to dilate and pushing people to click, share, and demonstrate?

Moving beyond the liberal reading of leaks and hacks as spreading knowledge in order to raise consciousness and awareness and fix the empire or reform the state, this book focuses on knowledge and texts that shake up and unsettle, that recode the relationship between aesthetics and politics by offering new critiques of power, author function, and public engagement. Leaks do not just flow across borders in some transnational utopia of information and circulation, but rather break down, expose, shatter, submerge, wound, and destroy. It is the effects of the leaks, and their dangerous and threatening pathways, I trace and examine, focusing on key examples from the Arab world that inform our understanding of digital-age writing and activism in the region and beyond. I argue that the leak is both translatable and untranslatable, emerging from transnational spaces of hacking, writing, and contestation, and from local traditions of shaming and scene-making such as *faḍḥ*. Assange is not an author or political critic in the tradition of the intellectual speaking truth to power but rather a scene-maker and a function of leaking—an imagined origin of a new genre and a model of contestation that shapes local and global politics, information flow, and fiction.

Approaching leaking as an affective condition, media scholar Wendy Chun argues that leaking is the way information circulates, and meaning is produced in the digital age. The leak is not the exception or the isolated event, but instead the default of communication, storage, and relationality in the age of machines.

> [F]rom WikiLeaks to Facebook disasters, we are confronted everywhere with leaks. This leaking information is framed paradoxically as both securing and compromising our privacy, personal and national. Thanks to these leaks, we now

> understand the extent to which we are under surveillance; because of these leaks, we are exposed. This leaking information and the problems/solutions it exposes/provides are often presented as oddly personalized and humanized. Snowden is a hero or a rogue agent; Anonymous are advocates or vigilantes; slanegirl is a victim or a slut. But to what extent is leaking information an issue of personal human agency? . . . *[N]ew media are not simply about leaks: they are leak.*[61]

Wendy Chun (along with co-author Sarah Friedland) removes the leak from the liberal narrative that ends in civilization and redemption according to Assange and Zizek's explanations (read, justifications). Instead, Chun reads leaking as a habit and a condition that disperses the author and his or her intentions. By uncoupling the act from the teleological outcome in the liberal narrative, Chun opens up the leak to the transnational, undercutting the romantic narrative of digital subversion as heroic ethos that only seeks to reform the broken system. This articulation requires an exploration of the involuntary, the visceral, and the habitual as practices and aesthetics with particular histories that are yet to be acknowledged as political and literary in the digital age. Given this articulation, how do we read the body, which is now embedded with machines, as a leaking body that is both threatening and threatened, unable to control its flows, language, narrative? Is the inability to "sit in silence" tied to leaking as a digital condition that produces or reveals new texts and models of consciousness? What conceptual and historical trajectories must we draw on to decipher the flows, narratives, and contestations of the leaking body and the leaky text in the digital age?

The digital condition that Chun identifies allows us to read modes of involuntarism as political affects coming from the present and the past, and arising from new technologies and their effects on bodies, writing practices, activism, and acts of leaking, hacking, and scene-making both online and off-. Multivalent fields of interaction and models of confrontation, chaotic freedoms, fluctuations, and disturbances could not be made to coalesce into a neat rubric of the subject and of its corresponding liberal state achieved with the expulsion of the colonizer, with the fall of the dictator, or with the advent of democracy. The leak as discharge, release, and insurgent text flowing through multiple digital and bodily ports and portals relies on a regime of privacy and secrecy, containment and security, but also on a digital regime of circulation and exposure. The leak is both the result of the circumstances of disclosure (its context) and the result of the formal, informational properties of the disclosure (its substance).

Exploring the relation between different modalities of leaking, I argue that the leak is a political intervention, an overflow, and a condition all at the same time. *Leaks, Hacks, and Scandals* engages leaking as a reconfiguration of the subject and of the public, and as a new literary and political practice that fundamentally breaks with traditional models of writing and the critique of power (*engagement*, novel, author, public, intellectual, etc.) tied to the project and theorization of modernity. Whereas leaks have been associated with WikiLeaks and hacktivism, I push this association to include embodied, affective, and involuntary yet political acts tied to the inability not to click, share, respond, or tweet. Activists and authors leak, hack, and expose through storytelling, swearing online, and demonstrating, thereby refiguring writerly and political traditions and cultures of debate, and displacing or recoding the position of the traditional intellectual.

The leaking subject, I argue, is a figure and a theoretical framework, a history and a code of writing, a condition and an array of political practices. In this sense Wael Abbas's swearing at rivals on Twitter and his compulsive uploading of videos of abuse and violation are also tied to his own body: wounds, limbs, and an uncontrollable tongue, heart, and fingers that prevent him from "sitting in silence," as I discuss in chapter 2. As for Chelsea Manning, she is described as compulsively grabbing files and leaking them to Julian Assange in a state of overflow and as a critique of power, as I discuss in chapter 1. The leaking of information, images, and emotion forces us to reflect on the "subject" as a theoretical category and historical construct referring to a coherent self with a particular model of subjectivation. *Leaks, Hacks, and Scandals* thus refers to specific authors and activists but also to a history and a narrative of subjectivity associated with *adab* that is being recoded in the digital age.

The leak exposes fictions of power, making a scene of their porousness and spills. Acts of hacking and revelation, "releases" and "leaks," form multiple trajectories: trickles and tsunamis, flash floods and flash mobs. Such is the language and register of the leak that I explore in this book. The practice and condition of the leaking subject consists of body fluids, stories, narratives, secrets, and fragmented texts. Scholar Laura Marks examines the leaking body in the work of Egyptian filmmaker Sherif El Azma, reading fluids as affects that try to give meaning to that which is not discursive.[62] Leaks make legible forms of knowledge, writing, and affective interventions. Thus, tracing the narrative of the leak requires an engagement with "affects," enacting and exposing breaks and fractures in discourse and in subject positions, and thus creating the possibility for new connections, movements, and significations. Affects characterize acts of writing and performance yet form a new readership looking for meaning and operating along different models of desire that move people to follow, share, and rebel. These affective acts expose, inscribe, and bring to light texts and histories that shock and titillate, and engulf and overwhelm. The reader or viewer is drawn to follow the trickle of revelation, to desire the rupture, to be submerged by it, and to expose the misdeeds of those in power. Following the narrative of the leak involves a process of desacralizing power and delegitimizing its founding myths or fictions (religious, political, literary). Far from appealing to a passive viewer, leaking involves a digital performance that unsettles yet seduces viewers and readers to click and follow the serialized and sensational text that shames and exposes. Leaking encourages and manipulates this reader to experience information as scandalous, linked to corruption and abuse, but also to sadistic forms of pleasure. Leaking involves a process of exposure (*faḍḥ*) that makes a scene, causes a scandal, and brings to light the affective economy that threatens and gives pleasure. In this light I examine images of limbs and texts cropped online, engaging the return of the archaic as a genre in Arabic literature and as a temporality and fantasy of death and enslavement. In this context I argue that the narrative of a modern Arab subjectivity is leaking. This subjectivity depends on a particular constellation tied to the *Nahda*, including the citizen of the liberal Arab state-to-come that Albert Hourani theorized,[63] and the novel as the central element that enlightens and civilizes this citizen.

TRIALS OF *ADAB* IN THE DIGITAL AGE

Leaks, Hacks, and Scandals picks up where my previous book left off. Ending with the analysis of the work of a new generation of Arab authors such as Ahmed Alaidy, *Trials of Arab Modernity* (2013) identified a vulgar, angry, and violent narrative targeting Arab modernity, history, and *adab*—the site of the civilizing process through high culture and perfectibility as theorized by Mathew Arnold in *Culture and Anarchy*, and critiqued by Sonallah Ibrahim in his novella *The Smell of It*.[64] The new author, I argued, explodes like a "sewer pipe" in the text. In *Leaks, Hacks, and Scandals* I explore the reference in *Trials* to "[u]pdating and upgrading one's server [as] forms of *prise de conscience*"[65] as constitutive of a digital consciousness, or what Wael Abbas calls *al-waʿī al-miṣrī* (Egyptian consciousness or awareness), produced by activists and authors who not only broke with Alaidy's 1967 "generation of Defeat"[66] but also with subsequent generations of defeat following 1990 and 2003 and who were taken by surprise by the Arab uprisings.

Exposing porous boundaries of languages and genres, narratives of the subject and of power, the leak as new fiction breaks the association between "literature" and the novel that is meant to produce privacy/interiority and national identification. In the new landscape I explore, the literary is tied to digital models of awareness, information, knowledge production, and entertainment. In this light Assange and WikiLeaks can and should be read in relation to new Arabic writing and tweeting, emerging from and responding to the collapse of a political and social ideal—a symbolic in the Lacanian sense. This symbolic made possible or fostered a particular kind of interiority or the private that emerges in relation to an overarching community, a community of the privates, a multiplicity of singularities engaged in collective reading practices centered on the novel and the newspaper as edifices.

The collapse of interiority and privacy, which I began theorizing in *Trials of Arab Modernity* and that I fully develop in this book, coincides with a larger ideological collapse: the liberal narrative of the state as an egalitarian and transparent structure, and of Arab modernity as a cultural and national project embodied in the nation-state—a structure that was physically and symbolically dismantled by the US invasion of Iraq in 2003, for instance. These national narratives, tied to eighteenth- and nineteenth-century literary genres, reading practices, and political models, are no longer capable of interpellating subjects who read novels and print-media to develop political consciousness and experience secular time. Instead we are witnessing the resurgence of the tribal, the sectarian, the vindictive, and the mythological, both online (cyber-raiding, trolling, video games) and off- (the Iraq invasion, ISIS). In this new landscape a portal has opened up, unleashing the fantasies of archaic violence and group formation, and further eroding idealized models of community, justice, and the law.

This book starts with a theoretical history, reading leaks as a form of embodied release of data and stories that conjures up classical storytelling genres. I argue that the leaking subject is both erased and inscribed through a *mise en abîme* in an open text attributed to a Scheherazade-like figure, a fictional character posited as author, to be celebrated or shunned, exiled or imprisoned. In this context social-media platforms become stages for literary texts and live performances that reproduce the traditional cafés of Arab storytellers.[67] I also examine hashtag campaigns on Twitter as forms of tribal mobilization that call on followers to partake in a scene of archaic violence. Specifically, I show how the process of "tagging" or "hashtagging," which is meant to call into discourse particular topics for discussion online, ultimately reenacts models of warfare and street scenes wherein fights and confrontations take place in the *ḥāra* (traditional neighborhood) of Naguib Mahfouz's novels and among the flash mobs of the Arab uprisings. Throughout the book I examine the intertwinement *of* and the mimetic relation *between* fiction and digital culture, the Arab tradition and cyberculture, online exchanges and street protests, and the local and the global.

Leaks, Hacks, and Scandals focuses on new writing from Egypt and the Gulf, exploring these writings' fascination with and appropriation of digital media. Recent transformations in literary cultures and digital technology make me particularly interested in Egypt—the old "center" of Arab nationalism and literary production—and in the Gulf, which is giving rise to a new subjectivity tied to the global and the digital, with literary prizes and dating apps supplanting the traditional cafés and meeting places of Baghdad and Beirut. This book does not seek to be comprehensive, covering cyberphenomena across the Arab world. The examples I focus on from Egypt and the Gulf chart a particular redefinition of what Arab culture *means* in the digital age, pointing to the changing meaning of Arab culture (novels, authors, education, etc.) and of *adab* as a model of subjectivity in a context shaped by technological development and political upheaval. This meaning, which was tied to *Nahda* (Arab modernity) models and shaped by pan-Arab discourses and ideologies associated with Egypt and the Levant, changed as a result of new media, prize culture centered on Gulf countries, and the like. The scope of the argument is not historical or ethnographic but comparative and theoretical. Specifically, the book argues that even Egypt, the site most associated with the Arab modernity project or *Nahda*, is undergoing fundamental changes that are not simply due to the rise of the Gulf as economic, political, and cultural sponsor from the 1990s onward. Thus the subtitle "Arab Culture in the Digital Age" is meant to showcase the transformations in the very notion of "Arab" (secular, pan-Arab, Nasser, *Nahda*) and "culture" (*adab*, education, civility, the novel) in the age of leaks, hacks, uprisings, the rise of fundamentalism, and Gulf cultural sponsorship.

The Arab cultural production I examine cannot be reduced to specific historical events, such as the Arab uprisings and their ensuing turmoil. The digital, I argue, is not a medium that simply expands or makes available unchanging texts or events that could now simply be downloaded or watched through live streams online for wider reach while remaining *essentially* intact.[68] Rather, I investigate how the Internet operates as a space of confrontation and exposure that breaks down and reconstitutes the text, and refigures its author function, reading practice, literary-critical significance, and reading public against the backdrop of radical displacement of the traditional sites of Arab modernity around which theories of aesthetics, of the political, and of the subject have been developed. Examining scenes of shaming and exposure alongside their specific histories both online and in classical Arabic sources, my work sheds light on tactical moments of disturbance that open up, make possible, and reveal a new reading of the aesthetic-political relation.[69] I explore acts of last resort that confront literary opportunism, authoritarian practices, and the fantasmatic as perverse reenactment of an imagined past.

Leaks, Hacks, and Scandals confronts the question of digital vulnerability and porousness that connect author to character and author to text. I investigate the text's imagined unity when it is reduced to fragments online, cropped and annotated by various users. I understand fiction as consisting of the multiple forms of storytelling including the novel, but also of sites for thinking the literary and the fantasmatic. The proliferation of writing and speaking through icons and avatars—leaking, as Wendy Chun would argue—leads to the amplification of the capacity to partake in fiction. Specifically, I argue that cyberspace and cyberwriting do not bring about the end of literature but instead its activation. Fictionalization and reading fiction stage the power of these new media as they operate alongside traditional models from Aristotle's *Poetics* to Mieke Bal's *fabula*.[70] This framework presents leaks and social media not only as the field of media and cybernetics experts, but of literary and cultural critics as well.

My book engages digital humanities by examining how a digital configuration of knowledge could not simply reproduce an encyclopedic epistemological ideal (or knowledge/power model) transposed online, but also signal an alteration in the meaning and experience of knowledge.[71] Scholar and digital artist Laila Sakr examines the Tahrir hashtag (Twitter debates centered on the January 2011 revolution in Egypt) by developing a framework for studying social media against the backdrop of Arab uprisings and beyond. Sakr writes that "social media platforms served as the database architectures for the accumulation of data on a scale heretofore unknown. This over-proliferation of data challenges one's research methodology—the impossibility of knowing or representing such a mass of information requires new ways of investigating and interpreting."[72]

Sakr's call to rethink traditional methodologies emphasizes new forms of knowledge production centered on the "over-proliferation of data" that leads to an impossibility to "know" and "represent."

Questioning the modes and implications of digital knowledge extends to such scholarly projects as the digitization of medieval manuscripts and multivolume compilations. This process not only subjects them to contemporary rules of searchability and accessibility, but also unsettles our contemporary disciplinary divisions and nomenclatures such as authorship and copyright, literature and history, thereby requiring a new approach to thinking about classical and modern genres and the very notion and division of classical and modern. In his introduction to the anthology *The Digital Humanities and Islamic and Middle East Studies*, Elias Muhanna poetically captures the possibilities that this new field offers: "Databases collapse time and space in dramatic ways. The trope that persists, hidden, through the centuries can now be traced effortlessly, as though one were fanning through an old manuscript and spotting the tunnels grooved into its pages by bookworms."[73] This description mimics a burrowing that captures the materiality of the digital, breaking down temporality and setting the critic on a trail under and above ground, requiring different movements and contortions of the body to access new meaning. The movement alters the text and the object of inquiry, intervening in the genre and in the body of the old text and that of the virtual rendering that pretends to represent it whole, with its pages ungrooved by bookworms. The "dramatic ways" in which the "collapse of time and space" occurs bring forth an event that alerts us that something from those classical knowledge production and writing genres has reappeared and materialized through a portal opened in cyberspace that now affects and shapes our current practices. The digital forces us to engage the classical tradition and its rhizomatic genres that—due to this engagement with the predisciplinary and premodern—change and shape our contemporary reading and critical practices.

Twitter is one of the key sites of investigation in this book. Discussing the coverage in January and February 2011 of the Arab uprisings, Zizi Papacharissi argues that Twitter is the new platform for news storytelling: "The storytelling infrastructure of the platform facilitated a hybridity of news values that blurred personal with objective, emotion with meaning, opinion with reporting, and affective with cognitive flows of information."[74] Twitter is thus a framework that brings together narrative genres and political contestation, transforming the nature of publics and public spheres, and the nature of knowledge as such. To anchor a new experience of knowledge, to capture the tunnels grooved into social networks and computer screens, Laila Sakr produces a visual simulation of the encounter with the digital, depicting a person going through Twitter's fields and fibers and fully inhabiting this platform.[75] In his turn, Abdallah al-Ghadhdhami describes Twitter in the Saudi context as an "unsafe house" and a "glass house," where everything is exposed.[76] Breaking the coherence of the subject in this digital landscape, al-Ghadhdhami argues that the fingers of the tweeter move on their own, shattering the framework of writing and editing associated with debates in the public sphere, and collapsing the human/machine distinction. In this new environment users and activists leak, write, respond, share, reveal, expose, and gossip through the machine as it leaks and reveals through them. The activist and author on Twitter are thus unable not to click, hold anything back, or keep their mouths shut when they see abuse and violation, or when they feel attacked or offended.

BOOKMARKS

While the first part of the book focuses on the making of the leaking subject as critic of power and performer of scandal, the second part examines the narrative of the leak. Specifically, the first two chapters deal with the body and affect, while the last three chapters deal with fiction and how it is affected by the consciousness of the leaking subject. Chapter 1, "On Leaking: From *The Arabian Nights* to WikiLeaks," offers a theoretical reading of the leaking subject, showing how the leaker's body, which produces flows and narratives, is marked as threatening and contaminating, and thus needs to be excluded from the community and placed in solitary confinement. Starting with *The Arabian Nights* and moving to contemporary leaking events involving Aliaa Elmahdy, Rupi Kaur, Chelsea Manning, Julian Assange, and Edward Snowden, this chapter traces the transformation of the leaker into superstar traitor and hero, and the making of the leak as encyclopedic knowledge in the digital age, adding *wiki* to leaks. I argue that acts of leaking are bodily, literary, and political, thereby exposing the porousness of national boundaries, fictions of power, security systems, and gender codes. From leak as symptom or lack associated with an unsettled symbolic that needs to be reactivated through redemption and ritual purification, we move to leak as affect that exposes both the leaking subject's body and the excesses of the body politic: abuse, secrets, jouissance.

Examining the leaking subject as leaker of torture videos and images of abuse, but also as a scene-maker gushing invectives and insults that burst out and knock down rivals online, chapter 2, "What Is in My Heart Is on My Twitter," examines the confrontational practices of Egyptian activist Wael Abbas. Focusing on the production of publics from street mobs to online followers, I read comparatively the Arab cultural tradition of exposure and scene-making (*faḍḥ*), and explore the production of a new digital consciousness that upholds states of bodily and political fragmentation, fusing the heart with Twitter as in Wael's motto, which is reproduced as this chapter's title. I engage the notion of *adab* as both literature and model of civility tied to power's fiction and instruments of suppression, and explore its productive violation online. Twitter remains the stage of leaks and scandals in chapter 3, "The Infinite Scroll," in which I analyze the intersection of the revelation of political news and scandals with literary genres such as classical *akhbār* and contemporary ones such as celebrity gossip. Focusing on Saudi tweeter Mujtahidd who boasts two million followers, I compare his revelation of "state secrets" to otherworldly revelations that draw on Sufi concepts of sight and knowledge, producing a constant trickle and an infinite text that engulf and bewilder readers. I argue that Mujtahidd moves beyond a marginal phenomenon online to designate instead a mainstream model for the production and consumption of fiction and news. I explore how the leaker and technology become intertwined, sharing, embodying, and reproducing each other's functions and texts that are simultaneously informational and literary, affective and scandalous.

Moving from leaking subjects as activists and critics of power, in chapter 4, "Fiction of Scandal Redux," I read new Arabic writing through the prism of hacking, leaking, and scandal. I argue that the literary fascination with the digital betrays the unsettling of the edifice of the novel as the traditional generator of political consciousness. Leaks and hacks transform the new literary text into a scandalous stage that reproduces street and online scenes and practices, affectively drawing in the reader. In this context the fiction of scandal is tied to obsessive browsing practices online, transforming the work into a bestseller and thereby intervening in the formation of the canon.[77] New technologies have permanently inhabited the novel, recoding its political potential and literary value. Continuing with the exploration of the meaning of literature in the digital age, chapter 5, "Cyber-Raiding," examines a Twitter campaign against Saudi author Badriah Albeshr. Contesting her views and literary production, Twitter activists mobilized to exclude her from a public forum, accusing her of apostasy for a few passages in her novel, *Hend and the Soldiers*. Circulating online, the blasphemous passages become sites of attack, tagging, and consumption, fragmenting the body and the novel of the Arab female author. I argue that this recoding of the text and of the author function is tied to a model of tribal warfare that erupts through a portal into the archaic in cyberspace. The digital in this chapter is explored both structurally and fantasmatically, given the current political state of the Arab world and the nature of the Internet, as a stage for the unraveling of certain forms of authority. Whereas Foucault and Althusser have located subjectivation in discourse, power, and the state, subjectivity in this context—leaking subjectivity—arises from the activation of *Jahiliyya*-like rituals that herald new forms of community, public, and political order.

In the conclusion, I reflect on my argument and ask what it would mean to move from the leaking subject to a postsubjective moment wherein the archaic no longer peeks through a portal on Twitter, but rather has returned with its beasts and monsters to permanently inhabit Arab cultural and political landscapes.

CHAPTER 1

On Leaking

FROM *THE ARABIAN NIGHTS* TO WIKILEAKS

> When we look at the term *data,* we generally do not recognize its Latin origin, as the plural form of *datum,* meaning "[a thing] given." The French word for data, *donnée* ("given," from *donner,* "to give"), retains the Latin sense exactly. If data are the "things" given, then what is it that gives data? Aside from having the speculation in mind that this givenness comes from God, we should recognize that since 1946, the word *data* has had an additional meaning: "transmittable and storable computer information." This second understanding of *data* suggests the need for a reconsideration of the philosophy of objects, because it can no longer be assumed to refer entirely to sense and noetic data. Instead, one should recognize this translation as taking on a material form and consider how this materiality constitutes a new form of "givenness."
>
> —Yuk Hui, *On the Existence of Digital Objects*

Faucets, bodies, taps, roofs, spills, streaming, letting things in or out, leaks perform the breakdown of containment, breaching the dam, regularly and incessantly, through fissures, holes, ports, crevices. Refugees leak across borders and expose in doing so leaky national boundaries and models of citizenship. Hannah Arendt theorized this in her work on refugees in the post–World War II period, asking what happens to human rights without a state to guarantee them? Arendt captures a biopolitical condition that seeks to reclaim rights beyond modernity's imagined communities.[1] Rethinking the political and the contestation of power from this perspective requires an examination of involuntary acts, compulsive acts, coerced acts, and acts of last resort by leakers who also become targets, refugees, exiles, and prisoners of their own leaks: fluids, secrets, videos, stories, war experiences.[2]

When WikiLeaks first started posting the correspondence of the American armed forces in Iraq in 2010 and 2011, the leaks were experienced as a deluge of data that risked submerging the public, the actors in these revelations, and the political structure altogether. The scandal was so great that it was compared to a "tsunami" that would bring about "the end of diplomacy as we know it."[3] The leaks—hundreds of thousands of messages and documents—were not individualized, with each text containing specific damning information.[4] Unlike the Watergate scandal in the early 1970s, contemporary leaks are associated with a radical bursting of the containable, of the dam that eventually cracks open to produce a flood, thereby drawing on the register of natural disasters. So when it was revealed in July 2015 that the US government was hacked, compromising the personal information of employees and contractors, CNN headlined: "Government data breach affected over 22 million."[5] The reaction of the CNN presenter was "Wow!" when hearing from her colleague that it was "five times more than they had expected or announced."[6] The article on the news site went on to describe the unprecedented "magnitude of this security breach,"[7] framing the event as earthquake.

As bundles and zip files of data unfolded on websites and airwaves, the leaks depended on a logic of anticipation, propelling someone like Julian Assange to the position of leak master (as in "master of ceremonies"), who announces that on this day thousands of leaks will be revealed, or that what was revealed was only the tip of the iceberg. The announcer of the catastrophic turned the public into terrified yet avid readers of a diluvial text that consumes, submerges, and fills every hole. Though the timing of the leak is part of a practice that creates anticipation, the revelations themselves could not be sorted, understood, or contained in terms of their circulation, effect, and meaning.[8] The leaks have become transnational, involving multiple locales, languages, and political contexts, requiring deciphering, editing, and translation projects. When the Panama Papers leak hit in April 2016,[9] it was announced as the biggest leak ever: millions of documents implicating world leaders in corruption scandals from the United States to Russia. It was an operation that took a year of preparation, with hundreds of journalists, editors, and translators working together to produce the story. The Panama Papers became a topic to which newspapers such as the *Guardian* and *Le Monde* devoted entire sections, reporting on them for days as more and more information was revealed.[10] Once unleashed, the leak becomes an apocalyptic scene of revelation, a tsunami, a deluge, a body of texts that is simultaneously translatable and untranslatable.

In Arabic, the register of leaks is expressed through terms such as *tasrīb* (leak) leading to a *ṭūfān* (flood), capturing the erasure of the trace, the origin, or the source. A 2015 *Al-Jazeera* article about the leaking of a torture video from Lebanese prisons describes how the minister of justice "ordered a criminal investigation of that which was leaked (*fī mā tasarraba*) on social media as pictures showing the torture of detainees."[11] Here, the leaker is unknown, as if it had dissolved in the act of leaking. In fact, the Arabic noun *tasrīb* belongs to grammatical form II (*al-wazn al-thānī* as in *taf'īl*), which has no actor or the actor is unknown, drawing attention to the leaked rather than the leaker, and presenting the act of leaking—or the leakage—as autonomous, happening by itself, as if it were an act of nature (like earthquakes and tsunamis), or part of a digital condition. With the leaker erased or unknown, the leak becomes merely given—*donnée*, data—thereby complicating our understanding of agency, authorship, intention, and text. Who leaked the videos? Of course, we have seen with WikiLeaks how leakers become superstars, villains, and heroes, thereby fixing their authorial intentions and assigning them specific liberationist projects or evil and traitorous schemes.[12] This process, however, is often established retrospectively through a production that involves leak masters and state apparatuses, public opinion and popular culture.[13] But most leaking occurs through compulsive and ongoing processes that trickle and expose. In the prison video example given above, the leaker is not identified as a conscientious objector to government policies but rather needs to be read as an economy, a network, a default condition, and a digital ecosystem of giving (*donner*), sharing, uploading, exposing, and watching. As if leaking acts on its own, is itself *given*, source and origin at the same time. It is the leak that makes the torture known and legible but also unacceptable and therefore requiring an investigation.

In this chapter I explore leaking as bodily function, tying it to fiction and author function. Engaging the theoretical framework of the leaking body from *The Arabian Nights* onwards, I examine how leaks became WikiLeaks, thereby questioning their framing as an attempt to fix the empire or restore the violated subject of the liberal state whose rights and privacy have been suspended or tampered with. This chapter traces the transformation of the leaker into superstar traitor and hero, and the making of the leak as "true knowledge" or encyclopedic knowledge by adding "Wiki" to "Leaks." The Derridean *reste* of this transformation is the leaking body and the leaking fiction—the subject of my investigation throughout the book. I argue that as leakers occupy liminal states of juridical limbo such as embassies, airports, and solitary confinement, their bodies become marked and their subjectivity undone and reconstituted while simultaneously undoing and reconstituting the law that they purportedly violate. Thus, leaking washes away its origin as a condition of contesting, knowing, and belonging. Approaching leaks as bodily functions that subvert both political and discursive orders, I engage theories of fluidity and materiality by drawing on affect theory and feminist critiques of psychoanalysis. From leak as symptom or lack associated with an unsettled symbolic that needs to be reactivated through redemption and ritual purification, we move to leak as political affect that exposes both the leaking subject's body and the insecurities and violations of power: abuse, secrets, security holes, jouissance. It is this double exposure of the leaking body and of the body politic that I focus on in this chapter.

REGISTERS OF THE LEAK

In the Arab context leaking as an act of exposure and unveiling is often emphasized through the process of *faḍḥ* (exposing, making a scene) and *kashf* (unveiling, revealing). Media reports use the expressions *tasrīb yakshuf* (a leak reveals) and *tasrīb yafḍaḥ* (a leak exposes) to designate the operation and effect of the leak. *Kashf*, which I take up in more detail in chapter 3, is linked to the Sufi concept of *mukāshafa*, which marks the collapse of subject/object relation, the veil, or the Apollonian. It is the moment of visibility that frames *faḍīḥa* (scandal), engulfing seer and seen, actor and acted upon, setting the stage for a new mode of knowing and touchability. *Faḍīḥa* engulfs and breaks down the subject/object binary structuring the model of knowledge (who knows and what is known) and its dynamic of control and domination that Said critiques in *Orientalism* (knowledge as power) by drawing on Foucault. This epistemological collapse brought about by the act of leaking ushers in a new form of knowledge, which is fundamental to the critique of leaking as a way of enlightening the public in a cyberspace often idealized as a Habermassian public sphere.

The knowledge revealed by the leak performs *faḍḥ* (exposure) and *kashf* (unveiling), thereby exposing another text and other information that needs to be recognized, acknowledged, seen under a new light, touched. This "other text" or "other object of knowledge" requires the kind of lighting as in the hacking example discussed in the introduction, thereby setting the stage for a new model of reception and critique of power. This critique, which makes a scene of power through the leak and makes power recognizable and exposed in the event of leaking, is coextensive with a textual production, a story, and a scandalous fiction that acts affectively on the viewer or reader. This fiction emerges from the leaking event and makes the knowledge that the leak reveals legible and affective at the same time, touching bodies and altering narrative course, subverting power relations and the codes regulating gender, the sacred and the profane, the private and the public, and the knowable and the unknowable. The event of leaking reveals a scene, a drama, and a web of interconnections that tie in fiction and affect, bodies and texts, and aesthetics and politics.

The intertwinement of bodily conditions, the critique of power, and fictions revealed in the event of leaking are best captured in two tales from *The Arabian Nights*. In addition to reading the *Nights* itself as a collection of leaks, which obliterates and fictionalizes its source or moment of origin—an "anonymous" text or a text "given," *donnée*—leaking bodies are a constitutive part of the narrative as such.[14] "The Story of the Lady and Her Five Suitors" shows how the body, when confined and panicked, leaks, subverting hierarchies and power relations. The tale is about a woman who invites the chief of police, the judge (Kazi), the minister (Wazir), and the king to her house for an amorous encounter in exchange for the freedom of her alleged brother—in fact, her lover. Scheduling their visits one after the other, she commissions a chest of drawers that would each fit a man from a carpenter who would join the fray at the lady's house. When each man arrives, she asks him to take off his official garb and don a house robe, obtains his signature on a release form, and orders him to hide in one of the drawers once a knock at the door is heard. After locking them all up, including the carpenter, she frees her lover from jail and escapes with him.

> Meanwhile, the five abode each in his compartment of the cabinet without eating or drinking three whole days, during which time they held their water until at last the carpenter could retain his no longer; so he urined on the King's head, and the King on the Wazir's head, and the Wazir on the Wali, and the Wali on the head of the Kazi; whereupon the Judge cried out and said: "What nastiness is this? Doth not what strait we are in suffice us, but you must make water upon us?" The Chief of Police recognised the Kazi's voice and answered, saying aloud, "Allah increase thy reward, O Kazi!" And when the Kazi heard him, he knew him for the Wali. Then the Chief of Police lifted up his voice and said, "What means this nastiness?" and the Wazir answered, saying, "Allah increase thy reward, O Wali!" whereupon he knew him to be the Minister. Then the Wazir lifted up his voice and said, "What

> means this nastiness?" But when the King heard and recognised his Minister's voice he held his peace and concealed his affair. Then said the Wazir, "May God damn this woman for her dealing with us! She hath brought hither all the Chief Officers of the state, except the King." Quoth the King, "Hold your peace, for I was the first to fall into the toils of this lewd strumpet." . . . And they fell to talking with one another, diverting the King and doing away his chagrin.[15]

The tale presents a sadomasochistic encounter wherein the woman seduces the men, ties them up, and leaves. The men lose control of their body functions and begin to leak on one another. Pissing on the king's head is the outcome of confinement that accentuates the subversive aspect of leaking. As the men leak, they become aware of each other's presence and of the power dynamic that had just been unsettled. Leaking makes them legible to one another and creates recognition through voice recognition not the garb; through desire and the power of the woman over them and not through their fixed positions in the political hierarchy; and through fluids seeping through cracks in the wood and not through visual recognition. The collapse of the visual paves the way for the emergence of leaks (pissing) and sound (talking) as the framework of political subversion and the production of new models of recognition that tie in subjects to one another. Leaking thus makes something known and heard, thereby exposing and making a scene of the subversion of power, which recognizes its downfall in the event itself. In the absence of the official garb and the symbolic power of kingship, a new intersubjectivity predicated on leaks (leaking subjects versus subjects of the king) emerges in this story.

Simultaneously, the story exposes the subversion of the codes regulating sex and desire. The alleged brother who is in jail emerges at the end as the woman's lover. The leak and the political subversion it enacts coincide with the breakdown of the codes of *haram* and *halal*, the permissible and the illicit. Thus the exposure of political authority in this tale coincides with a more radical subversion of sexual codes of love and the prohibition of incest. Leaking thus conditions a critique of political structure and of social order predicated on codes and prohibitions fundamental to patriarchy as such. The symbolic is unsettled in this leaky story, fundamentally forcing us to rethink what it means to desire, what objects of desire are sanctioned and which ones are not, blurring the boundaries between the permissible and the reprehensible, only to expose the ways in which these boundaries are established in the first place. The fiction of the "brother in jail" foregrounds the event of the leak only to be undone by it in the end. The fictional development of the imprisoned brother who becomes the liberated lover is both mediated by the leak and makes the leak possible. The question of gender and the position of the woman vis-à-vis the structure of power, and her ability not only to negotiate with it but to subvert it completely, emphasizes the relation between the bodily and the order of fiction as the leak exposes and intervenes in the political.

While leaking, both as a bodily condition and dramatic effect, subverts power and reshuffles amorous and intersubjective relations through a new mode of knowledge and recognition in "The Lady and Her Five Suitors," in "The Steward's Tale" leaking produces a fiction that critiques power as well as the exclusion of women as the basis of patriarchal community formation. Further questioning the limit and the boundary that separate the permissible from the forbidden, and the sacred from the profane, "The Steward's Tale" is about a girl who serves Lady Zubaida, wife of Caliph Harun al-Rashid. When the girl falls in love with a merchant in the souk, her mistress asks her to bring him to the harem so she can meet him and make sure that he is fit for her beloved servant. They devise a plan to smuggle him into the harem, hidden in a wooden chest along with other chests carrying clothes for Lady Zubaida.

> The chief of the eunuchs started up from sleep and cried out to the young lady, "Don't delay. You must open these chests." It so happened that the chest he was about to start with was the one in which I was, and when they brought it to him, I lost my senses and in my panic wet myself until my urine began to run out of the chest. Then the young lady said, "Chief, you have ruined me and ruined many merchants by spoiling the belongings of the Lady Zubaida, for the chest contains colored dresses and a jar of Zam-zam water. The jar has just tipped over and the water will make the colors run."[16]

In this tale fear produces an involuntary act of leaking, which is simultaneously fictionalized by the girl accompanying the chest into the harem. Akin to Christian holy oil, Zam-zam water in Islam comes from the divine spring in Mecca that God created for Hagar when she was lost in the desert after having been repudiated by Abraham.[17] When Muslims go to Mecca for Hajj, they bring back bottles of this holy water. To fictionalize piss as Zam-zam water exposes the exclusion of women from the tribe, narratively substituting the man's leaking body for that of the woman. The girl's interpretation or fictionalization of the leak—making it legible as story—blurs gender positions as in the previous tale, showcasing how leaking becomes affective, thereby unsettling the boundary between inside and outside, and holy and sacred. The leak thus operates as a literary comparative device connecting multiple temporalities, stories, and orders of narration from the biblical and Quranic narrative to the tales of the *Nights*. Narratives of tribal and religious identity that uphold the symbolic power of kingship, maintain social and political hierarchy, and regulate gender codes are subverted in the event of leaking, which is mediated by the literary *mise en abîme* characteristic of the *Nights*. Collapsing temporal distinctions by reading the past through the present and the present through the past, the leaking event and its fictionalization reveal a new comparative practice and critique of power that bring together affect, fiction, and the political through a drama involving fluids and stories, secrets and revelations.

Invoking the exclusion of women, from Hagar's expulsion in the biblical and Quranic narrative to the harem laws and boundaries, the leak calls attention to the porousness of and breaches in the fiction of power. Affectively mediating the lover's infiltration of the forbidden harem, the leaking of bodily fluids interrogates the political by interrogating the symbolic system that has traditionally considered the gendered leaking body as a *site* and *sight* to be suppressed, veiled, and locked up in the harem. The leak as affect, in this context, simultaneously exposes the "security holes" of the harem and of the religious narrative that confer identity and borders, thereby unsettling them as coherent fictions of the law and tradition. Thus, the patriarchal narrative of subjectivity is breached by the acts of infiltration, leaking, and fictionalization. Staging fiction against fiction, the event of leaking in this tale is coextensive with the violation of the law (bringing a man into a harem) and the making of a scene of the violation at the origin of the law (excluding women from the tribe and locking them up in the harem).

Leaking exposes models of exclusion and confinement (drawers, chests, cabinets, harems, incarceration, imprisonment) and subverts the mechanisms of containment (borders, limits, doors, seals) through which exclusion and confinement are maintained. It also associates leaking with a body function that is triggered in key moments to produce these subversive effects, which occur involuntarily—tied to sensorial processes involving fear, panic, and overflow—yet are politically affective. The dialectics of leaking and containing the leak expose the mechanism of prohibition and the failure or porousness of this mechanism at the same time. This exposure is always accompanied by an act of subversion of that which it exposes, reveals, and makes a scene of. In other words, in order to understand the constitution of the leaking subject and the reaction to contemporary leakers, it is necessary to trace leaking to an anxiety about bodily loss of control and social and political violations on the one hand, and to a history of failed attempts to contain and suppress these violations, on the other. Specifically, the leaking body has been ideologically produced as a gendered body and site of lack that needs to be contained but that could never be contained.

The leak is out of control. It is also uncontainable, triggering multiple meanings and narrative proliferation. An economy of fiction (tale, tellers, listeners, publics, canon) foregrounds and mediates the leaking event as the two tales from the *Nights* show, thereby intervening in other fictions and narratives of codification from ancient myth to the Bible to more recent examples. Fiction is thus integral to the leak as a mode of storytelling, narrative flow, and political intervention. Gender, as we will see in more detail in later chapters, becomes the battlefield of the leaking text and authorial position. The female body and the woman author, chick lit and *The Arabian Nights*, are key sites of investigation that reveal both models of anxiety about the female body, and about the circulation of stories and texts that threaten political and patriarchal orders. In order to understand the production of the contemporary leaker's body and understand the threat that this body represents through its leaking of secrets but also of stories, it is necessary to anchor leaks in the literary and cultural tradition that has cast body functions as threatening to the community and requiring isolation, containment, and sequestration.

MARKED BODIES

Narratives of contamination and impurity from Zoroastrianism and the Old Testament to psychoanalysis have systematically sought to contain and neutralize the leaking body. In the Arabian ode leaking women have generally been associated with tears of lament.[18] Fluids work metonymically in relation to one another, from tears to sweat to blood, intermingling and foreshadowing one another, staging yet interrogating the relation to killing, loss, and vengeance that structure kinship in the tribal order (e.g., al-Khansāʾ). This model of substitution continues to play out in modern Arabic literature as well: In Adania Shibli's *We Are All Equally Far From Love,* for instance, the main protagonist, Afaf, hides her menstruation from her father, as she lies in bed, vomiting, crying, and sweating.[19]

The association of the female body with leaking has traditionally excluded women from the community as a way of preventing the body from revealing its leaks and thus contaminating the social. Women from the Kalasha tribe in modern-day Pakistan live in a special house (*bashaleni*) during their periods.[20] According to Islamic jurisprudence, while going through the cycle of menstrual bleeding (*ḥayḍ*), women "cannot validly perform central ritual duties such as prayer (*ṣalāt*) and fasting (*ṣawm*) [or] have marital relations."[21] In the Old Testament the concept of *niddah* refers to the " 'menstruating woman'; literally, 'one who is excluded' or 'expelled.' "[22] Some of the oldest and most complex laws in the Bible prohibit a married woman from intimacy with her husband for almost twelve days during her menses. She can only be readmitted to the community through ritual ablution (*mikveh* or "immersion in ritual bath").[23] The impurity is tied to the anxiety of contamination that requires symbolic sequestering or exclusion of the leaking body. Referring to *niddah*, Charlotte Fonrobert explains that "the first option is *n-d-d*, 'to depart, flee, wander.' The second option is *n-d-h*, 'to chase away, put aside,' a cognate from the Akkadian *nadu*, 'to throw, cast down.' "[24] Fonrobert quotes Jacob Milgrom's view that "'*niddah* came to refer not just to the menstrual discharge but the menstruant herself, for she too was 'discharged' and 'excluded' from her society by being banished to and quarantined in separate quarters' (Leviticus 1–16, 745)."[25] Fonrobert problematizes this model of impurity and exclusion, suggesting a more nuanced understanding that contests the association of leaks with contamination and isolation as a structure that informs gender codification and the configuration of spaces within or outside the law, the public, and the social.

Feminist theory has engaged with representations of women in religious and tribal narratives but also in psychoanalysis, which in turn draws on the mythological to construct and maintain the boundaries of the modern subject. Critiquing Freud, Luce Irigaray states that "[n]o one must overflow his container, or make so much as a ripple. A motion or emotion. Which is 'impossible' in a (suitable) place."[26] Irigaray argues that women are forced to hide and suppress their leaks in the phallocentric economy that devalues blood in favor of ink, the penis, money, and gold. This logic of valuation and substitution could be seen in Arabic literature from pre-Islamic women poets onward. Structures of anxiety around gender are exposed in the kinds of leaking and in the fictional economy discussed here. Feminist activists culminating with FEMEN have confronted this anxiety and exposed it through staged performances and art projects.[27]

"L'ART NE CÉDERA PAS À VOS RÈGLES!": RUPI KAUR AND ALIAA ELMAHDY

In March 2015, Toronto-based poet and performance artist Rupi Kaur posted an Instagram photo of herself lying in bed, fully clothed, with a stain on her pajamas and sheet, denoting menstrual blood. When Instagram deleted the photo, Kaur replied: "You deleted a photo of a woman who is fully covered and menstruating stating that it goes against community guidelines ... I will not apologize for not feeding the ego and pride of misogynist society that will have my body in underwear but not be okay with a small leak."[28] Kaur's reaction to the deletion of the photo, which was part of a series for a visual rhetoric project, emphasizes that although women can be freely objectified, a "small leak" becomes unsettling. The "small leak" according to Kaur puts in question the imagined community online, undermining its covenant (guidelines), and generating a radical act of erasure. Kaur concluded: "Their patriarchy is leaking. Their misogyny is leaking. We will not be censored."[29] According to Kaur, leaking is not only associated with her body but with the misogyny of the community guidelines upheld online. The photo of the leaking body thus exposes the leak in the phallocentric model that only accepts the representation of the female body as an object of desire mediated through the male gaze. Leaking de-eroticizes the body, thereby exposing both the leaking of the body and of the system that seeks to suppress it.

Kaur's leak as double exposure (*faḍḥ*) had immediate consequences that were duly noted by the artist and the media. When Instagram reinstated the photo after it had deleted it twice, Kaur declared victory. In subsequent reporting on the story, the *New York Times* subtitled its article "A photo of a woman on her period unleashed an online revolution," explaining how Instagram apologized and reinstated the picture.[30] The newspaper's subtitle presents the leak as something that continues to wreak havoc, this time unleashing a revolution that overtakes the online community. The suppression and reinstatement of the photo highlight the affective power of leaking that intervenes in the political and exposes systems of exclusion and prejudice, but also reveals their porousness and insecurities. This dynamic of leaking and suppressing the leak has been key in exposing and shaming authority both online and off-, both on Instagram in the case of Rupi Kaur, and in the cultural and political contexts that align fears and anxieties playing out in a North American cyberspace with those in the Middle East.

In November 2011, less than a year after the fall of the Mubarak regime in Egypt, a blogger and activist named Aliaa Elmahdy put naked pictures of herself on her blog, *A Rebel's Diary*, in order to protest the authority of SCAF, the military council that was ruling Egypt at the time.[31] Circulating online, the images immediately drew the ire of fellow activists and opponents, some calling her the devil while others accused her of betraying feminism and the cause of liberalism.[32] The reaction to Elmahdy's photos excluded her from the community representing Egypt's wide political spectrum; some dismissed her intervention as a dangerous stunt, others as "child play"[33] that needed to be distinguished from "true" revolutionary action. And when Aliaa protested naked in front of the Egyptian embassy in Sweden, where she had gone to live in 2012 after receiving death threats and risking jail time, calls to strip her of her Egyptian citizenship were made.[34] Accompanied by two women activists from the group FEMEN, Elmahdy protested the new constitution under Mohamed Morsi by writing on her body, "Sharia is not a Constitution," while holding a fake Quran to hide her vagina.[35] Elmahdy's nudity in this performance was seen as a tarnishing of Egypt's reputation but also as grounds to exclude her from the national community altogether. Exposing the body thus exposed a discourse that defines citizenship and the community in such a way as to outcast the exposed female body, experiencing it as a threat to the political that is, in Marwan Kraidy's terms, "at once biological and digital."[36]

In August 2014, Elmahdy pushed her protest further, this time directing it against ISIS by publishing online photos of herself menstruating on the group's flag.[37] In this performance female nudity and menstrual leaks converge to enact a radical act of *faḍḥ* (exposure, scene-making), linking digital leaking with body leaks. Marwan Kraidy reads Elmahdy's act as "subverting notions of femininity and dirtiness to depict Daesh [ISIS] itself as a monster. By doing this through her own bleeding, unbounded body, al-Mahdy warned that if women were prohibited from being abstract individuals, then at the very least they can turn symbols of women as abject bodies into a political weapon."[38] In the staging of the menstrual performance, leaking becomes premeditated, meant to shock, soil, and in so doing, make a scene of the shocking ISIS's soiling, enslaving, and killing of *other* bodies in the name of Islam. The act of leaking operates as a political intervention through an activation of body leaks and the transformation of the female body into a scene and scandal of the violent and archaic system through which ISIS acts. The political effectiveness of this performance ties together the leak as involuntary and premeditated, as bodily and political, and as a condition and an image circulating online all at the same time.

In one of the entries on her blog regarding an art exhibition in Tunisia in June 2012 that sparked demonstrations by religious conservatives, Elmahdy joined FEMEN Tunisia to proclaim her solidarity with artists Nadia Jalasi and Mohammed Ben Slema, headlining her post with the declaration: "L'art ne cédera pas à vos règles! [Art will not submit to your rules]"[39] The exhibition, which showcased mannequins of veiled women surrounded by stones inscribed with Arabic text, was interpreted as drawing an association between Islam and the stoning of women, thereby sparking the vandalizing of the gallery, violent riots, and a lawsuit against the artists for disrupting public order.[40] The title of Elmahdy's entry invokes the leak as the act that triggers violent suppression. The word "règle" in French means "rule" or "ruler;" when in the plural form ("règles"), it means "period" or "menstrual cycle." On one level Elmahdy's announcement implies that art will not submit to your rules, i.e., the rules of the Islamists who were becoming increasingly vociferous following the fall of Ben Ali and Mubarak. On another level the comment should be read in relation to Elmahdy's menstruating over the ISIS flag. In this context menstruation ("règles") subverts the rules ("règles") associated with a patriarchal order seeking to stifle artistic expression and exclude and enslave women.

The choice of the verb "céder" is doubly important in Elmahdy's entry as it implies to "compromise," " submit to," and "abide by," thereby problematizing notions of voluntarity and involuntarity that tie in political action, bodily function, and the digital condition of leaking. In *L'éthique de la psychanalyse* (*Séminaire VII*), Jacques Lacan counters Kantian ethics with the ethics of desire, where the categorical imperative becomes to not compromise one's desire or "céder sur son désir."[41] "Céder," "céder sur," and "céder à" involve notions of surrendering, giving up, compromising, ceding, but also occupying and controlling. Lacan engages with the Freudian structure of desire through the Oedipal denouement on the one hand, and on the other hand, with Freud's death drive or Thanatos in *Civilization and Its Discontents*, which pulls eros into the inorganic state of being prior to the advent of the symbolic (meaning, language). With this in mind, Elmahdy's statement needs to be read as upholding the ethics of desire but also as desire's subversion through women's nudity and menstruation. In this context leaking no longer functions as symptom or lack imagined from the position of the symbolic, but rather as affect that intervenes in the political and subverts it. The rules ("règles") are those of the Freudian super-ego but also of menstrual blood that flows and makes a scene, thereby causing a public scandal, and triggering threats of imprisonment, death, and eradication. The Lacanian injunction and its subversion thus point to the involuntary and to the law of desire, which take shape through a rule or an injunction that is itself put in question in the event of leaking. This complex staging and undoing of the law characterize the framework through which leaking operates to contest and expose the body of the leaker and the body politic at the same time. The fiction of the Lacanian subject, which bears within itself the unyielding injunction of desire, is exposed (*faḍḥ*) as "fiction" in the event of the leak.

LEAK *CONTRA* LACK

Elmahdy's use of "règles" necessitates an engagment with psychoanalysis, and with the work of Jacques Lacan specifically, in order to theorize the leaking subject yet resist reducing the leaking subject to Lacan's injunction—its "règles." Jacqueline Rose argues that "for Lacan, the unconscious undermines the subject from any position of certainty, from any relation of knowledge to his or her psychic processes and history, and *simultaneously* reveals the fictional nature of the sexual category to which every human subject is none the less assigned."[42] She continues: "Lacan's account of subjectivity was always developed with reference to the idea of a fiction."[43] "The symbolic order … for Lacan … is not some mythical moment of our past, it is the present order in which every individual subject must take up his or her place."[44] In this context the leak as discharge is not only a material object in the world but also something that transforms the leaker, affecting and being affected by it. Coinciding with the fiction of the leak rather than with the fiction of the symbolic, the discharge activates femininity both in the male and the female leaking subject. In leaking, the subject's gender and sexuality are altered and redefined by the event of the leak, thereby intervening in the political and ushering in a text with a new aesthetic—a new fiction—that imagines a different relation among subjects, and between subjects and power. Models of interpellation and intersubjectivity are recoded in the event of the leak.

Leaking inscribes the body, and marks and outcasts it yet activates it affectively. Leaking operates through the inscription of skin and surfaces, from the

CD surface inscribed with classified information passing as "Lady Gaga songs" in Chelsea Manning's Iraq leaks, to the bodies of Manning and Assange oozing and leaking these "songs" (classified information) in cyberspace as we will see below. Leaks proliferate through loose connections and partial (digital) objects as intensities and fluxes, reconstituting the subject as a condition of reconstituting the social and contesting power relations.[45] This process designates the work of *faḍḥ* as making a scene *of* and *through* the leaking body, which not only undermines the structure of power (symbolic order, patriarchy) but also exposes the fiction through which these structures interpellate and assign roles and codify gender. The *faḍḥ of* and *through* the leaking body exposes the involuntary and voluntary functions of leaking in the *Nights* and in the performances of Elmahdy and Kaur. The voluntary and involuntary event of leaking emerges from the intersection of politics and fiction.

The leaking subject who exposes a fictional model that is unable to hold in its excesses and violations is at work in online leaking as well. Fluids transform into data and secrets online, subjecting leakers to outcasting and persecution. The leakers who have been unsettling models of news and communication from the mid-2000s onward, both in the United States and in the Arab world, reveal a public now engaged through modes of political awareness or consciousness tied to browsing practices and digital habits. This public has an antipathy to the secret and to the opaque in the digital age. It is from these new fictional models and what scholar Geoffroy de Lagasnerie calls "éthique du voyou" (thug ethics) that a reengagement of a cynical public *who knows it all but does not care* is taking place.[46] The leaking subject hacks systems and circulates information that submerges both the leaked and the leaker, the secrets of authoritarian regimes and the body of the leaker. The leaker's body becomes confined to spaces of extrajudicial detention, embassies and airports, all of which lie outside the state and, in some cases, beyond the gendering fiction of the symbolic (Chelsea Manning). From Elmahdy and Kaur, who are pushed outside the national and online community, to the leaker of classified data pushed beyond the law, the leaking subject makes a scene of systems of exclusion, authoritarian practices, and violations, exposing in the process the unsettled fiction of power. To bring something to light, to make it visible—be it gender exclusion or human-rights abuse—is to resort to making a scene (*faḍḥ*) for a public that relates to a new kind of knowledge and information, revealed under a different light, in order to produce a spectacle that shocks and titillates.

EXPLOITING SECURITY HOLES: MANNING, ASSANGE, SNOWDEN

In *Trouble in Paradise: From the End of History to the End of Capitalism*, Slavoj Zizek situates the leaking subject within the ethics of psychoanalysis in which perversion is not simply dismissed and criminalized but rather upheld as "règle." "For Jacques Lacan, the axiom of the ethics of psychoanalysis was: 'Do not compromise your desire.' Is this axiom also not an accurate designation of the whistleblowers' acts?"[47] By invoking Lacan's injunction not to compromise one's desire as a framework for thinking about whistleblowing, Zizek is unable to fully account for the kind of relation between the involuntary and voluntary as the constituents of the political subversion that I argue for in this chapter, wherein desire is not simply tied to the model of misrecognition fictionalized through the relation to the Other and language (Lacan), but also operates as something inscribed on the body, leaking in and out through cracks, fissures, and security holes.

In 2010, stationed in Iraq during the American occupation, twenty-two-year-old Chelsea (then Bradley) Manning sent classified information to Julian Assange about violations by the US military in Iraq. Manning also provided WikiLeaks with "260,000 classified United States diplomatic cables."[48] Describing Manning, Adrian Lamo, a hacker with whom Manning corresponded and who would later denounce Manning to the authorities, claims that Manning "was just grabbing information from where he could get it and trying to leak it."[49] Depicting a process of assemblage, "random grabbing" is a compulsive act that is not focused, targeted, or centered on a particular piece of information or violation that needs to be exposed. When "he was arrested in Kuwait on May 26, 2010," Manning was "accused of exploiting gaping security holes on the military computer system by downloading the secret material onto CDs that he marked as Lady Gaga songs."[50] The "gaping security holes" that the leaker "exploits" and the material he transfers onto CDs become exposed in a scene that marks the body of the leaker and the body politic at the same time. The holes reveal and are revealed on the body of the leakers and in the system itself. The holes are thus not structural, built into the body (lack), but come into being and become known, perforated, recognized, and made legible in the act of leaking. Security holes on the body of the leaker are activated as sites of contestation, information, and writing. This is not to say that the leakers have no agency or that they are simply gaps and holes through which excess fluids of power flow. On the contrary, the leakers themselves "exploit" these gaps by leaking and making a scene of their bodies as passageways and streams for these leaks to become affective.

The security holes that Manning exploits make a scene of the system as excessive and overflowing, and therefore leaking in an act that exposes simultaneously the violations of the US occupation of Iraq, and the US occupation itself as a leaking fiction and a violation to be made a scene of. The fluids (cables, data, e-mails, videos) leaked out by Manning to Assange and then from Assange to cyberstreams transform the body of the leaker, through its imprisonment in solitary confinement at first, and then through its cross gendering into Chelsea Manning when in prison. Classified information is recoded as songs by cross-dressing and gender-bending artist Lady Gaga[51] as it is burnt onto the CDs leaked to Assange. The leaking event inscribes the digital body (the CD surface) and the human body (Manning), burning and perforating holes that leak fluids and data, subverting the "règles" of security systems and gender codification, leaking in and out, releasing classified information and hormones. This proliferation of the leak renders the body porous and dangerous in terms of the instability it reveals about both the system ("security holes"), and about the "règles" as both rules and cycle through which the system controls its flows and those of others through codes of gender and sexuality as well as information and honor codes (is Manning a traitor or a hero?).

Reporting on Manning's initial detention in solitary confinement for ten months, Glenn Greenwald wrote: "In sum, Manning has been subjected for many months without pause to inhumane, personality-erasing, soul-destroying, insanity-inducing conditions of isolation."[52] The leaking permanently marks the body of the leaker who is now forced into complete isolation and erasure. And when Manning's trial began, Greenwald said that the military decided to subject her to the worst punishment: life without the possibility of parole.[53] Greenwald captures the desire to see Manning disappear, erased, banned from the community, and denied a plea deal as a vindictive act.[54] In this context leaking does not simply put the leaker outside the law, but also the law outside of itself, exposing and making a scene (*faḍḥ*) of punishment, torture, invasion, occupation, and killings as extrajudicial and vindictive. The leak as scene and rupture thus operates against the "règles"—from acquiring and sharing information illegally, to unlawful persecution and imprisonment that revert to a pre-Foucauldian incarceratory model. The leaker is not the subject of correctional and disciplinary practices, but rather a leaking subject trapped in his/her own body, which is marked, punished, isolated, and deprived. The materiality of the body is emphasized in this process, thereby exposing an archaic reversal in the imagined liberal model that codes power and knowledge, punishment and information, gender and sexuality.

The unusual punishment to which the leaker is subjected and the juridical limbo into which he/she is thrown seek to not only contain but also eradicate the contamination of the social and the political brought about by the leaks of Manning, Assange, and later Snowden but also Elmahdy and Kaur. The vindictive punishment is a desperate yet scandalous (*fāḍiḥ*) attempt to erase the new text, contain the proliferation of the leak, locate its origin, and suppress its "règles." Just as the leaking in the tales from *The Arabian Nights* exposes the leaker's body and the gaping holes in the harem security system (religious narrative, gender and sexuality codes, sacred/profane), the event of leaking in this contemporary example makes a scene of the fiction of power. The link between these two events is conceptual rather than cultural or historical, tied to questions of the law, its makeup and violations. This link is centered around bodily functions, the making of gender and sexuality, and the voluntary and involuntary as characteristics of those functions and acts that determine punishability and exclusion. The event of leaking thus involves a fiction that exposes the makeup and the porousness of the fiction or narrative of the law, be it political, tribal, or religious. The leakers are seen as contaminating, rogue, unpredictable, nomadic, dirty, unable to control or contain their bodies, mouths, and revelations, thereby constituting the real danger to systems of control and containment, namely to the symbolic as it has been theorized through an engagement with mythological structures and literary narratives from Oedipus onward.

Julian Assange, the Australian activist and hacker who founded WikiLeaks in 2006, is portrayed in articles and reports as having led a nomadic life since childhood, a Huckleberry Finn at the margin of the law, moving from town to town with his mother and her partner, who worked for a theatre company.[55] Assange, who hacked NASA and the Pentagon at the age of sixteen,[56] grew up on stage, which he came to enjoy as an adult as well, reveling in the attention and limelight as he mines and leaks data only to redistribute it to the "unknowing" and "uninformed" public. Starting out as a Robin Hood of the digital age, Assange as fictional character and actor subverts models of security, ownership, news, and authenticity. Assange's leaking is hailed and celebrated yet pathologized and criminalized.

Visiting Assange at the Ecuadorian embassy in London in 2013, Zizek describes Assange's restricted living conditions, constantly guarded and bugged. Referring to the sexual misconduct allegations against him, Zizek asks: "where does such a ridiculously excessive desire for revenge stem from? What did Assange, his colleagues and whistleblowing sources do to deserve this?"[57] Assange found himself in juridical limbo at the embassy starting in 2012, resisting extradition to Sweden to answer to an allegation that he had ejaculated during intercourse as part of a consenting sexual act. The allegation is that Assange, by refusing to use protection, could have infected his partner with a sexually transmitted disease. The body leak read as contaminating along with the leaks spewing from his website push Assange into a space outside the law in ways that Zizek reads as vindictive, excessive, and inexplicable. As in the case of Manning, the treatment of Assange reveals forms of excess and revenge as the law's deployment and violent reaction to the leak that risks contaminating through its proliferation the social and the body politic. The double act of leaking (the sexual misconduct allegation and WikiLeaks) exposes the leaker's outcasting and exclusion, and the law as vindictive. In this context the revenge against Assange and Manning—the whistleblowing and leaking duo of the Iraq cables—exposes the Iraq invasion itself as a campaign and fiction of revenge beyond the law, and the war on terror and the system of mass surveillance set in place after 9/11 more generally as rooted in revenge rather than legality. Leaking reveals a scene of vendetta and fantasy—a fiction of the law engaged in tribal warfare, or in sadistic practices of torture and punishment, as we will see in the next chapter with policemen filming and leaking their abuse of detainees in Egypt under Muabarak, and in chapter 5, in the Twitter campaign against Badriah Albeshr through cyber-raiding on Saudi Twitter. Leaking thus constitutes a transnational event and a comparative text, connecting the Arab world to the United States, and fiction to politics.

In *Rogues: Two Essays on Reason*, Jacques Derrida exposes the porous boundary between rogue and democractic states, elaborating on the notion of democracy to come (*à venir*). Derrida calls attention to the fundamental contradictions at the heart of democracy, which requires sovereignty to govern in the name of the *demos* or people, and upholds freedom and singularity yet imposes equality. Emerging from his response to the political environment and discourse following 9/11, Derrida argues that the democracy associated with the liberal state is never a closed system but always leaking out and being leaked into as an outcome of its necessary contradictions and deferals.[58] This is what Derrida calls the "autoimmunity of democracy," which renders porous the relation between rogue state and the liberal democratic state, the Arab world and the United States. The act of leaking in this context exposes in the moment of establishing the boundary with the rogues (*voyous*)—as both states but also leakers—the vulnerability of this boundary and the fiction of the boundary that is itself invested in fantasmatic modes of self-recognition (free world versus rogue states, liberal versus Islamic, etc.). Emerging from this framework is the agent of the leaking process, a rogue figure (*voyou*) or *roué*, who acts like the fold—lying outside of democracy yet conditioning its advent. The *roué*, whose name is semantically tied to being on the *roue* ("the wheel," a premodern torture machine), is also the agent of delinquency, perversion, and subversion, who acts roguishly yet freely, and in that movement performs and prefigures the democratic yet prevents its closure.[59] It is in this sense that the leakers discussed in this chapter could be viewed, operating at the limit of the law, negating it yet making it possible.

Geoffroy de Lagasnerie argues that the actions of Manning and Assange but also Snowden, the NSA whistleblower on mass surveillance, herald a paradigm shift in the Foucauldian sense (a reference to *Les mots et les choses*), forcing us to rethink the political, the law, and modes of subjectivation. He suggests that these leakers' punishment is so great and incomprehensible—like being put on the *roue* in Derrida's sense—that it implies that their actions fundamentally destabilize the system rather than operate as crimes that could be contained or incorporated dialectically and punished accordingly. De Lagasnerie draws on Agamben's "state of exception" in which he describes the nonjudicial state of the enemy combatant that places the detained person outside the law and the judiciary altogether, producing a "sujet déchu" ("fallen subject"), stripped of all rights.[60] De Lagasnerie describes jouissance as the experience of those in power in withholding the information from the public, and that leaking therefore constitutes a narcissistic wound, which explains the (inexplicable) excessive and violent reaction to leakers.[61] The leaking event thus reveals multiple scenes, bodily and political, involving massive and fragmented texts that flood and overwhelm, and a monstrous regime and practices that hinge on the wrathful and the archaic from Foucault's Place de Grève to drone warfare.[62]

Edward Snowden is the computer consultant and whistleblower who provided Glenn Greenwald in June 2013 with a cache of NSA data that exposed the amplitude of the government surveillance system targeting not only suspects but ordinary citizens as well. Snowden, who now lives in juridical limbo in Russia, discovered when working with the CIA a "Strangelovian cyber warfare program in the works, codenamed MonsterMind."[63] It is said that General Keith Alexander, head of the NSA during the Snowden leaks and whose motto is "collect it all," acted like Jean-Luc Picard, having transformed his work space into the command deck of the *Enterprise*, endowed with an immense screen to enact the notion of 24/7 control and surveillance of the world.[64] This sci-fi fan and trekky, who invited visitors to sit in the "Picard chair," has also been represented as a "loose cannon" and a "cowboy."[65] For Alexander, a notion of space and cyberspace as a fictional and architectural utopia enabling the operation of total knowledge intersects with the narrative of the outlaw (cowboy, loose cannon) who cannot control his gun, his actions, and his amassing of data. In this context madness is no longer the characteristic of the "rogue agent" who snaps and leaks but rather the attribute of a government that is supposed to control its fantasies (violations, fluids, secrets) but is unable to do so.[66] To invoke the Lacanian axiom, it is thus the government agency that is unable to compromise its desire ("céder sur son désir"), and is thereby reduced to the compulsive grabbing and collecting of data. Thus two fictions of the outlaw emerge: the NSA (Alexander) that cannot cede its desire, and the whistleblower (Snowden) who cannot cede his desire to hack and leak. This is also tied to the digital compulsion to amass and store information, which is a condition of leaking, as Wendy Chun argues. Read at the intersection of US and Arab politics, leaking as overflow and scandalous excess collapses "monstrous" Arab despots—as we will see in the next chapter—with a "monstrous" system of total knowledge unable not to amass data and not to vindictively punish those who leak it. In both cases models of involuntarity, uncontainability, and compulsion transform the leaker into leaking in and leaking out, embodying yet simultaneously exposing the leaking fluids of power. The relation between Arab dictatorship and liberal democracy is porous. The leak in this case puts in question both material boundaries (bodies, geographies, regions) but also time and histories, undermining the narratives through which these models are produced or imagined as distinct and delineated (democracy versus dictatorship or rogue state). The leaking events expose the portals through which the bodies and fluids that connect these regions and temporality flow.

In *Containment Culture: American Narratives, Postmodernism, and the Atomic Age*, Alan Nadel reads the Cold War through the US rhetoric of containment, which turned the United States into "the universal container," both in its foreign and domestic policy but also in its "rhetorical strategy that functioned to foreclose dissent, preempt dialogue, and preclude contradiction."[67] Building on Lyotard's notion that "the power to produce knowledge exceeds the power to comprehend it," Nadel argues that "political power thus resides in containing the resulting surplus, and the name that Lyotard gives to the strategies of containment is *metanarratives*."[68] Nadel engages George Kennan's theory of containment, developed in a 1947 essay in *Foreign Affairs*, in which the latter coins the word "containment" by representing the Soviet personality as suffering from psychological disorder, but also, as Nadel argues, as being schizoid-like.[69] The schizoid bypasses individuation at the Lacanian mirror stage or through the Freudian Oedipal structure. The schizoid is reduced to nonindividuated limbs and fragments that never coalesce into a whole and coherent subject. Nadel situates "containment" in relation to the fluids of the "contradictory" flowing body that can only be contained. The strategy of containment treats the other as "Aristophanes' Lysistrata,"[70] and its only aim is to contain the contaminating flow of its leaks. Nadel continues that the Soviets, given this containment model, are akin to the orientalized Other suffering from gender and sexual fluidity that needs to be suppressed and closeted with its boundaries (and binaries) clearly marked. Drawing on Eve Sedgwick's *Epistemology of the Closet*, he writes: "In distributing the potentials for domination and submission, allegiance and disaffection, proliferation and self-containment, loyalty and subversion—all of which require clear, legible boundaries between Other and Same—the narrative of American cold war takes the same form as the narratives that contain gender roles."[71]

Despite the emergence of evidence regarding Assange's collusion with Russia starting in 2016, the leakers including Manning were already imagined and interpellated as leaking subjects given the Cold War model of containment that Nadel so brilliantly identifies. The inability to control one's body, contradiction, seduction, and gender disphoria are all staged in the practices and treatment of leakers that need to be isolated and contained through imprisonment, exile, or worse. Though Nadel focuses on the strategies of containment, I engage here the uncontainable leaking subject and the ways in which the fluids in need of containment end up exposing the impossible and fantasmatic attempt to contain them. The leak and the attempt to locate and stop the leak and its subjects expose the leakiness of the fiction of power or old fiction, which includes *adab* and *ta'dīb* in the context of Arab regimes, or the containment strategy and "know it all" fantasy in the NSA context. Invested in controlling and wiping spills and breaches, the attempts to contain Soviet body fluids and the revelations of contemporary leakers make a scene of the fiction and practices of power, exposing the porous boundaries of the liberal state as well as its ideology, vindictive practices, and archaic logic. This reveals a strategic continuity in deploying containment, both in the context of the Soviet Union and the contemporary Middle East, thereby connecting the Cold War on the one hand to the War on Terror and the two Gulf Wars on the other, thereby moving from the ideological conflict with the Soviets and communism to Islamic fundamentalism and terror, both represented as uncontainable and schizoid-like. The focus on the leakers' actions and justifications in this context helps to elucidate the political stakes of the leaking subject, who exposes the ways in which these fictions are produced, imagined as separate, and sustained through acts of war, containment, surveillance, torture, and imprisonment.

THE *WIKI* IN WIKILEAKS

In a 2012 *Rolling Stone* interview, Julian Assange stated that in addition to 9/11, which unleashed mass surveillance laws, "[t]he creation of WikiLeaks was, in part, a response to Iraq ... the clearest case, in my living memory, of media manipulation and the creation of a war through ignorance." Then he added: "The question is, where has the United States betrayed Madison and Jefferson, betrayed these basic values on how you keep a democracy? I think that the U.S. military-industrial complex and the majority of politicians in Congress have betrayed those values."[72] Assange displaces betrayal from the leaker to the leaked, from Manning to the US government, representing the latter as having betrayed its founders and spirit of the law. This betrayal extends to the functioning of the political structure (see, elections) that falls short of restoring the shattered ideal. In an interview with Google executives Eric Schmidt and Jared Cohen published in *When WikiLeaks Met Google*, Assange says: "You can have a lot 'change' in the United States but will it really change that much? Will it change the amount of money in someone's bank account? Will it change contracts? Will it change void contracts that already exist? And contracts on contracts? And contracts on contracts on contracts? Not really."[73] According to Assange, there needs to be a distinction between an ideal of justice tied to the founding of the liberal state and the US Constitution on the one hand, and an excess and perversion of that ideal through practices involving political corruption, extrajudicial incarceration, mass surveillance, and the violation of human rights on the other.[74] In this sense, leakers and whistleblowers in Assange's narrative are not consciously set on eliminating the law altogether but rather on exposing and making a scene of a compromised ideal or an unsettled symbolic that needs to be restored and reactivated. The perversion of the *roué* thus masks a true belief in a distorted ideal invested in forms of rights and freedoms.

Leaking as performance and event of revelation centered on the body exposes the rupture and the reaction to the rupture, ushers in extralegal practices, and reveals new (or old) fictions and definitions of the law and justice. Commenting on Manning's trial, Greenwald writes: "The government has insulated its conduct from what is supposed to be the legitimate means of accountability and transparency, judicial proceedings, media coverage . . . and has really erected this impenetrable wall of secrecy using what is supposed to be the institutions to prevent that. That's what makes whistleblowing all the more imperative; it really is the only remaining avenue that we have to learn what the government is doing . . . the only thing that shines light on what they're doing."[75] Describing Manning's actions, Greenwald says: "That's a whistleblower in the purest and most noble form: discovering government secrets of criminal and corrupt acts and then publicizing them to the world not for profit, not to give other nations an edge, but to trigger 'worldwide discussion, debates, and reforms.' "[76] According to Greenwald, the insistence on a properly functioning government has to revert to measures of last resort. The system's overflow with secrets and violations pushes subjects to commit acts of last resort, and then prosecutes them and tries to erase them when they do. Far from advancing a causal logic wherein the leaker or whistleblower, as Greenwald would suggest, is an idealist or hero as opposed to traitor, I argue that the event of leaking as exposure (*faḍḥ*) is both digital and political, voluntary and involuntary, and sets in motion a proliferation that could not be reduced retrospectively to an identifiable political narrative following the intentions of its "authors" and their stated political ideals.

Like *faḍḥ*, leaking is an act of last resort that is meant to restore a dysfunctional system or compromised ideal. WikiLeaks as well has been characterized as "publisher of last resort."[77] That said, this act of last resort needs to be aligned with a new condition of grabbing and leaking in the digital age tied to compulsion and involuntary actions as well. What needs to be emphasized is the event itself as it unfolds rather than a focus exclusively on the cause ("what caused the Arab Spring?") and the structure. It is important to investigate the scene of *faḍḥ* that involves compulsion and a digital condition as well as instances wherein people are pushed or coerced into acts of last resort where leaking takes place, as the examples from *The Arabian Nights* and Elmahdy demonstrate. In this context, the whistleblower/activist is the scene- or scandal-maker (*faḍḍāḥ*) who risks death and undergoes erasure as he/she confronts and exposes the withdrawal or erasure of the law. This double exposure of oneself and of the violation is staged in the act of leaking, and more specifically, in the act of whistleblowing in the case of Manning and Snowden. The excess of the reaction (expulsion, isolation, incarceration, juridical limbo, suppression) mimics the excess of the law that has gone beyond itself through "unlawful" acts. Leaking as a scene of *faḍḥ* occupies a space outside the law in order to confront yet reestablish the law as other, misrecognized, irredeemable. The act of leaking opens up a possibility for rethinking the law altogether and not simply restoring it to an ideal origin in the constitution of the liberal state. In this sense leaking moves beyond its justificatory narrative to produce its own meaning that could not be fully contained.

UNTAMING THE LEAK

The leak's power consists in the very act of revelation as violation against violation, rupture against rupture, which engulf character, author, reader, and story. Thus, we need to deconstruct the notion of the "new" in Zizek's "new Encyclopédie,"[78] and open it up to the power of *faḍḥ* (scandal, scene) as an affective and biopolitical fiction countering the fiction of the law, or the law as fiction such as *adab* in the Arab context. Leaking is not a process of showing and informing conducted by those who know how to enlighten those who lack knowledge or are in the dark. Rather, leaking consists in making a scene and exposing the inscriptions and perforations on leakers' bodies, as with the Lady Gaga CD, through their own gaping holes, which are pushed into spaces outside the system of knowledge altogether. As such, leaking cannot be controlled once set in motion. Leaking and whistleblowing subvert the legality of the law by exposing it and confronting it with its own violent and vindictive fiction—its fiction of origin of the state and of the self, or the fiction of modernity. Moreover, leaking introduces a condition of materiality that needs to be distinguished from the ideality of the law and the political more generally. Wael Abbas's quest for "real freedom" and "real democracy" explored in the next chapter, which is embodied in the mouth, in the tongue, and on the body, prevents us from considering leaks as the redemptive coalescing or the return of a healed subject finally in control of the needed information to awaken from his/her deep slumber. In trying to determine and fix the meaning of the leak—to direct it like an arrow in a political fight—Assange ignores the advent of models of consciousness and subjectivity that could not be sutured through a "redemptive" liberal moment in the digital age. The leak always operates through what Derrida calls "dévoiement," a straying movement and a leading astray of the narrative of power. In this respect leaking is both an act by individuals who often remain anonymous and also a text and fiction countering and exposing the fiction of power. The leak engulfs the leaker and exposes power's excessive, overflowing, tribal, religious, and fantasmatic fiction. Leaking as an event and as a text offers a new model for the way fiction interrogates the political in the digital age, exposing its unraveling rather than correcting its functioning. The leak is a perverse text, superfluous yet incriminating, decipherable yet untranslatable.

Leaking interpellates publics by forcing them to take account of that which they could be shielded from through traditional media. It interpellates people as spectators in a scene of *faḍḥ* in which they too become engulfed, sending videos of abuse to the YouTube channels set up by leakers and hackers. The public participates in the affective economy of the leak as contributors and avid consumers and readers who are shocked and titillated yet always following the leak. Quoting Zizek again: "We didn't really learn from Snowden (or from Manning) anything we didn't already presume to be true—but it is one thing to know it in general, and another to get concrete data."[79] "Concrete data" as *donnée*, as a material and affective "given" following Yuk Hui's opening quotation, is tied to the question of materiality that leaking makes possible, that the leak reveals as in the tale of "The Lady and Her Five Suitors," wherein the king becomes exposed and humiliated in the act of leaking. This concrete data is the data of *faḍḥ*, an affective scene anchored in the uncontainable body of the leaker who cannot but click, hack, write, respond, and violate in order to face the violation. This body becomes a bruised body but also a body that is pushed outside the law and its codifying power, coerced into liminal spaces such as embassies, airports, diaspora. As we saw in "The Steward's Tale," the leak is always coextensive with a story that needs to account for it, ushering in a new fictional order and "règles" that make this concrete data legible, allowing it to proliferate and go viral.

CONCLUSION

This chapter has established that leaking is a process tied to the body, which becomes a *site* and *sight* from which the fiction of the leak flows, exposing the fiction of power as vindictive, fantasmatic, monstrous. Whistleblowers are both anonymous and the new celebrities trapped in their fame, burnt, marked, harassed, imprisoned. Their hostage bodies need to be smuggled in and out of countries and across borders like the information they smuggle on CDs, zip drives, and videos. The body that exposes is dangerous and in danger. The leaker and whistleblower let knowledge out through pores and holes that stink and flow. The body cannot escape what it leaks. Therefore the leak is not excrement but rather that which marks the body and gives it meaning, determines its belonging and unbelonging, its location in jail or exile, and its gender. The question of gender is fundamental to the anxiety surrounding the leaking body both in terms of what it discharges and what it reveals, requiring an elaboration on the porous boundary between the sacred and the profane as a way of framing the subversive potential of the leak. This dovetails with the topics of women writing and harassment, with which I engage in the last two chapters of the book, in which anxiety about leaking and women's fiction is a key site for investigating the subversive economy of leaks with regard to gender roles and public participation, especially in the Gulf.

The leak brings the body into fiction and into a new economy of knowledge. To be informed in the digital age is to acquire the desire of the leak, which involves pleasure, pain, and horror. Information as leaks could not be fully comprehended, understood, and read. The leak thus draws on the literary yet contests its power of representation. There is a materiality in the leak that could never be subsumed in the figurative, demanding an investigation of bodies, ports, portals, and affect. Leaks are tied to fiction as stories and founding narratives yet could not be reduced to it, requiring an investigation that simultaneously engages the metaphorical and the material, thereby forcing us to rethink what fiction means in the digital age. Is the virtual the fictional, or does fiction designate a new order of reality and materiality in the digital age—a hyperreality perhaps? These are questions I take up throughout the book.

Leaking exposes an affective text that arrests and unsettles, countering its readers' fatigue and cynicism. Snowden wanted to "out" himself after leaking the documents to claim the act.[80] "I only have one fear in doing all of this," he said, "that people will see these documents and shrug, that they'll say, 'we assumed this was happening and don't care.' The only thing I'm worried about is that I do all this to my life for nothing."[81] The scandalous effect is not produced by the simple act of revealing the secret, which readers might already know, as Zizek claims, but rather by the scene that is made of this secret. "Shining light" on the revelation brings it into discourse in such a way that it outs the system itself. Thus, Snowden fears not being able to make a scene or enact the scandal (*faḍīḥa*), which requires a story and an affective scene that shake things up, as in outing the king who is locked up in the lady's cabinet in the tale from the *Nights*. When Greenwald got the first batch of leaked documents, he exclaimed: "My heart was racing. I had to stop reading and walk around my house a few times to take in what I had just seen and calm myself enough to focus on reading the files."[82] Provoking fear and excitement, the experience of reading the leak as "a major explosive story"[83] or "explosive revelation"[84] unsettles and fascinates. The fiction of the leak explodes and splinters, moves the body and triggers affects for both readers of the leak and the people translating and making those leaks legible and available, such as Greenwald or the journalists who worked for a year to decipher and translate the Panama Papers. This transfer of affects from leaker to reader, and from leaker to reporter to reader, is key in identifying an affective fiction that requires a reader-manual like the one Greenwald and other journalists provide by editing and covering the leaks in traditional media (newspapers, TV).

Making the heart race or causing a drop in blood pressure as Ahmed Naji's detractor claimed upon reading his text, *Using Life*, characterizes the effects of the narrative of the leak or leak as narrative that is both literary and material, producing affective reactions that shake and knock down. As biopolitics and fiction of scandal in the digital age, leaking unveils and exposes fictions of power across political and cultural contexts, from the United States to the Arab world. However, no longer restricted to ideological narratives of opposition, leaking emerges from the intolerance of abuse, the secretive, and the opaque. Unable to control and contain the leak, leakers are no longer authors in a text whose meaning they can define and control because leaking moves beyond the construction of the leaker as author, public intellectual, criminal, traitor, or hero, as we will see in the case of Wael Abbas. Wael's leaks and scene-making practices are inscribed on the body, in the mouth, bursting out as words and invectives, torture videos and images of abuse circulating online. These leaks arrest readers and interpellate them as consumers of scandal from which they are unable to turn away, making them read more, anticipate, follow.

CHAPTER 2

What Is in My Heart Is on My Twitter

To scandalize is a right. To be scandalized is a pleasure. And the refusal to be scandalized derives from a moralizing attitude.

—Pier Paolo Pasolini, interviewed by Philippe Bouvard, October 31, 1975

I usually don't like to talk about myself, but if you ask anyone who follows mainstream Egyptian media, you will only learn that I don't shower; that my ear is cut off; that I'm ill-mannered [*qalīl al-adab*]; that my parents didn't raise me well; that I'm queer; that I'm impotent; that I'm a loner; that I'm debauched and decadent; that I'm a drunk; that I'm a stoner; that I'm an atheist; that I'm an agent for pay; that I'm a sleeper cell; that I'm a member of the Muslim Brotherhood; that I'm a spy; that I work for Qatar; that I work for the US; that I'm on the run in London . . . and countless other filthy rumors.

—Wael Abbas, *Min Awrāq Nāshiṭ Ḥukūkī* ("From the Papers of a 'Scratchy Activist' ")

In April 2006, Wael Abbas—whose star as an activist was on the rise—participated in a solidarity protest organized by the Centre for Socialist Studies and by a number of political activists in solidarity with the basement dwellers of Imbaba [in Cairo]. Wael Abbas was a familiar figure to a number of these activists, including Khalid Abdul Hamid, who leaned over to Wael during the demonstration and said: "There are people who have something to show you." Abdul Hamid took him aside and introduced him to two Imbaba residents who showed him [on their phone] a short video of a police officer assaulting a fellow Imbaba resident. Wael copied the video via Bluetooth and uploaded it online. This was the first torture video to be posted on the Internet [in Egypt]; it shows an officer beating a citizen on his scruff, and thus the video became known as 'the scruff' [*al-qafā*].

—Ahmed Naji, *Al-Mudawwanāt min al-Būsṭ ilā al-Twīt* ("Blogs: From Post to Tweet")[1]

The exchange between Wael Abbas and the two demonstrators narrated in the quotation above characterizes the *exchange* of an illicit substance, threatening to the law and to those "trafficking" in it. The video transfer links two scenes: the exchange of an illegal substance at a demonstration in 2006 and a scene of abuse leaked on video. This exchange or transfer marks the moment that separates yet connects digital and analog, Bluetooth and Wi-Fi, and Internet and the street. It is this limit, transition, and connection that I examine in this chapter by exploring the ways in which the illicit and nondiscursive object leaked out of a police station is always already transferred and circulated, moving and producing its own audience. This process serves to create a new political consciousness or awareness, the exploration of which helps to frame the rise of the Arab activist blogger that I read as the leaking subject. This subject produces an affective textuality and imagery online that keeps the audience titillated, outraged, and informed. A new public and imagined community arises from these practices that break with the Andersonian model and the theorization of modernity centered around the novel, the author, and eventually, the intellectual speaking truth to power. New configurations of writing and critique, circulation and representation tied to the digital, are fully explored in what follows.

The most famous "Wael" to emerge from the Egyptian uprising of January 25, 2011, which led to the fall of President Hosni Mubarak, is Wael Ghonim, a Google executive who founded the "Kullena Khaled Said" (We Are All Khaled Said) Facebook page and helped support online organizing and communication before and during the uprising.[2] International media has focused on this upright, *mu'addab* (civil, respectful, well-mannered, polite) media executive who was detained by the police and is best remembered for his appearance on TV, crying and recanting his actions. The focus on Ghonim contributed to the perception of the Arab uprisings as Facebook and Twitter revolutions, granting social media the lion's share of responsibility in triggering and enabling a political movement that led to, initially, the toppling of autocrats across the region. This perception has also generated a counternarrative, namely that the uprisings were not at all *caused* by the Internet and new media at the service of "neoliberal" subjects such as Ghonim, but are in fact rooted in traditional activism led by unions and civil-society organizations, mobilizing against economic disenfranchisement and state corruption.[3] The social-media hypothesis and its refutation generated a false binary, deflecting from a critical investigation of the intertwinement of digital culture, new writing, and the critique of power emerging from sites and practices that are local and global, tied to online leaks and video uploads, and to the traditional practices of *faḍḥ* and scene-making both online and on the street.[4]

The lesser-known "Wael" (outside of Egypt, that is) is Wael Abbas (b. 1974), a human-rights activist and citizen journalist who founded in 2004 the blog *Al-Waʿī al-Miṣrī* ("Egyptian Awareness" or "Egyptian Consciousness") along with a YouTube channel, and in 2007 a Twitter account with over 300 thousand followers.[5] Wael, who is referred to as *qalīl al-adab* (ill-mannered, disrespectful, impolite, uncivil, rude, *roué*)[6] in the quotation above, was one of the first to capture and report on government violations, organizing protests and flash mobs from the mid-2000s onward, and taking and receiving videos of abuse and police brutality, which he would then post online, starting with "The Scruff" (*Al-Qafā*) in 2006, the same year that WikiLeaks was founded. Picking fights with authority figures and fellow activists alike, Wael swears and expresses himself in colloquial Egyptian, using an abrasive language characteristic of many bloggers.[7] During his coverage of a Kefaya protest in 2005 to which I will return in chapter 4, Abbas's blog received half a million hits in two days.[8] In 2009, he tweeted Barack Obama's speech at Cairo University as well as the election protests in Iran known as the Green Revolution. A fierce critic of Mubarak, the Muslim Brotherhood, but also of military rule and the 2013 coup that toppled the Brotherhood and brought Abdel Fattah al-Sisi to power, Wael has maintained a credibility that earned him the respect of his peers both locally and abroad. He has won many awards, including Human Rights Watch's Hellman/Hammett Award in 2008, and he was named Middle East Person of the Year by CNN in 2007, and "Blogger of the Year" by the BBC in 2006.

Wael confronts political figures and actively engages in slinging matches with rivals online, perfecting the art of invective and boast, and mixing a vehement human-rights activism with performative speech that spares no one. With the motto *illī fī albī ʿalā twītrī* ("what is in my heart is on my Twitter"), he tells it like it is, exposing in the process scenes of abuse through reports and videos. "Digitizing" the Arabic expression, "what is in my heart is on my tongue," which implies that one cannot but say what one feels, Wael presents Twitter as tongue- and heart-like. This direct link between the tongue, the heart, and Twitter denotes a relation of immediacy that unsettles the boundary between technology and its users, man and machine, turning social media into a body organ, and handheld devices into prostheses.[9] While transparency is traditionally framed as the demand and the right of the citizen of the liberal state to information, the transparency linking the heart and the tongue to Twitter arises from an inability to hold anything back, and from a digital condition and compulsion tied to constant checking, typing, and posting, starting with Wael's video *Al-Qafā* ("The Scruff") in 2006.[10] The relation between technological development on the one hand, and unscripted and almost involuntary speech and graphic content that violate the codes of *adab* (civility, propriety, manners, literature, culture) on the other, coincides with the movement of the uncontainable leak, or the leak as a default condition in the digital age. Political engagement thus needs to be read at levels involving body functions and the compulsion to say and show everything, to expose (*faḍḥ*) and be exposed (*mafḍūḥ*), and to scandalize and to be scandalized at the risk of one's own life.

Investigating the interplay of leaks and scene-making in Wael's posts and language, which are often decried or dismissed as vulgar and offensive, I problematize the charge of *qillat adab* (uncivil, disrespectful, impolite, rude), exploring it both as practice and performance that is amplified by new media technology yet coincides with, is grounded in, and arises from local, affective models of protest and contestation. Tracing a trail of invectives and bruises, torture videos and online attacks, I argue that the activist-blogger is no longer tied to the disciplining project (*ta'dīb*) of the liberal state discussed previously, or to the "lonely intellectual" speaking truth to power.[11] The *waʿī* (consciousness, awareness) generated by Wael's practices and confrontations is not that of the *mu'addab* (disciplined, docile, civil, respectful) and the intellectual/*adīb* (intellectual/author) in the public sphere who seeks to heal a fragmented subject and nation,[12] but rather the *waʿī* that captures and exposes a state of fragmentation that is both bodily and political, digital and narrative, emerging from the intersection of the Internet and the street, the body of the activist-blogger and that of tortured and abused people in leaked videos and images that circulate through his accounts online. It is the *waʿī* of the leaking subject—Wael's *waʿī miṣrī*—that moves and interpellates a new public who cannot turn away from the fiction of scandal.

WAEL ABBAS: *ADAB* VIOLATIONS

When the Tahrir uprising erupted in Egypt in January 2011, proregime commentators on TV referred to protestors as "ill-mannered kids" (*awlād qalīlīn al-adab*), inquired about their parents, and ordered them to return home. This characterization betrayed an anxiety about the gradual erosion of the legitimacy of a regime sustained through forms of coercion, censorship, and faux *adab*. In this light Paul Amar argues that "a human-security governance regime . . . aim[s] to protect, rescue, and secure certain idealized forms of humanity identified with a particular family of sexuality, morality, and class subject."[13] Particularly, the discourse of *adab* as fiction of power, civility, cultural production, and law abidance that has operated as the backbone of Arab authoritarianism, systematically deployed to stifle dissent, is sustained through a security governance regime that still draws on morals and *adab* to legitimize its power. This discourse, though it could be traced to classical *adab* or belletrism,[14] emerges most directly from a *Nahda* civilizing project best captured by Butrus al-Bustani's 1859 speech on *adab* and its plural, *ādāb*, defined as the series of developments in education and cultural production meant to forge the civilized—and civil—subject of the modern nation-state, namely the *mu'addab*.[15] Marwa Elshakry argues that *adab* "literature" in the nineteenth century "came to imply new norms of civility and a new kind of moral science,"[16] while "*tarbiya*" became a "national domestic order" that leads to "the production of healthy, hygienic, well-behaved, moral, and productive subjects."[17] Eventually, *adab* crystalized with Taha Hussein in the twentieth century as a literary canon but also as a framework for the production of the *mu'addab* and *adīb*, the enlightened and docile subject of the *Nahda*, and its intellectual and author respectively.[18]

The violation of *adab* as "literature," culture, and morality but also as civility in Norbert Elias's sense[19] gradually became the ground for excluding authors and activists from public discourse, banning their books, and incarcerating them. In 1966, Yehya Haqqi's critique of Sonallah Ibrahim's *Tilk al-Rā'iḥa* (*That Smell*) for its violation of the codes of *adab* contributed to the withdrawal of the book from circulation.[20] In *Egypt's Culture Wars: Politics and Practice*, Samia Mehrez discusses a series of cases involving Egyptian state intervention to suppress "indecent literature," engaging Sonallah Ibrahim's confrontation with the regime of moralistic censorship under then-minister of culture Faruq Husni.[21] In 2015, the case brought against author and blogger Ahmed Naji, which alleged that his novel *Using Life* violated public morality (*khadsh al-ḥayā'*,[22] a violation of *adab* codes) for its graphic content, causing a reader palpitations from a drop in blood pressure, reactivated this deployment of *adab* as *ḥayā'* or *tahdhīb* (disciplining), namely that which ought to govern writing, speech, and behavior. While *adab* became an ideological model for the fiction of power, providing it with symbolic legitimacy to control literary and cultural production, *ādāb al-'āmma* (public morality)[23] became the gauge that allowed states to intervene in *adab*'s name, such as in Naji's case.

Whereas *adab* has been identified as the handmaiden of power, *qillat adab*, or what Emily Apter refers to in a different context as "fiction mal élevée,"[24] has been marginalized, shunned, and excluded. The violations of the codes of *adab* or *qillat adab* (incivility, rudeness, disrespectfulness) are affective texts and performances that could be traced to scenes of *faḍḥ* as scandal and public shaming, and *radḥ* (verbal mudslinging) to name a few.[25] From the vulgar mudslinging in Egyptian movies to camp as entertainment in a larger context, these unruly affects of *qillat adab* have been traditionally sidelined as working-class and/or gendered phenomena that could be suppressed whenever it suited the regime, or decried when erupting in texts such as Naji's, leading to censorship if not incarceration. "Such scenes," argues Edward Said, "are often dismissed as catering to some vague mass cult (of voyeurism? lower-class sensationalism?)."[26] In the context of the Egyptian uprising in 2011, Elliot Colla analyzed the use of insults in protestors' slogans, reading this *qillat adab* as "a political weapon [striking] at the legitimacy and rectitude of the powerful."[27] Colla argues that these insults could not be reduced to a linguistic analysis, and thus require a theoretical framework engaging with performance studies, and, I would add, affect theory.

Going back and forth between the street and social media, the poetics and affective economy of insult, *qillat adab*, and *faḍḥ* have found in cyberstreams and circuits the ideal habitus through which they burst out in fights and mudslinging matches, but also through graphic and inappropriate content leaked and posted online. The proliferation of *qillat adab* as inappropriate, graphic, or offensive content marks a loss of control that exposes leaky boundaries, both political and bodily. *Qillat adab* as I define it denotes the practice and the condition of the leaking subject that is itself breached, uncontainable, and leaking from the "heart to Twitter," thereby exposing the leaking of power's legitimizing fiction. This subject is constituted by affective scene-making (*faḍḥ*), and often compulsive actions and reactions, thereby requiring new conceptual tools for explaining political confrontation in the digital age.

EQUALITY IN INSULT

In addition to posting videos of abuse and exposing human-rights violations, Wael Abbas is the go-to person for confronting regime figures and supporters, insulting them and revealing their hypocrisy. Courageous and aggressive, Wael perfected the *kussumak* (literally, motherfucking) insult in his online exchanges, ushering in a poetics of invective that could be traced to Naguib Surur's *Kussumiyyāt*, the unpublished expletive-filled poem that exposed social and political corruption under Nasser following the Arab defeat against Israel in 1967.[28] Examining *qillat adab* in this context helps to explain the kind of political subjectivity associated with the subject leaking from the heart to the tongue to Twitter.

In the tweets in figure 2, Wael deploys his signature *kussumak* to advance what we may consider a theory and praxis of insult, expounding on its political and legal significance. He claims the right to insult the Muslim Brotherhood, who were about to come to power, just as he had insulted other political figures and groups before them. Foreshadowing the 2013 coup and the ensuing Rabʿa massacre, Wael's tweets imply that *shatm* (insulting, swearing) is the condition of the Muslim Brotherhood's entry into the political arena, hence denying them any appeal to the sacred. This exchange debunks the secular/religious binary as the framework often used to explain Arab politics. Wael engages the Brothers as equal subjects in a new political process predicated on *shatm*. In this framework the production of the political subject requires an act of desacralization wherein nothing is taboo, from insulting the mother to insulting the imam. "To insult and be insulted" ushers in equality that turns the vulgar and uncivil confrontation online into a political system of exchange that the Brothers "better get used to." The aesthetics and politics of *shatm* in this case remove political subjectivity from a false binary maintained by the regime (Mubarak's and al-Sisi's) through the slogan: "It's either me or the Brotherhood," namely a choice between "stability" and "chaos." This binary relies on an artificial opposition between the ideological narrative of the state upholding *adab*, discipline, and Arab nationalism as tamed speech and fiction of power on the one hand, and Islamism as this narrative's imagined (and orientalized) Other.[29] Breaking with this binary, *qillat adab* emerges in Wael's case as the framework for a political engagement involving the leaking mouth and heart of the abrasive blogger, circulating videos and images of abuse online and engaging in slinging matches with fellow bloggers and rivals.

The right to insult and be insulted in Wael's case involves not only the right to free speech finally achieved after the fall of Mubarak, i.e., it's not a political right acquired after the redemptive revolutionary event of January 25. The right to insult is constitutive of political subjectivity through affective speech. Jokingly, blogger and activist Nawara Negm, who spars with Wael online, captures this affective quality of insult, which counters the cooptation of the activist as *adīb* or *muthaqqaf* (intellectual).

Wael إقَندي Abbas @waelabbas 22 Mar

انا شتمت حسني مبارك والبرادعي وأيمن نور وحمدين صباحي !!! مش هاعرف اشتم شيخ ابن متناكة براحتي ؟؟؟ ياخي أحه !!!

Wael إقَندي Abbas @waelabbas 22 Mar

احنا بتوع سياسة وبنشتم في بعض على طول ومتعودين لما بتوع الدين يتحشروا في السياسة ما يزعلوش بقى لما نشتم كس أمهم ولا على راس كس أمهم ريشة ؟؟؟

Wael إقَندي Abbas @waelabbas 22 Mar

إني أرى 1954 جاية تاني والعسكر ها يدبح في الإسلاميين ويركب تاني والإسلاميين الوحيدين اللي فاكرين نفسهم أقويا وكلنا ها نتناك في النهاية !!!

Wael إقَندي Abbas @waelabbas 21 Mar

المساواة في الشتيمة عدل ومحدش كبير على الشتيمة وعلشان كده كس ام الاخوان المسلمين تاني ! اتعودوا بقى !

Wael إقَندي Abbas @waelabbas 21 Mar

عاوز اقولكم كس ام الاخوان المسلمين مش علشان حاجة بس علشان يتعودوا عالشتيمة زيهم زي غيرهم!

Figure 2. Wael Abbas tweets in Arabic and translation. Wael Abbas, March 6, 2012, https://twitter.com/waelabbas.

I insulted Hosni Mubarak and [Muhammad] el-Baradei and Ayman Nour and Hamdeen Sabahi!!! Now I'm not allowed to insult a son-of-a-bitch imam as I please??? Fuck that!!!

We who do politics insult each other all the time and we're used to it. When those who do religion stick their noses into politics let them not get upset when we insult their fucking mother's cunt [*kussumuhum*], or is their mother's cunt holier than thou???

I see 1954 happening again and the military will slaughter and fuck over the Islamists who now think they're so strong, and in the end we're all gonna get screwed!!!

Equality in insult is justice and no one is above insult, and because of this I say motherfucking [*kussum*] Muslim Brothers again! Get used to it already!

I want to say motherfucking [*kussum*] Muslim Brothers for no reason other than to get them used to insult like everyone else!

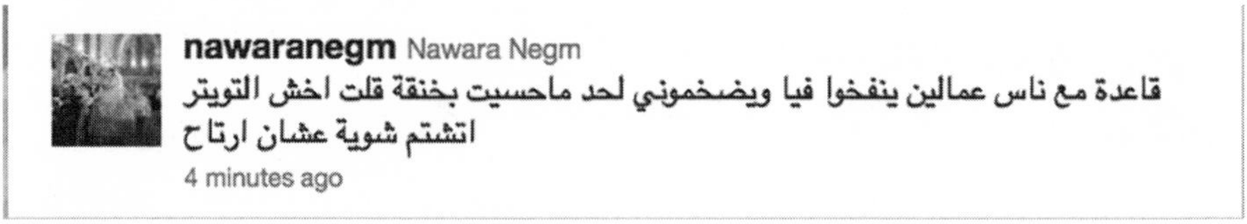
nawaranegm Nawara Negm
قاعدة مع ناس عمالين ينفخوا فيا ويضخموني لحد ماحسيت بخنقة قلت اخش التويتر اتشتم شوية عشان ارتاح
4 minutes ago

Figure 3. Nawara Negm tweet and translation. See Nawara Negm, May 28, 2011, https://twitter.com/nawaranegm. For a brief biography of Negm, see http://thecairopost.youm7.com/news/9683/wiki/nawara-negm.

> I was hanging out with people who kept inflating and boosting me so much so that I felt stifled, so I thought I'd go on Twitter to get insulted to feel relieved [*artāḥ*].

In the tweet in figure 3, the practice of *shatm* deflates, relieves (*artāḥ*), and brings someone back to her correct size. *Shatm* in Nawara's tweet as well becomes a form of desacralization that interrupts the transformation of the activist-blogger into spokesperson, figurehead, and icon. *Shatm* keeps it real. The position of the intellectual as *muthaqqaf* or *adīb* in Taha Hussein's model or in that of the revolutionary hero turned media expert is subverted through these exchanges and confrontations. The intellectual as embodying the conscience of the nation[30] and whose demise Zeina G. Halabi theorizes,[31] makes way for the blogger or tweeter who exposes affectively the discursive production of "the intellectual" through *adab* and *taʾdīb*. Attacking and knocking down the other as in a street fight, the vulgar and uncivil blogger "un-performs"—or, to use Halabi's term, "unmakes"[32]—the *muthaqqaf* (intellectual). Unable and unwilling to claim an *adab*-centered moral high ground, activists who insult and are insulted confront the abuses, hypocrisy, and violations that they witness and in the face of which they cannot remain silent. This "inability to remain silent" as in the hacking example discussed in the introduction, links in Wael's case the heart to the tongue to Twitter through an economy of affective immediacy.

Wael's performance as loose tongue, equal opportunity offender, and exposer and critic of power is captured in a hashtag aimed at discrediting him. The hashtag, which was started on Twitter in September 2013 and is entitled, "What do you know about Wael Abbas?,"[33] gathered hundreds of comments, with people both praising and insulting him.

The tweets in figure 4 reinforce the perception of Wael as an insulter who does not distinguish between parties as long as they deserve and need to be insulted. The *shatm,* however, is not only a gauge for the righteousness of the critique but also for the ability to engage in a new exchange practice predicated

بحب شتايمه فشخ >> بتشفي الصدور حقيقي وبتجيب المفيد م الاخر وع بلاطه يعني 😂
#ماذا_تعرف_عن_وايل_عباس

A royally profane brazen brute schizo with a filthy but credible tongue who loves cats and whom I actually respect #ماذا_تعرف_عن_وايل_عباس

#ماذا_تعرف_عن_وايل_عباس احمد فؤاد نجم النثر للعصر..مش ضرورى تكون موافقه 100% ولا اى انسان حولك ممكن توافقه بالنسبه دى.. عيبه ..عاملى بلوك!

#ماذا_تعرف_عن_وايل_عباس المثقف صاحب أطول لسان 😬 اللي بيختلف مع الاخوان لكن بيدافع عن مظلومهم ممكن تختلف معاه لكن في النهايه#دكر بالصعيدي

دايما بيشتم بس الصراحه اللي بيشتمهم يستاهلوا الشتيمه 😂 #ماذا_تعرف_عن_وايل_عباس

#ماذا_تعرف_عن_وائل_عباس الاخوان بيشتموه والسيساوية بيشتموه و ده في حد ذاته يخليني أتأكد انه صح

Figure 4. Series of tweets in Arabic (with emojis) with hashtag "What do you know about Wael Abbas?" July 2015, https://twitter.com/hashtag/%D9%85%D8%A7%D8%B0%D8%A7_%D8%AA%D8%B9%D8%B1%D9%81_%D8%B9%D9%86_%D9%88%D8%A7%D8%A6%D9%84_%D8%B9%D8%A8%D8%A7%D8%B3?src=hash.

I fucking love his insults. They really relieve the chests [*bitshaffi al-ṣudūr*] and get straight to the point [*ʿa balāṭa*].

Ahmad Fuad Negm of prose in this age … you don't have to agree with him 100% for you can't agree with anyone to such extent … his only fault … is that he blocked me.

The intellectual [*muthaqqaf*] with the sharpest tongue [*aṭwal lisān*] who disagrees with the Muslim Brothers but defends those among them who are treated unjustly. You can disagree with him but in the final tally he is a real man [*dakar*].

He's always insulting someone but honestly those he insults deserve to be insulted.

The Muslim Brothers insult him and so do al-Sisi supporters, a fact that confirms to me that he's in the right.

on equality in insult. To insult and be insulted implies entering the rink wherein the courageous Wael can distinguish himself and gain and confer legitimacy, thereby recoding the rules of *adab*, debate, and political subjectivity based on a new sense of morality and consciousness. The critic and activist fights like a *dakar* ("real man" in the primordial and visceral sense), both in reference to his principled position and to his aggression and readiness for street fighting. Vulgar and abrasive speech in this case operates both as critique of power and subversion of traditional models of political legitimacy sustained by *adab* both as a narrative of power and as a practice of civility.

One tweet depicts Wael as "the intellectual with the sharpest tongue" (*aṭwal lisān*) or, more precisely, "foulest mouth." Moving from the pen (of the *adīb*) to the tongue or the mouth (of the blogger), Wael is thus "the intellectual" who violates the codes of civility or *adab* as speech and fiction of power, thereby introducing a new poetics and politics of confrontation. The blogger is an insulter who fights, exposes, blocks, and humiliates, yet vindicates in the process.[34] Wael's *shatm* goes straight to the "heart" both as body part that is either wounded, broken, or relieved, and to the "heart of the matter" (*'abalāṭa*), emphasizing the blow that knocks someone on the ground in a moment of exposure, leaving nothing veiled, hidden, suppressed, unsaid. The tongue, the mouth, and the heart function as semi-autonomous entities that are associated with the blogger yet are not reduced to an identifiable intellectual narrative of opposition that would reify him/her. The different body parts do not coalesce into a coherent whole but offer instead leaking portals from which words, insults, and videos burst out and overwhelm opponents and spectators.

The practice of insulting moves the audience affectively, transforming the engagement into a spectacle involving curse words and blows. Watching Wael insult political figures leads to vindication (*shafī al-ṣudūr*, but also *tashaffī* or *shafī al-ghalīl*), which relieves one's chest, where the heart is, producing both a deep fulfillment as in Nawara Negm's "*artāḥ*," and enacting the humiliation of rivals and regime supporters. Wael moves his followers because he has the power to relieve them and give them pleasure rather than simply expressing their views. He provides them with a sense of comfort and takes revenge by exposing and beating up the opponent on their behalf, or even blocks them if he so chooses. As he attacks and exposes himself to attack, he renders the audience's position tenuous, never stable or outside the fray.[35] This dialectic of *shatm*, which operates affectively, places Wael in the position of the vindicator and defender of the one who is treated unjustly (*maẓlūmhum*) regardless of his or her political affiliation. Taking matters into one's own hands thus involves violent encounters, "doing justice," and a truth-telling that recodes the truth of the intellectual speaking it to power.

Wael's performance online and the way it is perceived in this hashtag conjure up a form of street confrontation that needs to be distinguished from that of the *balṭagī* (thug) who takes the law into his own hands, beating up and bullying others.[36] *Balṭagiyya* (thugs) have become infamous in the reporting on the Arab uprisings, designating the regime's henchmen unleashed to intimidate and beat up demonstrators. In Wael's case, the form of vindication needs to be aligned with the actions of the neighborhood *futuwwa* (the strong and courageous one) who defends the weak from the attack of the bullies yet is as violent and aggressive as the latter. He is also the *faḍḍāḥ* or *faḍḍāḥa* at the same time, the street scene-maker, a role often performed by a woman in a working-class context, physically attacking and insulting rivals, shaming them for all to see, often as a means of last resort.[37] This scene-making involves acts of violence by stepping outside the law in a vindicating and affective spectacle made up of performers and audience.

The intersection of *faḍḥ* as a critique of power and as a fighting style online is best captured in Wael's fight with activist Nawara Negm in 2011, which unfolded both online and off. After a raging slinging match where she threw her shoe at him, they moved to Twitter, where everything was fair game including insulting the parents. Once done, Wael declared: "We are now satisfied with this amount of *sharshaḥa* [humiliation, exposure, insulting, scene-making]," and added immediately afterwards and in English: "my feminine side."[38] The *dakar*-like fighter online with a "feminine side" alludes to a model of street fighting that involves invective and scene-making. This characteristic is emphasized by one of Wael's detractors, who says: "It's like hiring a woman to make a scene for a man, that's what Wael does."[39] This observation, meant to embarrass the activist and human-rights defender, captures the class and gendered aspect of *faḍḥ*, thereby revealing another scene of confrontation that has been deployed in fights online against rivals and regime figures.

In Wael's case the practice of *faḍḥ*, as in the leaking event discussed in the previous chapter, is anchored in the body, recoding the construction of the subject along a particular *Nahda* or modernity narrative, both in the European context and in the Arab world. This reconfiguration of subjectivity, which coincides with an exposure of the fiction of power, subverts gender codification and ethical codes. The unpredictable scene of *faḍḥ* leads to the rethinking of the liberal narrative that considers the Arab uprisings as a redemptive act and a restoration of a democratic ideal in line with *Nahda* principles. It also unsettles the model of interpellation through processes of education, disciplining, morality, and gender and sexual codification. The possibility of change lies precisely in the unraveling of the familiar and recognizable liberal model of the state–citizen relation, mediated by discourses of power theorized by Foucault or Althusser. In this light the Arab uprisings activated and multiplied the sites of collapse and exposure (*faḍḥ*) of the fiction of power and of its ability to interpellate.

EXPOSURE, SCENE-MAKING, SCANDAL

In Arabic grammar, *faḍḥ* (exposure) is a verbal noun, i.e., a noun that has the power of the verb. The *Oxford English Dictionary* defines "exposure," the English equivalent to *faḍḥ*, as: "The action of exposing; the fact or state of being exposed.... The action of uncovering or leaving without shelter or defence; unsheltered or undefended condition.... The action of bringing to light (something discreditable); the unmasking or 'showing up' of an error, fraud, or evil, of an impostor or secret offender.... *Indecent exposure*, the action of publicly exposing one's body in an indecent manner.... The action of bringing to public notice; the condition of being exposed to the attention of the general public, publicity."[40] In *Lisān al-ʿArab*, Ibn Manzur defines *faḍḥ* as the act of "exposing a misdeed."[41] Ibn Manzur emphasizes the visual aspect of *faḍḥ*, comparing it to "the sudden advent of morning light that exposes (as in exposure to light) the true shape, color, and contours of an object."[42] So the object becomes known in the moment of *faḍḥ* but also *faḍīḥa* (scandal, scene), which could be a scene online or a street scene involving a gathering crowd, as in Wael and Nawara's fight. This scene involves body language, gestures, anxiety, and fear of being engulfed by the scene itself, which could leave one damaged or dead.

Faḍḥ is often associated with the power of the slighted and the disenfranchised who, with no recourse to a system of justice, use their body to stake a claim. For instance, in the film adaptation of Naguib Mahfouz's *Miramār*, a slighted lover, Safiyya, makes a scene (*faḍīḥa*) for Sarhan after she learns that he took advantage of her, betrayed her, and left her for another woman.[43] Showing up at the hotel where he is staying and peforming her scene as an embodied *faḍḥ* in front of everyone including Sarhan's new girlfriend, Safiyya humiliates him publicly and leaves, saying at the end: "*Immā warrītak*" (I will show you!), thereby threatening him with more scenes and retributions in the future. Exposed and humiliated, Sarhan then explains to the audience of the scene that he had had a relationship with Safiyya but it ended, and that she had come "*tishahhar fiyya ʿashān akhāf min al-faḍīḥa wa-argaʿ lahā tānī*" (to slander me so I fear the scandal and get back to her). In response, Mariana, the hotel owner says: "*di vulgera khālis, kwayyis matgawizztūsh*" (she's a very vulgar woman; I'm glad you didn't get married). Expressions like "you will see" (*ḥatshūf*) and "I will show you" (*immā warrītak*) situate the performance of *faḍḥ* in a visual scene, a drama that unfolds through gestures, invectives, and body postures. The *faḍḥ* performance of the "vulgar woman" is raw and violent as it exposes a violation that is not acknowledged and that could not be acknowledged—seen and shown—except through another violation, a physical performance of *faḍḥ* that brings the violation to light and makes it legible and scandalous simultaneously.

The class- and gender-inflected space of the "vulgar" in the narrative of modernity and its rules of "civilized" engagement is rehabilitated and reappropriated in the culture of scene-making, mudslinging, and leaks online. These *faḍḥ* practices expose abuse, torture, and violation that are unseen, dismissed, or unacknowledged by systems of justice, both legal and patriarchal. Wael's *faḍḥ* makes something legible by bringing it to the attention of others in a spectacle of invectives and exposure, fights with rivals and videos of abuse online. Crossing gender codes, he is both the *dakar* (real man) and the "vulgar" *faḍḍāḥa* (scene-making woman). *Faḍḥ* in Wael's case is not only an act of last resort but also a condition tied to the inability not to swear and make a scene, not to respond or answer back as his tongue is tied to his heart and Twitter.[44] Thus, *faḍḥ* is a powerful weapon that could be used to confront and expose violations but also to slander and expose others. In fact, *faḍḥ* has been used as a form of "shameful outing" linked to nakedness and homosexuality in club- and hamam-arrest scandals from Cairo to Beirut.[45] The *faḍḥ* in this case is turned into a normative weapon in the hand of state actors or media outlets in order to extol the virtues of *adab* through a scandalous story that everyone follows on TV, in newspapers, and online. Just like leaks, *faḍḥ* is not intrinsically and consistently the weapon of the disenfranchised. Rather, it produces a dangerous space of possibility, rendering those engaging in it vulnerable, subject to attack and injury, physically and emotionally exposed, yet providing new trajectories for thinking critique, confrontation, and reception.

An affective economy of blogging and tweeting helps explain the dialectic of insulting and being insulted, exposing and being exposed, blocking followers and rivals yet bringing them into the fray. This economy shapes the political landscape enabled by social media yet remains rooted in Arab and Egyptian cultural models and poetics. Situating Wael and other bloggers' practices within this context of protest and its corresponding genres, which we see in Mahfouz's novels and filmic adaptations, for instance, allows us to connect exchanges online tied to digital technology and compulsion on the one hand, to traditional forms of confrontation on the other, thereby moving back and forth between the street and the Internet, the novel and Twitter, and local cultural practices and scandal.com culture.

AFFECTIVE TRANSPARENCY

In his discussion of the rise of political blogging in Egypt in the mid-2000s, Ahmed Naji captures the affective and scene-making quality of blogging. He states that the first political blogs to appear were in 2003, the same year that the United States invaded Iraq.[46] Listing their characteristics, Naji writes:

> Excitability [*infiʿāliyya*]: unlike the press and media, which pretend to be neutral and objective, the blogger eschews neutrality, and more often than not leaves more room for his emotional outbursts [*infiʿālāt*]. For this reason blogs such as Malek [Mustafa's][47] shocked [*ṣadamat*] many readers, and brought the issue of sexual harassment to the spotlight. If this incident were to be published in a neutral, impassive language it would have turned into an insignificant news item relegated to the miscellaneous-events page [of a newspaper].[48]

Naji characterizes the excitability (*infiʿāliyya*) and affectivity of blogs as that which distinguishes them from traditional print media. Blogs, according to Naji, "knock down," "deliver a blow," or "shock" (*taṣdum*). Capturing street fighting and confrontation, the language of bloggers, who are often activists themselves, emerges from physical encounters with police at demonstrations, suggests Naji.[49] He makes the link between these encounters and the language and content of the bloggers' posts, as if arguing for a transfer of affects that moves from the street to the online space and back, shaping and recoding cybercommunication and circulation. Bloggers' affective content brings together action (*fiʿl*)[50] and outburst (*infiʿāl*) in an emotive economy that invests the digital text with intensity and the force to act, expose, and make a scene. The blogger's words burst out and knock down as they are expressed or forwarded, generating other actions and reactions. Naji's excitability and affectivity thus reproduce the inside and make it visible as language and story that grab and draw in the audience. The message of the text acts violently upon the reader; when the text comes on the screen, the reader "gets the message." The affective power of blogs as digital texts thus emerges from the space that separates yet connects the Internet and the street, the digital arena and its corresponding reality, and the story reported and the events that make up the story as such.

A key player in this early wave of blogging, Wael cannot hold anything back; he is breached, leaking speech, images, and videos. Keeping in mind his motto ("what is in my heart is on my Twitter"), all that is inside not only makes its way to Wael's Twitter feed but must unavoidably do so. In Wael's case the relation between the heart and Twitter is not only sufficient but necessary. The blogger is no longer external to the medium through which ideas take shape. The origin of the digital contribution has shifted from the mind to the heart and the tongue, from the traditional site of thought to the "unruly" site of emotions and outbursts amplified by new technology.[51] The heart, this now "involuntary" or loose organ (or "cannon") no longer associated with the romantic narrative of subjectivity, becomes part of an affective political engagement, leading one to read incivility simultaneously with truthfulness as that which is in the heart yet leaks out of it through a new circuitry and ports. The medium itself becomes incorporated into an economy rooted in uncontrollable body organs (heart, tongue, mouth), collapsing the boundary between the inside and the outside, the body and the digital, the blogger and the blog.

In *Excitable Speech: A Politics of the Performative*, Judith Butler problematizes the relation between speech and the body, engaging the question of interpellation and subjectivation involved in hate speech, injurious speech, and naming.

> In the law, "excitable" utterances are those made under duress, usually confessions that cannot be used in court because they do not reflect the balanced mental state of the utterer. My presumption is that speech is always in some ways out of our control. . . . Untethering the speech act from the sovereign subject founds an alternative notion of agency and, ultimately, of responsibility, one that more fully acknowledges the way in which the subject is constituted in language, how what it creates is also what it derives from elsewhere. Whereas some critics mistake the critique of sovereignty for the demolition of agency, I propose that agency begins where sovereignty wanes. The one who acts (who is not the same as the sovereign subject) acts precisely to the extent that he or she is constituted as an actor and, hence, operating within a linguistic field of enabling constraints from the outset.[52]

Butler's formulation offers a key framework for distinguishing sovereignty and agency in the formation of the subject. She argues that even the speech that is "out of our control" still emerges from within preexisting apparatuses, discourses, and power. Political subjectivity operates through models of interpellation that exceed the speech of the sovereign subject. Wael's model of immediacy, captured by his motto and practices online, frames the emergence of a new political subjectivity wherein equality is *shatm* (insulting). In this context affective performances of scene-making could not be reduced to the processes of interpellation that constrain and prefigure the speaking subject. Wael Abbas's model, which ties in tongue, heart, chest, and screen, privileges emotion, action, outbursts, confrontation, and body parts acting in unison and independently, leaking in and out, releasing content and making online followers (the public) feel vindicated and comforted but also threatened and overwhelmed. Though subjectivity as a narrative is always already tied to discursive practices, historicity, and state apparatuses, the leaking subject emerging from the digital and street context that I explore in this book emerges from processes of viral circulation, the disjointedness and unsuturing of the subject that misrecognizes itself and is misrecognized through speech acts and address, introducing the digital as constituting streams and body parts that operate interchangeably with the leaking subject made up of tongue, heart, chest, and Twitter.

In Wael's case the model of transparency that shows the inside and targets the inside of others (their heart, chest, etc.) leads us to read the relation between the heart and Twitter as that which bypasses the mind as the site of editing, taming, and containment. This taming is encapsulated by such expressions as *lisānak ḥiṣānak, in ṣuntuh ṣānak* ("loose lips sink ships"), which is at the basis of an idealized civil debate (*adab*) and model of communication (*adabiyyāt).* Bypassing the mind as the site of control if not censorship, and breaking with the decorum and discipline of the imagined national narrative, Wael untames the tongue (*lisān*) (or lips) to perform *infiʿāliyya* (excitability, affectivity) in speech, reporting, and political engagement. In the process Wael owns, if not fully embodies, the social medium now referred to as *twītrī*, "my Twitter," akin to the heart and other body parts. In this sense Wael and bloggers more generally no longer "use" the Internet but are in fact constitutive of it, while it becomes constitutive of them as they are connected to it through screens, handheld devices, tongues, hearts, circuits, ports, and connections (Bluetooth, Wi-Fi, etc.). The collapse between the machine and the user, which we will see in the context of Mujtahidd and Twitter in chapter 3, removes the Internet and social media from the register of Western tools and inventions that are then exported eastward or southward, according to a particular narrative of borrowing from the West, importing Western products, or translating or adapting Western culture. Wael and his fellow bloggers are not agents of the West or modern subjects using Western tools, but rather embody cyberspace and reproduce its functions including scene-making and revelation, thereby marking the advent of new forms of immediacy and subjectivity that need to be theorized on their own terms. In the case of Wael, this immediacy or transparency is constitutive of *qillat adab* as the exposure of so-called graphic and inappropriate content that not only violates the codes of *adab* but also shows a radical inside tied to the body of the blogger, to the bodies of those whose pain and torture he/she exposes, and to the bodies of those who follow Wael and share his images, videos, and insults.

The affectivity that recodes body parts (tongue, heart, mouth, lips, chest) by removing them from traditional narratives of subjectivity ushers in an "affective transparency" as in a spectacle or street scene. What Wael exposes is regulated by the compulsion of clicking and sharing pictures, posting, responding, and insulting, but also by the reaction of the activist who cannot see injustice and keep his mouth shut and lips tight. Political engagement and activism emerge from traditional means of organizing and civil-society work, including the Kefaya movement, with which Wael was associated, but also from this inability to stay silent or keep one's tongue and fingers tucked in, and from the inability not to click, respond, comment, share, or forward. This political and digital compulsion involving the values and practices of the tough guy (*dakar, futuwwa*) and scene-maker (*faḍḍāḥ/a*) on the one hand, and the affectivity of blogs on the other, contributes to an economy of exposure and confrontation that vindicates, relieves, comforts, and gives pleasure.

The interplay between political affects and the involuntary and the vulgar could not be collapsed with a model of transparency in the liberal sense, reduced to the end of political corruption or to the suspension of the emergency laws in Egypt as the uprising of 2011 was meant and expected to achieve. Nor can it be fully interpreted through the Foucauldian lens of discursivity and the linguistic turn more generally. Instead, the affective transparency practiced by Wael and others creates openings and shows something that could only be exposed by violating the law as an extension of the fiction of power. This transparency is tied to what Wael calls "real freedom" and "real democracy," namely a series of practices that deterritorialize and reterritorialize "freedom" and "democracy."[53] Affective transparency becomes a new mode of showing and seeing the inside (heart, chest), and of showing and seeing, as in "I will show you!" and "You wait and see!," which are threats of exposure, of scene-making, and of physical violence. This new seeing and showing also remove us from the model of ocularcentricity and the economy of the gaze discussed in the introduction; ultimately, these practices produce and arise from a new *waʿī miṣrī* (Egyptian consciousness or awareness) that recodes the relation between consciousness and subjectivity, publics and texts.

DIGITAL CONSCIOUSNESS

The affective transparency that consists in spilling the beans and showing the inside is fundamental to the formation of digital *waʿī*. Wael describes the advent of this *waʿī* as a process of capturing a visual and political moment "on the street" that needed to be shown online. He claims that he bought a new camera and wanted to get people interested in politics by taking and posting pictures and videos of demonstrations and protests, and random abuse and violation scenes.[54] Becoming aware of the violations of the Mubarak regime coincides with becoming conscious as political subject through a new digital consciousness. Mediated by handheld devices, online communication, and presence on the street, this consciousness or political awareness thus operates at the level of the heart, chest, and tongue, and involves action, reaction, outbursts, and leaking. Wael's filming and tweeting of an attack on himself and his posting images of his bruises best capture the modality of the new *waʿī* that connects body parts to technology, and the subject to the political in the midst of the proliferation of images and experiences of abuse on the street and online.[55]

In April 2009, Wael live-tweeted on his handheld device an attack on himself by a neighbor who happened to be a police officer, and then his ordeal between the police station and the hospital from beginning to end. As he was being led to the station, followers were not only tracking him online as he was constantly updating his feed, but some of them also showed up in person and followed the car transporting him. The act of violation and the ensuing ordeal thus took place in real time, unfolding through updates on Twitter that moved people affectively and physically, and gathered supporters and followers from Egypt and abroad. This attack also left traces, marks on the skin, inscribing the body through a trail of wounds to be further circulated and shared online.

In his account of the events, Wael wrote: "Fate willed that I should drink from the same cup of police brutality, thuggery, and abuse of power from which those I defend drink."[56] Wael's bruises connect the body of the exposer of abuse to those whose abuse he usually exposes, as Ahmed Naji claims when explaining the affective nature of the bloggers' language and *qillat adab*. The violation and the exposure of the violation become inscribed on Wael's skin and in his mouth, where the sharp tongue is. The bruises shown in figures 5 and 6 are not only tied to Wael, the foul-mouthed activist critiquing the regime, but also enter into a continuum of bruises and traces of abuse that connect different body parts exposed online. The attacked blogger becomes bruised body parts to be shown

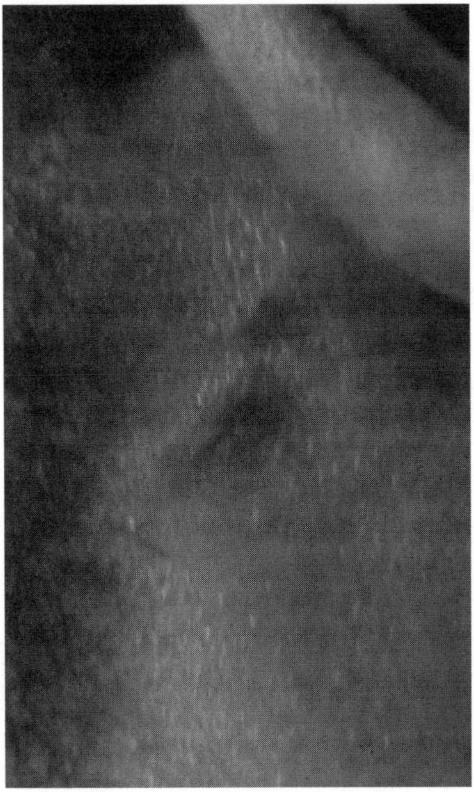

Figure 5. Bruise. Wael Abbas, April 2009, http://misrdigital.blogspirit.com/archive/2009/04/index.html.

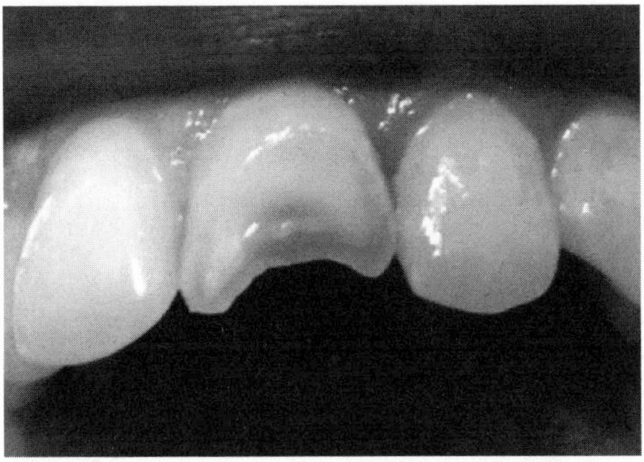

Figure 6. Broken tooth. Wael Abbas, April 2009, http://misrdigital.blogspirit.com/archive/2009/04/index.html.

and exposed through the different takes that are then circulated and commented on. The close-ups of the broken tooth and the bruised skin point to that which is outside of itself, entering a web of connections, circuits, and scenes, part of other acts and experiences of abuse occuring at police stations or on street corners. The close-ups are not only evidence of the attack but also traces through which different forms of identification—assemblages—take place through the inscription of bruising on the bodies of those who "drink from the same cup of police brutality."[57]

The blogger with his motto of radical transparency (*illī fī albī ʿalā twitrī*) transforms the *lisān ṭawīl* (sharp tongue) from a metaphor for the outspoken and abrasive critic into a material object in the mouth, close to the teeth, the broken tooth. The position of the critic is not outside the fray but is situated in a materiality that flares up and takes shape through these inscriptions. Wael appears and becomes materialized online by insulting and getting insulted, exposing and getting exposed, and showing bruises and getting bruised in the process. Wael's tongue, mouth, lips, heart, and teeth undo the docile (*muʾaddab*) subject of the liberal state and the latter's disciplinary narrative invested in the containment of speech, actions, and critique, or what Milad Doueihi calls "affect management" as a civilizing process online.[58] The inappropriate, the graphic, and the gross transform and produce Wael through acts of leaking and exposure, images of bruised skin and broken teeth, bringing about the leaking if not fragmentation of a subjectivity produced through *adab* and *taʾdīb* (*adīb*, *muthaqqaf*) that Nawara railed against by craving insults on Twitter.

Wael tweets his ordeal as he is transported to the police station, leaking on his mobile device as his wounds flare up, and as he moves in the car with followers moving behind him. The subject manifested through his involuntary and exposed organs is leaking from the car both in terms of what he reveals through live updates on Twitter, and as a material and digital condition, thereby leaving a trail of statuses and wounds that proliferate and multiply online. Leaking is a practice and condition of leaving a trail to be followed but one that could never lead back to a source allowing the subject to coalesce, recognize itself, and feel whole again. Just like the uprising of 2011 need not be a redemptive event that mends a broken nation, the trail of leaks and graphic content (images, videos, invectives) creates possibilities for thinking of subjectivity in new ways. This leaking subjectivity, which requires equality in insult, links different bruises and experiences of abuse, and produces a new—and wide—audience that follows (as in "followers") and participates in the dramatic scene online and on the ground.

The collapse of the boundary between critic and object of critique extends to the boundary between spectacle and spectator. Jasbir Puar and Patricia Clough reflect on virality, which I tie in to proliferation and fragmentation or *tafashshī*, as a new intersubjectivity. They argue:

> In its effect on subjectivity, memory, desire, and history, virality suggests a move away from identity; it is a move away from those sorts of representational forms or strategies that privilege interiority, depth, and integrity. Virality proposes its own strategy of creativity in its being attracted to or aligned with what Gilles Deleuze called the "virtual." ... The viral brings a porosity of boundaries, with the ease of crossing them, or the requisite to cross them with the expectation of transformation.[59]

Wael's showing of his bruised body parts is coextensive with tweeting as a performance and live coverage of the event attended by tweeters who are not only following and offering support from behind their screens, or swearing at the attackers online, but in fact materializing at the police station. Tweeting in this context constitutes coverage of an instance of abuse that doubles as a live performance, with material effects on the audience. Through his movement in the car and his status updates, Wael leaves a trail behind like Hansel and Gretel's bread crumbs, fragments of a new narrative to be picked up, made legible, and consumed by others. Leaking from inside the police car and station thus produces outrage and intervention, mediating material presence with people coming into the scene on the ground. This is the *fiʿl* (action) of affective tweets or the *infiʿāliyya* (excitability, affectivity) of bloggers and tweeters to which Naji refers. Tweeting or blogging is the making of a scene as indecent exposure (*fiʿl fāḍiḥ*) of body parts, wounds, and speech, and of a fiction of power that is incapable of interpellating subjects as whole, coherent, docile, and disciplined.

REGIME IN FRAGMENTS

While notions of *qillat adab* and leaking have been associated with the blogger who confronts rivals, Wael's leaks link *qillat adab* to the regime itself. The regime seems unable to control its fantasies and practices, which are continuously exposed through videos of violations in police stations and on the street that the torturers themselves often leak out compulsively from police stations and torture cells. This is reminiscent of the Abu Ghraib leaks of images of torture, and of Manning's and Snowden's leaking and exposure of the fantasmatic workings and violations of power from the Iraq war to NSA practices. Introducing Wael as a guest speaker at the University of Michigan in 2013, Juan Cole stated that although Egyptians in the 1980s complained about Mubarak in private and jokingly disrespected him, "in more recent years, they're angry and they feel that the man ruined their lives, and he's a monster ... and that sea change in their attitudes towards Mubarak partly came out of the realization of what his secret police is doing to people, and I think it was Wael who changed their minds in some way, revealing the reality."[60] What kind of reality did Wael reveal and in what way? "Revealing the reality" of violation and abuse involves the kind of affective transparency, scene-making, and live coverage discussed above. It also involves the leaks filmed by Wael or others, which he then uploads and circulates online, thereby overwhelming systems of secrecy and containment and drawing in more and more viewers and bystanders who can no longer turn away or stop watching.

While Wael leaked the assault on himself, police officers sometimes leak videos of detainees being abused for deterrence and perverse pleasure. Wael's most famous video, *ʿImād al-Kibīr,* shows officers attempting to sodomize a detainee with a broomstick at a police station.[61] However, what is exposed both on the body of the leaking subject and in the videos he or she posts is not an identifiable form of violation that would amount to a scandal in the traditional sense, i.e., a scoop revealed by a journalist. Instead, what Wael leaks or what is leaked to and through him are mostly random encounters and events that collectively reveal the *inside* of a system of abuse and brutality. Like Rupi Kaur's pictures that were deleted from Instagram for their "graphic content," as discussed in chapter 1, Wael's YouTube, Facebook, and Yahoo accounts were briefly shut down for posting "gratuitous violence" and "inappropriate and graphic content."[62] Wael's images and videos, which violate the codes of *adab* (*takhdush al-ḥayāʾ*) at multiple levels, extend the notion of "inappropriate content" from swear words and invectives to scenes of torture and harassment, all collectively exposing the inside of the regime itself.

Police brutality videos such as that depicted in figure 7 often show detainees being sadistically beaten and humiliated. These videos expose slaps and bruises, a hand lifted or a hand that lands on the face or on the scruff (*qafā*), while the other grabs the collar of a detainee. These videos thus brought, on daily basis, the "insides" of the Mubarak security apparatus to the screens of Egyptians and people abroad. Wael showed a kind of violation that people realized took place

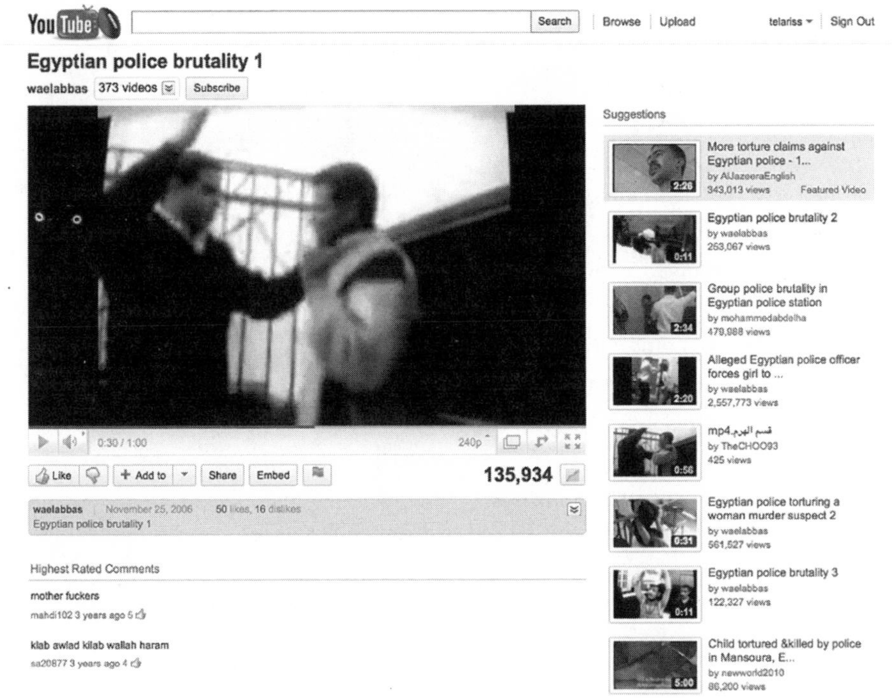

Figure 7. Police brutality (Wael Abbas YouTube). Wael Abbas, February 6, 2011, https://www.youtube.com/user/waelabbas.

but did not—refused to or did not have to—see, or did not realize was happening at such a grand scale. Collectively, these videos exposed the regime not only as indecent and *qalīl al-adab* (uncivil, inappropriate, rude) but also as monstrous, further eroding its legitimacy (morality, culture, narrative) and its power to contain what is seen and shown and by whom. We move with these images and practices online from the affective transparency as *qillat adab* and inappropriate content associated with the blogger, to the radical exposure of the regime itself as monstrous, something Snowden realized in the case of the NSA and Manning in the case of the US occupation of Iraq. Wael shows this monstrosity to a public that can no longer turn away from the screen, and that cannot help but click and view the video online, following the trail of the leak. The leaking and uploading of videos thus activate the violation, transforming it into a scandalous event and an unfolding drama that affectively draws viewers. A new economy of viewership and outrage that is conditioned by digital habits and compulsions, a taste for the secret, and a taste for the violent and scandalous scene (*faḍīḥa*), exposes the regime as monstrous. The new political awareness (Wael's *al-waʿī al-miṣrī*) emerges from this economy of leaking, viewing, and circulating in the digital age.

In *Moroccan Noir: Police, Crime, and Politics in Popular Culture*, Jonathan Smolin analyzes the emergence of sensationalism in tabloid journalism in the early 1990s in Morocco, focusing on the coverage of crimes and criminals. Smolin argues that this phenomenon, while reaching an audience beyond the educated readers of traditional journalism, was in fact manipulated by the state to rehabilitate the image of the police. However, Smolin argues, as "the state became more and more involved in the production of these images, it would increasingly lose its ability to manage the process."[63] This production of a new public is taken to new heights in the digital age, with real-time coverage and leaking of abuse videos from police stations by victims and perpetrators. From the sensational and drama-like unfolding of the coverage of crimes and trials in Morocco, we move with Wael to leaked videos and images of abuse circulating virally online from the mid-2000s onward. This ushers in a new biopolitics in which the regime becomes a multiplicity of batons and slapping hands forming a cornucopia of bruises and screams. We have moved from the docile Arab body, produced through *taʾdīb* as disciplinarity to the extreme form of *taʾdīb* as torture (*taʿdhīb*) and pure violence targeting body parts, bras,[64] mouth, face, and tongue, which are slapped, shut, cut, and filled. This is what is meant by Wael's exposing Mubarak as a monster who not only perfects his power of *taʾdīb* in the Foucauldian incarceratory sense, deployed discursively through *adab* to stifle dissent, but rather exceeds it and moves us to another relation to the body, the subject, and the human, dissecting their different parts. Therefore, the activist who exposes these acts online is no longer the "denouncing" public intellectual speaking truth to power, let alone the *adīb*, the conscience of the nation and the engenderer of its *waʿī*. Nor is he/she the author of prison literature who details the abuses of previous regimes both in Egypt and elsewhere in the Arab world. Instead, we have entered with the digital into the *waʿī miṣrī* that needs to be conscious of the fragments and leaks, torture videos and localized inscriptions on the body at the various police stations and street corners, exposing power in real time as leaking, uncontained, and monstrous. This paradigm shift brings about a new set of genres, writing, and viewing practices examined throughout this book.

The *waʿī* emerging from the practices of the bloggers working online and on the street, organizing demonstrations and sparring with rivals and authority figures on Twitter, requires us to explain the practices of power, to capture processes of dissection and carving up, and to identify models of resistance that could no longer reconstitute the subject as whole and healed or imagine a political system that would correspond to this healed and coherent subject. The subject is now permanently marked by what it leaks, from wounds and bruises to videos and data. It is no surprise that Mary Shelley's wretch in *Frankenstein* has returned as a model of a brutalized—and leaking—subjectivity in contemporary Arabic literature.[65] It is the subject whose fragmentation is constitutive of its subjectivity, never veiled, sutured, or redeemed, that the leaking subject reveals. Be it the blogger or the whistle-blower, the leaking subject is precisely the one who can see, show, and confront this spectacle and make a scene (*faḍḥ*) of it online and off, through images, words, invectives, and concrete data (*donnée*). The leaking subject is constituted in the event of leaking and showing, ushering in nonstructural models of subjectivity that have broken with systems of interpellation grounded in the fiction of power and in power as fiction.

Seeing and showing fragmentation, the leaking subject unsettles the interpretive models centered on the economy of the gaze that have been fundamental to the "production of subjectivity" (Foucault's panopticon) through *adab* as *taʾdīb* transposed from theories developed around European nation-states onto other contexts and locales. The *waʿī* of the leaking subject intervenes in the construction of the subject of the gaze and of systems of surveillance. Through Wael's performance of exposure and scene-making, *waʿī* emerges from the fragmentation of the gaze and the acceleration of sites and sights of circulation and scene-making. The camera that Wael uses not only records the violations of the regime as the author of prison literature would do but also puts in place the conditions of seeing and showing leaked videos that go viral and from which the public cannot turn away. His online accounts become receptacles for videos given to him—given, *donnée*—and coming to his sites from all over. Wael Abbas's *Al-Waʿī al-Miṣrī* is a gathering place of scenes and scandals, of slaps, scruffs, and bruised body parts.

Moreover, theories of digital exposure have focused primarily on privacy and surveillance to announce the end of the (veiled) subject.[66] Structurally, these theories continue to rely on the subject now unveiled and its privacy shattered. However, with the collapse of the boundary between revealer and revealed, knower and known, leaker and leaked to, everything can be shown and must be shown. Thus, we need to engage the consciousness of the leaking subject, leaking through ports and orifices the monstrosity and fragmentation of the regime itself, exposing it as batons, slapping hands, and drone strikes. Investigating the experience of information in the digital age and the levels of engagement that jolt viewers and followers who cannot but follow the trail of images, invectives, and wounds reveals a new trajectory for reading texts, publics, and critiques of power.

IDEAL PAST, CONCRETE PRESENT

When asked about his history of activism, Wael claims that since 2006 he has been organizing flash-mob protests against the government and practicing digital activism in order to bring about "real freedom, *real freedom*, real democracy!"[67] The "real" freedom and democracy that Wael seeks to achieve through digital and street activism are those of the leaking subject, requiring affective transparency, which involves the ability and the right to see the inside and to spill it. The "real" that Wael emphasizes is tied to the materiality and unruly affects through which the leaking subject exposes bruises and slaps, thereby producing a collective *faḍḥ* (exposing, scene-making). The "real" is in a dialectical relation to "ideal," to democracy as an idealized narrative that only operates at the level of discourse, or as an assumption in scholarly interpretations of the Arab uprisings, namely the "democracy" that would accompany the healed nation after the fall of the dictator.[68] "Real democracy" and "real freedom" are political and material conditions in Wael's landscape, linked to the tongue and heart as body parts from which words burst out, and sites that flare up and reveal bruising. "Real" democracy and freedom are embodied in an affective justice that gives pleasure and relieves (*bitshaffī al-ṣudūr*) yet also threatens. The performance of this justice exposes "ideal" justice as *adab* and *taʾdīb*, both as fiction of power and as an interpretive model tied to an ideal modernity, originating with Gutenberg or eighteenth-century salons, that allegedly survives with the Internet as a public sphere.

In Tawfiq al-Hakim's *ʿAwdat al-Waʿī* (*The Return of Consciousness*) (1974), the author/*adīb* laments the mesmerizing effects of Nasser on the Egyptian people.[69] Critiquing Nasser after his death, al-Hakim presents the return of *waʿī* as an awakening from a long spell that was exposed or made a scene of after the Arab armies' 1967 defeat against Israel.[70] The spell that the "worshipped ruler"[71] cast was mediated through TV and radio (*Ṣawt al-ʿArab*), the media technologies of the time. Nasser's appearances for hours on end, delivering speeches and addressing the people, were fundamental to his sacralization through the suspending of the critical faculty. In al-Hakim's model the leader shut down the mind (*ʿaql*) and the ability of discernment, and thus occupied the position of the father/leader in the Freudian reading that is tied to the nation-state, embodying its usurpation and salvation. The return of *waʿī* following the leader's death consists in al-Hakim's text in a *prise de conscience* that moves the subject from dreamscape to reality, from unthinking to rational thought. This *waʿī* is also intimately tied to the prevalent *Nahda* narrative of "awakening," which imagines a liberatory moment of consciousness that could be traced to dialectical models of subjectivity through their various articulations from Hegel to Marx to Sartre.[72] This *waʿī* has been the major framework that kept returning through a discourse on the *Nahda* during and before the Arab uprisings, especially with Islamist parties.[73] The *waʿī* that I'm theorizing, however, breaks with this model of awakening that is meant to reactivate the *Nahda* and put the nation back on the track of *adab* and *taʾdīb*. The hacked screen of the Lebanese ministry website discussed in the introduction will not be lit again because there is still no electricity. The pupils' work of dilating and contracting is ongoing.

Reflecting on Wael's *al-waʿī al-miṣrī* in the context of leaks and as *qillat adab*, one recognizes a narrative of subjectivity that has been undone and reconstituted affectively in the digital age, a process that I began exploring with Ahmed Alaidy's work in the last chapter of *Trials of Arab Modernity*. The affective *waʿī* emerging from Wael is the *waʿī* of the leaking subject that harnesses affectivity to shatter the fiction of *adab* and expose its porousness. The fall of the dictator does not bring about enlightenment and the return of the critical faculty, as al-Hakim imagines. The state of fragmentation is now permanent; it cannot be reversed, healed, sutured, or redeemed. It is this fragmentation in the body and in the text, in the nature of knowledge and in the formation of subjectivity, that Wael is able to capture without reverting to tired notions of the intellectual. This explains why Wael, Rasha Azab, or Nawara all resist the position of *muthaqqaf* (intellectual) who is stuck in the *adab/taʾdīb* dialectic. Wael's scene-making and crowd-gathering both online and through flash mobs break with *waʿī* as in *tawʿiyah*, as in national conscience produced by an idealized *Nahda* project or the nineteenth-century novel in Benedict Anderson's sense. The new consciousness is tied to exposure as in *faḍḥ* and the exposure to a new light through affective scenes that reach and move a new audience. This audience not only shares and comments online but also materializes on the ground to contest and confront. This is the link between digital activism from the mid-2000s onwards and what we saw with the Arab uprisings starting in 2010. The year WikiLeaks was founded and the year that the first video of abuse was leaked and shared online in Egypt, 2006, constitutes the technological and political link that connects the invasion of Iraq to the Arab Spring, the failure to safeguard the nation-state and uphold universal justice on the one hand, and the move to subversive politics that could no longer be reduced to reforming the state or healing the nation on the other.

In his analysis of the early stages of the Arab uprisings, Mohammed Bamyeh identified the emergence of a new form of patriotism or mode of "connectedness" among people that transcends nationalism as the exclusive model of citizenship.[74] The communal bonds that Bamyeh identified also operate along different lines from the traditional ideological requirements of revolutions. "The new patriotism consists above all in establishing a sense of connectedness to others in less artificial ways than before. . . . Old Arab nationalism was also distant from *concrete personal lives* in another way that is now being overcome by the new patriotism. The new patriotism has little to do with educational curricula such as those spearheaded by Satiʿ al-Husari in the first half of the twentieth century, which spoke more of an absent history than of a *directly felt present*."[75] This model is linked to the educational-political system but also to the reading practices involved in the process. It is also directly related to Ahmed Alaidy's call to burn history books in *Being Abbas el Abd* (2003) as an attempt to break with and move beyond the discourse of Arab nationalism that he and many of his generation perceive as a veil for practices of abuse disguised by the fiction of *adab/taʾdīb*, targeting culture and sexuality.[76]

The *waʿī* (consciousness, awareness) of Wael and of the bloggers is the *waʿī* of the multiplicity of singularities rather than the singularity of multiplicity. The *waʿī* that involves an awareness of fragmentation as fragmentation, and of leaks and bruises, lays the ground for thinking the political. In this sense the Arab uprisings are not a moment of cohesion invested in a narrative of redemption through a new *prise de conscience* in al-Hakim's sense, nor the event of techno-salvation referenced in Assange's justification as he claimed credit for the Arab Spring, but rather a series of processes and trails that lead to thinking the political and the collective while upholding a state of fragmentation and collapse that could not be veiled or suppressed. That is why models of containment such as incarceration and the building of walls and barriers after the uprisings in Egypt have become the state's modus operandi, embodying desperate attempts to contain the uncontainable, to preserve its cohesion and fiction of power in order to suppress the flow of people and leaks.[77] Wendy Brown argues that the "striking popular desire for walling today ... can be traced to an identification with and anxiety about this sovereign impotence.... The detachment of sovereign powers from nation-states also threatens an imaginary of individual and national identity dependent on perceivable horizons and the containment they offer."[78] In the Arab context *adab* and *ta'dīb* as the disciplinary power at the origin of the modern state and its docile subjects, now in need of containment, are no longer effective, either as a theoretical model or as an ideology that links Arab subjects to a not-so-distant "golden" age (*Nahda*). The digital age and the Arab uprisings and their ensuing chaos have permanently established the "concrete personal lives" and "directly felt present" to which Bamyeh refers as social and political conditions from which no redemption is possible. Confronting the leaks and upholding the fragmentation is the challenge to thinking subjectivity going forward.

CONCLUSION

The shift from the subject of *adab* to the leaking subject violating *adab* in this chapter has put in question the disciplinary production of subjectivity (*ta'dīb*) in the contemporary Arab context. Specifically, the leaking subject, posting so-called graphic and inappropriate content and leaking "from the heart to Twitter," is constituted through a different kind of consciousness (*wa'ī*), which is collective and rhizomatic, affective and constantly making a scene of its own unraveling as it makes a scene of the unraveling of power's organizing fiction, as we have seen in the previous chapter as well. The leaking subject cannot watch in silence or control his/her mouth, tongue, and heart. This affective economy of confrontation and revelation produces a multiplicity of trails that confuse and mitigate both the linear narrative of the historical subject and of the nation-state corresponding to this narrative. The leaking subject is not the coherent subject who is one with itself, nor is it the subject of lack, i.e., the veiled Lacanian subject covering a structural fragmentation. The leaking subject is produced affectively through bodily inscriptions and modes of compulsion to click, share, post, and circulate that cross and expose the porousness of national boundaries and disciplinary models. It is in reading leaking as breaches in the subject and in *adab* as a collection of narratives and organizing fictions of the self and of the state that we can begin to understand Arab culture in the digital age in ways that tie in the local and the global, revealing models of intertextuality, transnational critiques of power, and the affective production of publics.

Moreover, models of digital circulation move us away from the narrative of the activist as hero or traitor, as we saw in the previous chapter, but also from the narrative of the activist as foreign agent or intellectual, as we have seen in this one. Michael Warner argues that "for many people, 'public intellectual' has come to mean a quasi-journalistic pundit with a mass following. Older conceptions—such as that of the intellectual as the conscience of the age, adhering to conviction or historical memory whether anyone listens or not, keeping alive an alternative that may be reanimated in some distant future—have faded into the background."[79] Made up of tongue, heart, mouth, and teeth, the activist discussed in this chapter engages through digital consciousness and affective transparency, confronting fragmentation yet upholding its irreversible effects.

Not even the return of the despotic ruler, despite all the prisons he fills and the walls he builds, is able to relegitimize the broken symbolic and thus reactivate the power of *taʾdīb* and the fiction of *adab*. That said, and given the developments that occurred in Egypt since 2013 with the erection of walls and rampant incarcerations, one could legitimately wonder whether hacks and leaks make the system stronger, more monstrous, and more aware of its excesses and weak spots exploited by hackers and leakers.[80] In this light one could argue that the state itself became the hacker that now hacks the hackers.[81] This question will return in the coming chapters, taking different shapes and forms as leaks engulf and make possible, threaten and secure political systems, communication models, and literary canons.

In the next chapter I continue to explore the leaking subject on Twitter, moving from the bodily inscriptions, invectives, and videos in Wael's case to the complete disappearance and etherialization of the leaker and scene maker on Twitter. As Mujtahidd inhabits Twitter and reproduces its function of storytelling and revelation, he could no longer be traced to a body or a material site outside his leaking function and fiction of scandal. We move with Mujtahidd, a Saudi blogger leaking the "inside" of the Saudi government, into a radical embodiment that puts in question not only the human/machine distinction, but the worldly/otherworldly one as well. The leaked text in Mujtahidd's case is not only anonymous, *given*, and pointing to other bruises and violations, but also mystical, coming from Mujtahidd and from somewhere else.

CHAPTER 3

The Infinite Scroll

> I remained bewildered and perplexed, anxiously thinking about how a science [the telegraph], worthy of being considered divine since it is infinite, was not discovered before, knowing that [Arab] grammarians continue debating matters of rhetoric ad nauseum, wasting their lives arguing, contesting, and hypothesizing.
>
> —Ahmad Faris al-Shidyaq, *Kashf al-Mukhabba' 'an Funūn Ūrūbā* ("Revealing the Hidden in European Arts") (1863), from al-Azmeh and Trabulsi, *Introduction to Ahmad Faris al-Shidyaq*

In June 2015 WikiLeaks released thousands of internal communications revealing Saudi patronage of media outlets and politicians across the Arab world. The accompanying press release stated:

> [Today] WikiLeaks began publishing The Saudi Cables: more than half a million cables and other documents from the Saudi Foreign Ministry that contain secret communications from various Saudi Embassies around the world. The publication includes "Top Secret" reports from other Saudi State institutions, including the Ministry of Interior and the Kingdom's General Intelligence Services. The massive cache of data also contains a large number of email communications between the Ministry of Foreign Affairs and foreign entities. The Saudi Cables are being published in tranches of tens of thousands of documents at a time over the coming weeks. Today WikiLeaks is releasing around 70,000 documents from the trove as the first tranche.[1]

In this description the language of leaks revealed in "tranches of tens of thousands" as part of a "trove" of secret reports and correspondences emphasizes leaks as a treasure to be found and shared among its rightful owners, the unknowing public deprived of information and kept in the dark. To this effect Julian Assange declared: "*The Saudi Cables lift the lid on an increasingly erratic and secretive dictatorship that has not only celebrated its 100th beheading this year, but which has also become a menace to its neighbours and itself.*"[2] Assange's statement, which reiterates the "enlightening" power of WikiLeaks captured in the press release and discussed in the previous chapters, ties in the leak to a traditional Orientalist trope of the chaotic, mysterious, and despotic Orient, associating in this context the kingdom with "erratic action," "secrecy," "beheading," and threats to itself and others. But beyond the Eurocentric and Orientalist framework that underlines Assange's comment, it's the power of what is known and the model of deployment of the leak that is key for my purposes. The circulation and consumption of the leaks produce a new kind of knowledge, critique of power, and aesthetics, which I examine in this chapter.

Discussing the leaking of the Saudi Cables, political scientist Marc Lynch argues that leaks confirm what was already known: "Their [the leaks'] danger lies not in the new information that they reveal but in the *documented confirmation they provide* . . . It's one thing for everyone in the region to '*know*' about Saudi efforts to control the media, but it's something else to read the details in an official document—and to know that everyone else is reading them, too."[3] Emphasizing leaks as Zizek's "concrete data" or *donnée* discussed in chapter 1, Lynch's distinction marks the emergence of two forms of knowledge: a knowledge that is already known or assumed to be true, and an embarrassing if not scandalous knowledge from which no one can turn away. What distinguishes scandalous knowledge is the stage-making it involves and the fiction it generates. The knowledge and information brought about by the leak and its "documented confirmation" offer a text to be circulated and read. Mining caches of data and sharing troves of official documents in tranches introduces a principle of materiality and concreteness, thereby producing a scandalous text that grabs and hooks the public affectively.

The unsettling character of this documented, scandalous knowledge arises from yet another "knowledge" that embarrasses the regime, namely the knowledge that "everyone else is reading" the leaked documents, a collective act of reading online that reveals a secret that is not *really* a secret. Simultaneous acts of reading and knowing—knowing together, all at the same time—constitute the scandalous effect of the leak and make it embarrassing to those in power. These simultaneous and collective acts draw a fundamental connection between "what is to be known" and "how it is being known" on the one hand, and leaks and online reading and circulation practices on the other. In the process we move from the collective reading of novels and newspapers as the practice fundamental to the formation of political consciousness and a national public in the nineteenth century, as Benedict Anderson argues, to collective acts of reading the fiction of scandal—leaks that produce a knowledge with a specific aesthetics and scandalous, unsettling, and threatening effects in the digital age.

The practice of leaking embarrassing revelations read collectively and avidly is pervasive on Arab social media. An iconic revealer with over two million followers who has been feeding this reading frenzy is the Saudi "tweeter" (Twitter user, or in Arabic, *mugharrid*) Mujtahidd. This jinn-like figure, who is everywhere and nowhere, who knows and reveals all that happens behind the scene *as* it is happening, has been leaking by "showing the inside" of the Saudi government and royal family since 2011.[4] Called the Saudi "Julian Assange," Mujtahidd is the practitioner of a new form of knowledge that involves scandal, secrets, and fiction. While Wael was "showing the inside" of the Mubarak regime, Mujtahidd reveals sensational and secret information and weaves scandalous narratives that affectively draw Twitter followers, shaping their political awareness and interpellating them as consumers of news and scandalous fiction at the same time. In this chapter I explore how the leaking subject, the unknown Mujtahidd or Mujtahidd the "mystery," constructs himself as an online character (avatar), author, and knower. Drawing on classical Arabic prose genres such as *akhbār* (anecdotes, news, lore), I read the fiction of the leak in relation to the genres of serialized novels and TV series. I argue that the collapse between Twitter user and Twitter as such, explored in the previous chapter, is at work in Mujtahidd's case as well. Mujtahidd fuses with Twitter, reproducing it as function of revelation, writing genre, and *machine à scandale*. The leaking subject and technology become intertwined, sharing and embodying each other's functions and texts in ways that are simultaneously informational and literary, affective and scandalous, thereby producing a new kind of digital and political *wa'i* (consciousness).

TWEETS, LEAKS, *AKHBĀR*

The knowledge and information emerging from the proliferation and consumption of leaks needs to be situated in relation to debates in the Arabic tradition about the relation between eyewitnessing and reading, certainty and falsehood, and history and storytelling. Incorporated into histories, chronicles, biographies, and literary anthologies from the classical period onward, this knowledge could be found in the compilations of the Baghdad scholars from the ninth and tenth centuries and in the multivolume *Kitāb al-Aghānī* by al-Isfahani or al-Tabari's *Tārīkh*, which digital humanities scholars and practicioners have digitized and searched in more recent years.[5] The way this knowledge contained in such classical Arabic texts was produced and communicated, which today might involve acts of hacking and leaking presented in compilations on the website of WikiLeaks or organized and edited like the Panama Papers, raises aesthetic and philosophical questions about truth, form, and source. In this context an examination of classical genres and their media is key to understanding what I identify metaphorically—but perhaps not—as a portal that has opened in cyberspace, one that blurs distinct temporalities and strict and restricting epistemological frameworks that have previously prevented a certain kind of comparative work from being done, without which we are unable to understand contemporary phenomena and, for the purposes of this book, Arab culture in the digital age.

Leaks and news circulating online as anecdotes, fake news, and true reporting conjure up debates about the classical prose genre of *akhbār*. In the classical tradition *akhbār* refer to information arising from "the fact that the narratives are ascribed to eye-witnesses or reporters close to the events in question."[6] *Akhbār* are also inseparable from history (*tārīkh*), which was "made up," in part, of verifiable *akhbār*. In today's parlance the term *akhbār* (singular, *khabar*) means "newscast" or "the news" that one watches on TV or reads in newspapers and online, and it is also linked to technologies of communication from the twentieth century, such as the telephone. While *khābara* is "to telephone," *mukhābara* means "phone call," a phenomenon that would surely make Shidyaq marvel at its uncanny nature, as he did when he encountered the telegraph or "the Victorian Internet" in England in the nineteenth century. *Akhbār* are tied to communication technology but also to surveillance and security systems: the "Intelligence Services" or the "Secret Services" referred to in the press release regarding the Saudi Leaks are known as *mukhābarāt*, namely the holders of the secrets to be tapped or hacked and revealed as *akhbār*—leaks, fragments, anecdotes, gossip, hearsay, and tales. The term *mukhābarāt* refers to the shadowy secret police apparatus that surveils, arrests, suppresses, and makes dissidents and bloggers disappear. *Mukhābarāt* are thus tied to a form of information gathering and secret holding, and to the power of physical erasure of those who oppose both the regime and the system of secrecy, communication, and containment that sustains the regime and its fiction of power. Hacking the system of privacy by revealing and leaking secrets and information that produce *akhbār* coincides with a political hacking that undermines models of legitimacy and control.

The etymological leakage between news, communication, and security systems embodied in *akhbār* exposes epistemological and historical leakages and interplays that need to be exploited and widened to tease out and explain contemporary leaks. In the classical tradition *akhbār* were part of biographical writing and the historiographic tradition, including Ibn Khaldun (1332–1382 CE) and al-Jabarti (1753–1825/6 CE). *Akhbār* make up the chronicle, the compilation of lived experiences and past events that are always mined and interpreted, narrated, and recounted as happenings, occurrences, and *données* (data). *Akhbār* constitute the necessary components that make the telling of events a history, involving multivocal narratives in the same text. *Akhbār* have been defined as "vast compilations [that] make no effort to construct a unified narrative of events. On the contrary, they consist of a series of discrete reports varying in length from a line to several pages. These *akhbār* are not linked by a narrative thread; they are simply juxtaposed end to end, each being marked off from the others by its own *isnād* (chain of transmission). A compiler might select several reports pertaining to a given event, and these could variously repeat, overlap, or contradict one another."[7] *Akhbār* are thus "reports" that collectively fail to coalesce into a coherent narrative but instead operate comparatively as they are juxtaposed to one another, introducing different takes on the same event, with variations that move from confirmation and mimesis to fabulation and utter contradiction. *Akhbār* constitute a narrative that upholds its contested or unstable relation to truth. This narrative is made of fragments that don't need to coalesce or be subsumed into a coherent whole, not unlike the leaking subject theorized in the previous chapter.

> [H]istorical knowledge was constituted by statements which could be traced back to reliable authorities—ideally, to eyewitnesses of known veracity, but in any case to reputable persons who had obtained their information from good sources. The historian's task was thus simply to determine which *akhbār* were acceptable and to arrange these in a usable order. On another level, the events recorded by early Muslim historians were intensely controversial. Hence if they discussed these in their own words, they would inevitably be regarded as mere propagandists for one or another faction. Scholarly authority required a talent for self-effacement.[8]

Experiencing an anxiety about the source of *akhbār*—an anxiety about "fake news" in contemporary discourse—the historian has to sort out what is allegedly prejudicial or fabricated from what is allegedly true and objective, which derives in turn from a prior knowledge transmitted through a trusted and authoritative chain (*isnād*). *Akhbār* thus constitute a text that straddles the line between objectivity and subjectivity, partisanship and neutrality, thereby constantly putting in question what is true knowledge and how the latter could be reported and recognized by the reader. *Akhbār* as a composite text provide a key framework for thinking news and leaks proliferating on social media platforms, whereby authority is established through forms of repetition and circulation as opposed to through an appeal to traceable signifiers of truth or objectivity (from traditional *isnād* to Reuters and the BBC). Whereas WikiLeaks is constructed as a "trustworthy" leak source with accurate access to secret information, individual bloggers and online activists have to construct and maintain their own legitimacy, trustedness, and appeal by keeping readers and followers hooked to a fiction of revelations, secrets, and scandals.

Literary critics have analyzed classical *akhbār* as fiction and lore, thereby moving beyond the strict historical concerns for verifiability and accuracy.[9] In their "map" of classical Arabic prose genres, Stefan Leder and Hilary Kilpatrick argue that these genres have not received their fair share of critical inquiry in light of the predominant attention to classical Arabic poetry.[10] The authors end by calling for comparative approaches to engage this prose tradition. "The *qāṣṣ* [storyteller] of the early Islamic period, who admonished and entertained his audience with sermons and edifying tales and urged them on in war, made a distinct contribution to the development of Tradition and narrative material. His skill in relating fables may well have been at the origin of many accounts of people and events in the early Islamic period which were later included in the historical sources as *akhbār*."[11] In this formulation *akhbār* are not simply verifiable reports that make up the chronicle but also precursors and components of a prose tradition that depends on narrators operating both as historians and storytellers.

Muhsin al-Musawi develops this comparative framework and reads *akhbār* as a literary genre tied to anecdotes and storytelling that puts in question models of *isnād* (authoritative transmission) and authority as the exclusive grounding of historical knowledge. Referring to Ibn Qutayba (828–889 CE), al-Musawi argues that "the whole *khabar* practice [is] the most embryonic in Arabic literary tradition. Vague, undefined, or hedging reference helps to undermine and liquidate authoritative transmission with its imposed limitations on fiction."[12]

Liberating *akhbār* from the demands of "true knowledge" thus opens up their fictional potential, and, for our purposes, situates fiction as an essential component in understanding the flow of *akhbār* and in assessing their impact on publics and power in the contemporary context. Going further in his articulation and quoting yet another classical author, al-Musawi writes:

> ʿAmr Ibn Baḥr al-Jāḥiẓ (d. 869 CE) specifies the meaning of the *khabar* practice by saying: "Some thoughtful [wise] person said to his son: son, a human is a *ḥadīth*, discourse, [a subject of narrative]. If you can be a good one, be it." He further adds: "Every secret on earth is an anecdote about a human, or hidden from a person." The association between *akhbār*, secrecy, suppression, expression, human life and narrative is of great significance to any study of Arabic narrative, not only because of the emphasis on the dynamics of disequilibria as central to the art, but also because narrative is centered on human life, especially in times of social change and political turmoil.[13]

Comparing leaks to *akhbār*, which could not be separated from fiction at a time of tremendous "social change and political turmoil" in the Arab world, one has to engage with politics as well as aesthetics involving reading practices, public formation, and genre as essential characteristics that move us beyond the binaries of truth/falsehood and objectivity/subjectivity. The comparative connection between history, biography, and storytelling in the classical tradition frames and anticipates our reading of *akhbār* in the information age, wherein the distinction between literature and history no longer holds. Just like the process of digitizing manuscripts brings something of their order and genre into our contemporary practices, networks, and codes, contending with *akhbār* on Twitter exposes the blurring of genres through the dynamic interplay between the classical and the modern in the digital age.

The intertwinement of fiction and objective/prejudicial reporting in *akhbār* allows us to tie in contemporary leaks (*tasrībāt*, singular *tasrīb*) to the revelation of secrets not as that which is "unknown" or "already known" but rather to revelation as *ifshāʾ*, a literary performance online involving circulation and sharing as well as collective reading and "knowing" practices. This collective "knowing" ties in *ifshāʾ* (revelation) with *tafashshī* (proliferation, contamination, virality), thereby producing a dangerous and threatening proliferation that needs to be contained. Leaks emerge from a model of knowledge production constituted through breaches and ruptures. The leak as revelation, namely *ifshāʾ*,

sets in motion the proliferation of *akhbār*, events, and secrets. As they reveal information, leaks erase or reconstruct the origin of the leak retrospectively. The fiction of the leak, as we saw in chapter 1, makes the author or source no longer someone who could be situated, recognized, or fixed, thereby controlling the intention of the author and the intended meaning of the text.[14] That which is unleashed in the event of leaking is an untamed text that proliferates and engulfs through trickles, fragments, or "tranches by the thousands," as in the press release on Saudi Leaks. Arrested and put in solitary confinement, as in the case of Manning, or forced to mitigate his whereabouts, as in the case of Mujtahidd, the leaker becomes a function of revelation, unveiling, exposure, and fiction, thereby unsettling systems of containment and control.

The Arabian Nights belongs to the classical prose genres of storytelling that include *akhbār* and fables that accompany narrative development, inciting the audience's curiosity and leading to revelations that might endanger a character's life. The *Nights* is a text that ends up submerging the reader through a narrative proliferation that unfolds and multiplies over thousands of tales and *akhbār* narrated each night by a fictional storyteller to her murderous husband. Just like leaks, these collected stories have erased their origin, supplanting it with a function of revelation and storytelling associated with the author-character, Scheherazade, engaging in a process of *kashf* (unveiling) and *faḍḥ* (exposing), revealing secrets, and hooking the reader to the serialized text that unfolds over the course of the narrative. Referencing an unclaimed (unsigned) text by Abu Hayyan al-Tawhidi (d. 1023 CE) that mimics the *Nights*' literary structure, al-Musawi designates the dynamic of *al-mafḍūḥ wa-l-makshūf* (the exposed and the unveiled) as a fundamental function at work in the *Nights*, erasing the very author of the text yet retaining a fictionalized origin—an imagined origin subsumed in the nom de plume Scheherazade.[15]

This imagined origin that is itself fictional, constructed retrospectively as a narrative function of revelation and storytelling, is at work in the case of Mujtahidd ("the diligent one," "the intrepid knight," "the exegete"). While Wael Abbas's body becomes marked and bruised, imprisoned and exiled for the leak to flow, all that remains of Mujtahidd's body is the function of revelation and storytelling, his nom de plume—Mujtahidd. The Saudi tweeter who has been systematically revealing the inner workings of power and the secrets of Saudi royals, makes legible and scandalous behind-the-scenes information (assumed to be taking place) that unfolds as *akhbār* on his Twitter account. This leads us to read the digital context of leaking at the intersection of classical genres and their narrative logics, while seeking to identify new ways in which social media forums produce and accelerate affective forms of storytelling and revelation.

Moreover, building on al-Musawi's *akhbār* as constituting narratives "centered on human life, especially in times of social change and political turmoil,"[16] we revisit the notion of *akhbār* in Abd al-Rahman al-Jabarti's *History of Egypt: ʿAjāʾib al-Āthār fī al-Tarājim wa-l-Akhbār* (*History of Egypt*), which involves anecdotes and stories that coexist in a complementary fashion with *tarājim*, linked to *tarjama*, meaning both translation and life stories.[17]

> Cairo had, in fact, produced the last great work in a traditional mould, the *ʿA<u>dj</u>āʾib al-ā<u>th</u>ār* of ʿAbd al-Raḥmān al-<u>D</u>jabartī (1753–1826 [*q.v.*]). Al-<u>D</u>jabartī witnessed the catastrophic self-destruction of the Mamlūk beylicate in the late 18th century, the shock of the French occupation in 1798–1801, and the tumultuous changes forced on the country by Muḥammad ʿAlī (*r.* 1805–48 [*q.v.*]). He was an acute observer, but he regarded none of this as progress, and he was content to work within the chronicle/biographical dictionary framework bequeathed to him by the great Egyptian historians of the Mamlūk Sultanate.[18]

This assessment of the last Arab chronicler and practitioner of *akhbār* allows us to reflect on the political as well as the literary comparative context that frames the return of *akhbār* on Twitter and on the Saudi twittersphere, as I argue in this chapter. Completed in 1821, al-Jabarti's *akhbār* chronicle was banned because of its critique of the regime of Mehmet Ali Pasha, ruler of Egypt. Moreover, picking up where al-Jabarti left off—namely, at the threshold of the *Nahda*—Mujtahidd and the bloggers critiquing autocratic regimes today through their digital chronicles and activation of *akhbār* should be situated in relation to the *Nahda* as a national project that was meant to forge a new culture of *adab* and *udabāʾ*, novels and the public sphere, and to forge a new political consciousness. The consumption of *akhbār* on Twitter heralds larger transformations in political consciousness that are mediated through literary genres that have broken with the *Nahda* paradigms of the novel and the nation-state, and are increasingly shaped by classical poetry and prose genres and early Islamic history and folklore, as well as by the *Jahiliyya* or pre-Islamic period, as we will see in chapter 5. Understanding new communication and writing practices lays the ground for thinking the emergence of new communities tied together by the digital, fiction, and political turmoil from al-Jabarti's Egypt to Mujtahidd's Saudi Arabia.

GLASS HOUSE OF TWITTER

As we have seen in the case of Wael Abbas, Twitter operates as an embodied machine of proliferation, literary performance, and scandalous knowledge wherein the boundary between exposer and exposed, the leaker and the leaked to, collapses. In *Thaqāfat Twitter* ("Twitter Culture"), Saudi scholar and cultural critic Abdallah al-Ghadhdhami, who is very active on Twitter, offers a literary and linguistic analysis of Twitter primarily in the Saudi context. Al-Ghadhdhami examines figures of speech, excesses, and violations, and debates notions such as freedom of expression online while calling attention to its pitfalls. *Thaqāfat Twitter* is also a manual for online civility, thereby explaining how to act when someone is attacked, and the possible consequences of certain responses and reactions. Al-Ghadhdhami describes and warns against the collapse of a social contract and a code of ethics tied to civility and *adab.* His manual captures a fascination with new technology yet expresses fear and anxiety about the threats of erasure experienced in cyberspace.

Thaqāfat Twitter, both as a manual and as a personal narrative expressing anxiety about digital media, arises from a specific characterization of Twitter as a "house made of glass for whosoever enters it is no longer safe, and remains unveiled (*makshūf*) as much as he is unveiling (*kāshif*) of others."[19] Al-Ghadhdhami elaborates:

> Twitter is a formidable (*jabbāra*) cultural tool that performs dual yet complementary functions of unveiled unveiling (*makshūfa al-kāshifa*). It is unveiled because the account holder becomes unveiled (*makshūf*) as if he were bathing in a glass house, while his fingers precede his thinking, carried away with every outlandish tweet (*shaṭḥa*), only to end up in an exposed scene, standing on a curtainless stage. Twitter also performs the function of unveiling (*kāshif*) since you as follower are able to see everyone, unveiling them in a live scene through this unveiling tool. These dual functions of Twitter create a new kind of cultural curiosity since you will gain insight into a character's [Twitter user's] impulses (*nawāziʿ*) and hidden sides (*makhbūʾāt*) so that what was covered up (*mastūr*) and shielded (*mudāra*) becomes exposed (*yatakashshaf*). And that [outlandish tweet] for which you could have apologized becomes exposed by the function of unveiling, for the latter gives you no option but that of a publicly humiliating retreat.[20]

In this description al-Ghadhdhami brings together the dialectics of exposure and being exposed, and unveiling and being unveiled, situating them within a context of nudity akin to that of the bather in a glass house who sees and exposes others while being exposed him/herself. Twitter exposes "a character's impulses (*nawāziʿ*) and hidden sides (*makhbūʾāt*)," thereby revealing the repressed and the visceral akin to Naji's description of a blogger's excitability and affectivity discussed in the previous chapter. Thus Twitter is a stage and a scene (as in making a scene and being made a scene of, scandalizing and being scandalized) that draws the audience into a visual and interactive spectacle of seeing and being seen, exposing and being exposed. Twitter is also a hall of mirrors: drawing on the notion of *kashf* (unveiling) and *faḍḥ* (exposing, scene-making) and emphasizing their complementarity, al-Ghadhdhami asserts that nothing could be edited or erased on Twitter. Tweeting mimics *shaṭḥ*, which is a form of mystical writing—and the only possible form of writing on Twitter, one could argue—that makes the tweeter lose control of his/her text, unable to direct his/her fingers to edit or retract. Thus digital compulsion and radical, dual exposure come together in this description, which draws on the collapse of the veiled and the hidden, namely the breakdown of the space of the private altogether.

Al-Gadhdhami's characterization of Twitter could be tied to the Sufi tradition at multiple levels. The notion of *shaṭḥ*, which the poet and critic Adonis compares to surrealist, involuntary writing or automatism, is a "speaking in ecstasy," in a state of intoxication that gushes and reveals the truth of the mystic, marking a loss of control, fast movement, and transcendence.[21] Moreover, the notion of *kashf*, which is key to the *faḍḥ* that I develop throughout the book, operates in relation to the veil, *hijāb* and *sitr*, and consists in the lifting of the veil, which brings about the ability to see and to know.[22] Cyberautomatism tied to the uncontrollable fingers of the tweeter writing in a state of digital intoxication leads to *kashf* as radical unveiling. *Kashf* is traditionally associated with *mukāshafa* (lifting of the veil), i.e., the grace that God accords the Sufi who reaches a high level of learning and insight.[23] *Kashf*, in this context, marks the collapse of the veil or the symbolic that structures the subject/object relation. On Twitter *kashf* inaugurates a non-ocularcentric visibility that consists in a form of affective seeing as knowing and being one with what is seen and known. Like the naked bather in al-Ghadhdhami's glass house, the tweeter is engulfed by revelations and encounters online. *Kashf* and *shaṭḥ*, which operate at the intersection of Sufi models of knowledge and the digital, shape the framework through which communication, writing, and knowledge sharing function on Twitter. This new model of seeing and revealing is captured by Arab media language, and, for instance, by *kashf al-mastūr* (lifting the veil), which is the title of an *Al-Jazeera* program that ran in 2010 and 2011 that specialized in revealing documents and leaks regarding the political situations in Iraq and Palestine.[24]

The *kāshif/makshūf* dialectic that al-Musawi analyzes in the case of *The Arabian Nights* and that al-Ghadhdhami probes in the context of Twitter through the notion of "unveiling" or "revealing" is essential to the model of *fāḍiḥ/mafḍūḥ* (exposer/exposed) that I examine throughout. Specifically, the dialectic of *kashf* and *faḍḥ* stages the breakdown between author and audience, critic and object of critique. Going online is not dissimilar from going down into the street, where one is not safe, either as a blogger or activist, follower or mere bystander. The breakdown of these boundaries ushers in a new kind of critique and fictionality that is not "unreal" but rather operates along a different understanding of reality that I explore more fully in chapter 5. *Kashf* and *faḍḥ* thus help to frame Mujtahidd's mysterious character and function: someone who is unknown, who claims to know what happens in every meeting and behind every door. This ability to know and expose on Twitter is fundamental to the mystique and power of Mujtahidd. As the veil is lifted before his eyes (*makshūf*), the Sufi-like tweeter gushes out *akhbār*. Present in multiple places at the same time, Mujtạhidd's power of exposure produces a new kind of knowledge and writing—an infinite scroll that comes to him and comes out of his account as if through some portal to the otherworldly.

MUJTAHIDD: A JINN FROM ARABIA

Speculating about his identity, which remains a mystery,[25] and wondering how he is able to know what he knows, reporter Laura Secorun Palet, who interviewed Mujtahidd via e-mail, revealed that "[h]e admits being an 'Arab male' . . . Perhaps he's a member of the royal family or is being fed information and protected by someone who is. He claims to be in Saudi Arabia, though there's no way to prove that. . . . 'There's no doubt they know who he is,' says Caryle Murphy, a Saudi-based journalist and author of *A Kingdom's Future: Saudi Arabia Through the Eyes of Its Twentysomethings*. 'But it's likely there are some factions in the royal family who support what he is doing and others who don't.'"[26] Mujtahidd thus is an insider to power or is close to those who are.[27] While exposing others, his whereabouts and "true identity" remain unexposed, a mystery, the subject of speculation, wonderment, and marvel (*ʿajab*). In this context the *kāshif* (exposer, unveiler) is not also *makshūf* (unveiled, exposed) in al-

Figure 8. Mujtahidd's Twitter profile. Mujtahidd, October 1, 2015, https://twitter.com/Mujtahidd.

Gadhdhami's sense. In Mujtahidd's case the exposer has to remain hidden as a subject, which is key to the power of his tweets and to the mystery he represents—as if the author has to disappear for the text to live and for the author himself to be constructed and mystified as the origin of a new text, real but not real, truthful yet fictional. While in the context of Wael Abbas the exposer on Twitter is an embodied presence occupying center stage in acts of *kashf* and *faḍḥ*, in Mujtahidd's case the process of *kashf* and *faḍḥ* depends on a model of fiction that erases the materiality of the exposer, transforming it into a function of revelation, a ghost or a jinn inhabiting the "formidable tool" that is Twitter. The tweeter thus becomes a Scheherazade-like figure who is always outside the story, an ethereal presence that could not be tied to a principle of reality outside the virtual, as in Snowden's being reduced to a video presence appearing everywhere and giving interviews while remaining in Russia.[28] With Mujtahidd leaks and revelations permanently link the digital to the mysterious and otherworldly, staging Twitter as their privileged portal.

The production of Mujtahidd as the mystery of Saudi Twitter starts with his profile picture, as depicted in figure 8—an image of Monument Valley on the Arizona-Utah border. This image conjures up Native American land prior to the establishment of the United States. Mujtahidd is either hiding in Saudi Arabia or in London, or inhabiting Monument Valley, a real and fictional place from which he launches his cyber-raids into the hidden (*mukhabba*ʾ) of the Saudi regime. Mujtahidd thus could be anywhere and is in multiple places at the same time, occupying political, geographical, and fictional realties that come together in the virtual (reality), connecting the American and the Arabian deserts, American natives and Bedouins, ancient and modern heroic figures. Mujtahidd aligns the struggles and fictions of the original inhabitants of the land prior to the establishment of the Saudi kingdom and the discovery of oil, a moment that resonates with the work of Abd al-Rahman Munif, the dissident author who was stripped of his nationality for critiquing corruption and authoritarianism in the kingdom.[29] The virtual in this context is not opposed to the real—as in Wael Abbas's "real freedom" and "real democracy"—but rather constitutes it and becomes actualized through a fiction and a digital portal opened on Twitter that uphold its multiplicity, crossing space and time, genres and cultural and political contexts.

Mujtahidd, who is endowed with the power of seeing (*kashf*), has access to information and is able to speak up for a forgotten or oppressed tribe that has lost its land. This association is compounded by Mujtahidd's motto, *ḥārith wa-hammām*. While *ḥārith* means the tiller and the protector, *hammām* refers to the proud and hardworking one. These two adjectives are also male first names; in fact, they are the names that the Prophet Muhammad considered to be God's favorite names, as they designate those who are most truthful.[30] The motto of Mujtahidd thus doubles as a truth-telling function that comes from divine revelation. This allows Mujtahidd to align tribal resistance with an Islamic ethos that could be traced to the times and practices of early Islam and the sayings of the Prophet more specifically. This figure of the truth-telling and intrepid Arabian knight has now returned on Twitter to protect, labor, interpret, and struggle for the rights of the forgotten tribe. Mujtahidd's profile picture and motto, which ought to complement the name and picture on government issued IDs in terms of the visual format in which they're presented on his Twitter account, are replaced by a window or portal into a different dimension that is both fictional and prenational, activated on Twitter as spectral haunting, political contestation, and truth-telling that take shape as exposure and leaks. Mujtahidd's revelations are thus a comparative text, a scroll that comes from and brings forth new conditions of identification and of imagining one's relation to the past, history, and identity on the one hand, and to the nature of revelation and truth-telling on the other.

Scrutinizing Mujtahidd's nom de plume, one notices that the name "mujtahidd" (or, more accurately, *mujtahid*) means the "exegete" who draws on *ijtihād*, the Islamic jurisprudential model of interpretation of the revealed text, in order to understand the will of God and fulfill his commandments. Mujtahidd thus constructs himself as a practitioner of a particular kind of *ijtihād* that endows him with the power of writing, reading, and interpreting, and the power of seeing and exposing that which is hidden in the actions and intentions of others. Moreover, the word *juhd* in Arabic, from the same etymological root, means "effort" and "strain," giving us the infamous word *jihād* (struggle, often associated with holy war). Thus "mujtahidd" also means the "hardworking one" or the "studious one," namely the assiduous reader and exposer of events who will spare no effort in revealing on Twitter what he claims to know. Mujtahidd's identity is thus not located in the name but rather in the action that the name performs, and the extent to which this action is well done, far-reaching, insightful, thorough, and pervasive. In this context the leaker disappearing through leaking is inscribed in the function, scope, and the intensity of the labor of leaking that unfolds on Mujtahidd's account as reports and scandals that draw hundreds of thousands of eager followers of his infinite scroll, mesmerized by what is revealed and by the function of revelation—Mujtahidd himself. Practicing *ijtihād*, Mujtahidd is not simply offering an alternative truth that rearranges and counters that of the state and of the Saudi religious establishment. Instead, Mujtahidd's *kashf* and *faḍḥ* function as a system of counterinterpretation, with its own logic of knowing, writing, and exposing the political and the theocratic in cyberspace.

Further contributing to his own mystification, Mujtahidd refers to himself in the third person, as if he were a news source or witness to the events that he narrates in installments of 140 characters on the Twitter account bearing his name. With "no way to separate truth from fiction in his claims," he tweets about political corruption as well as royal family feuds and rivalries.[31] As in a Mark

Lombardi drawing, full of names, circles, and arrows flowing and sustaining an architecture of scandal that is both mysterious and clear, the picture that Mujtahidd paints is that of a mismanaged state, wherein the ruling class exploits riches with impunity.[32] Exposing oppression and disenfranchisement, his critical tone is sometimes Marxist, sometimes Islamic, and sometimes simply scandalous, that of a celebrity gossip columnist who revels in exposing public figures' abuses and "dirty habits." Mujtahidd's "mystery" and fictionality, his narrative style and bewildering access to *akhbār* that he reveals and that leak through him and his Twitter account, distinguish him from fellow activists and critics online, making his contribution worthy of investigation by political scientists and media studies experts—and especially by literary critics.

Mujtahidd has been tweeting since 2011. In fact, some of his tweets were collected and edited in a compilation entitled *Al-Kitāb al-Muʿtamad fī Taghrīdāt Mujtahidd* ("The Reliable Book of Mujtahidd's Tweets" or "The Trusted Source for Mujtahidd's Tweets"),[33] which was issued as an e-book on the occasion of his reaching one million followers. The 253-page compilation, which brings to mind the compilations from the Arabic classical tradition now put online and made searchable by digital humanities scholars, is divided according to characters—members of the royal family whose actions, scandals, and deals Mujtahidd exposes. The work includes a detailed table of contents and a list of links to articles at the end showcasing "Mujtahidd in the News."[34] This "reliable book" or "trusted source" further assumes that Mujtahidd and his tweets could be forged, doubled, and corrupted. The book title sustains the tension that mires Mujtahidd's *akhbār* and persona, straddling a narrow line between truth and fiction, true knowledge and mere slander. Beyond that, in ascertaining the book's trusted and reliable status, the title opens up the possibility for other books, other "mujtahidds" who might be out there, reproducing or mimicking the one true Mujtahidd. The title thus closes down yet opens up in doing so other trajectories and versions of *ijtihād* on Twitter. Thus, the book needs to be read not so much as a circumscribed compilation with a closed horizon but as an open text with the compilation merely representing a "best of Mujtahidd's tweets" chosen from the entire corpus of tweets by Mujtahidd himself, or by other mujtahidds, or by those pretending to be him or forging his work. This fact allows us to tie in the notion of *akhbār* introduced above by calling attention to the multiple versions of reports and accounts that are constitutive of a particular compilation or anthology, thereby mimicking and recoding classical prose genres. The fictional dimension of *akhbār* is thus not related to its un-truth or inaccuracy but rather to the possibility of multiple representations and texts that could be written and compiled. It is this aspect of fiction that becomes key for theorizing Mujtahidd as the leaking subject on Twitter.

Offering alleged details about the value of the Saudi royals' wealth and how it was acquired, and about shady deals and transactions involving ailing rulers, the "reliable book" is a history, a biography, and a chronicle of scandals. One of the major characters in Mujtahiddd's "best of" and the one to whom he devotes the longest section is Prince Abdel Aziz bin Fahd, son of the late King Fahd of Saudi Arabia (r. 1982–2005). Allegations of corruption and theft of public funds in Mujtahidd's tweets represent the prince as a spoiled brat. Mujtahidd paints a picture of emotional manipulation and blackmail, involving violations of royal family codes and "law," with elders protecting their favorite sons or nephews at the expense of the public good. For instance, Mujtahidd claims that bin Fahd was involved in acquiring a parcel of land close to the holy sites in Mecca although it was designated for public works. He also discusses how bin Fahd orchestrated a "mafia-style" kidnapping of his cousin, Sultan bin Turki, when the latter made public statements critiquing financial corruption in the kingdom.[35] The kidnapping occurred in Geneva in 2003, where the ailing cousin was lured to a family-owned house only to find himself drugged by masked men and flown to Saudi Arabia.[36] In Mujtahidd's landscape, the personal and the political, family feuds and the struggle for power, are intertwined, determining the fate of the country and the marginalization of the common person. His revelations about the royal family provide a drama to be exposed but also serialized as *akhbār* and episodes on Twitter, the "best of," which is compiled in a "trusted book."

Since the rise of King Salman to power in 2015, roughly coinciding with the beginning of the Saudi military intervention in Yemen, Mujtahidd, along with other dissidents in the Saudi Twittersphere, have set the lights of exposure on this war and on the main players involved in its unfolding. Exposing it as a series of costly and misguided failures derailing the country and the economy, Mujtahidd's tweets have taken aim at the king's son and heir, Mohammad bin Salman (MBS). Mujtahidd and other dissidents invariably paint this prince, who made international headlines for having embarked on a radical restructuring of Saudi economy since the fall of oil prices in 2015–2016 and who conducted a wide purge of rivals and opponents in 2017,[37] as the embodiment of reckless politics. Many of Mujtahidd's *akhbār* involve MBS's business dealings, interventions in foreign policy, and gradual takeover of strategic and lucrative ministries, including defense and oil. Mujtahidd's tweets allege that MBS is one of the main architects of the catastrophic war in Yemen. This costly war turned the Twittersphere into a highly contentious zone, with critics targeting government policies. Representing its struggle with rival Iran in Yemen and across the region as an existential one, the government responded by passing draconian laws to suppress dissenting voices.[38] In addition to the arrest and persecution of bloggers and intellectuals critical of the regime,[39] a series of hackings have sought to quell opposition online. Accused of being an Iranian agent, Mujtahidd's account was hacked in September 2015. The tweeter, in this case, is not simply someone who is ignored or marginalized; hacking Mujtahidd and cracking down on dissent expose the vulnerability of the image of stability and unity that needs to be maintained at all times and at any cost.

LEAKAESTHETICS

Mujtahidd's *kashf* and *faḍḥ* take the shape of storytelling and direct confrontation with public figures. He interpellates them on Twitter by using expressions such as "isn't it so . . . ," or "don't you admit that . . . ," or "do you deny that . . . ." These forms of address presume that these figures are on Twitter, if not also following Mujtahidd. Bringing them to justice, Mujtahidd acts like a digital prosecutor who reveals the compromising information and puts the accused on the stand. The person implicated in the affair is thus tried in a scene of *faḍḥ* involving cross-examination and public shaming. This scene, as we saw in previous chapters, generates its own audience, which comments, shares, condemns, contests, rejoices, and defends. Despite the tweeters' varied reactions to Mujtahidd's revelations, it only goes to show that they are all reading—if not following—his account.

In addition to the shaming of public figures, Mujtahidd employs a mode of storytelling (*qaṣṣ*) that is either limited to a short *khabar*, or extends to a long session that allows him to describe and connect various events pertaining to a certain affair or scandal. In this case Mujtahidd draws the reader in by telling a story with recognizable public figures, engaging the psychology of different characters, and acting as an omniscient narrator who's witnessed the violation firsthand. Mujtahidd introduces the tweets by using such openings as: "Tweets containing details about . . . ;" "Now we'll be discussing . . . ;" "We start the conversation about . . . ;" and "In a little while . . . ." What follows varies from revealing simple information ("tweets containing details about this particular case") to introducing detailed questions that frame the rhythm and structure of the tweets to come ("Coming soon, why did this prince take over this company? How does this minister perceive this prince? And how is this perception erroneous and why?").

In the tweets in figures 9a and 9b, Mujtahidd goes back and forth between brief revelations and extended descriptions involving storytelling, interpretation, and prediction. Throughout, he announces the tweeting session and introduces its main topics. In most cases revelations unfold over dozens of tweets, each of which is retweeted, liked, or commented on by followers. Through retweets, followers announce the session to others so that they can all attend and read, at the same time, Mujtahidd's scene of revelation. Mujtahidd calls the session *al-ḥadīth* (conversation) or *al-qiṣṣa* (tale), which is reminiscent of the classical prose genres discussed earlier. Sessions reveal details about a particular affair; Mujtahidd maintains the suspense by declaring that he will continue his story the next day, or he simply announces "the end." The end of the session is often followed by the moral of the story, which might consist of a psychological observation about a particular character or a prediction regarding future events. Mujtahidd's style and revelations, reminiscent of Seymour Hersh's iconic *New Yorker* essays covering American interventions in Iraq and Afghanistan, bring together contemporary leaks, journalistic genres, suspense genres, *faḍḥ* practices, and the classical Arabic prose genres of *akhbār* and *qiṣṣa*.

Some tweets, those "to be continued," draw on the model of serialization (as we will see with Rajaa Alsanea's feuilleton-style text in the next chapter), as if announcing a trailer for the next episode, creating suspense, and enticing readers/followers to be at the rendezvous. This serialization can be found in *The Arabian Nights*, operating diegetically with Scheherazade deferring the continuation of the tale until the next day in order to escape death, and extradiegetically with the storyteller (*qāṣṣ*) but also the *ḥakawātī* performing the *Nights* in some café in Baghdad or Cairo.[40] The *Nights* performer tells his audience that he will continue tomorrow and that, if they want to learn what happened to the gentle prince, they should attend the session at the given time. Mujtahidd thus plays both roles: he tells the story as a Scheherazade-like figure but also performs its telling to a group of followers gathered to attend his session online. Though the story itself plays on the desire of the reader through intrigue and suspense, the performance of the story operates affectively, generating retweets and likes, shock and disbelief, and "ahhh" and "ohhh" as in the reactions to the

@mujtahidd مجتهد · Apr 29

تغريدات فيها بعض التفاصيل عن عزل مقرن

↩   ↻ 152   ★ 142   •••

@mujtahidd مجتهد · Jun 30

نتحدث الآن عن قصة سعود بن عبدالمحسن مع أراضي الحرس والدفاع في حائل

↩   ↻ 148   ★ 134   •••

@mujtahidd مجتهد · May 4

نبدأ بالحديث عن
لماذا استولى محمد بن سلمان على أرامكو؟

↩   ↻ 206   ★ 156   •••

@mujtahidd مجتهد · May 4

بعد قليل
لماذا استولى بن سلمان على أرامكو؟
كيف ينظر عبدالعزيز بن فهد لمحمد بن سلمان؟
لماذا يطالب ورثة الملك عبدالله بالتحقيق مع التويجري؟

↩   ↻ 267   ★ 211   •••

Figure 9a. Mujtahidd's tweets and translation. Mujtahidd, https://twitter.com
/mujtahidd.

April 29, 2015: Tweets containing details about the deposing of Muqrin.
June 30, 2015: Now we'll be discussing the affair of Saud bin Abdel Muhsin
regarding the lands of the guards and the defense in Hail
May 4, 2015: We start the conversation about
Why did Mohammad bin Salman take over Aramco?
May 4, 2015: Coming soon
Why did Mohammad bin Salman take over Aramco?
How does Abdel Aziz bin Fahd view Mohammad bin Salman?
Why are the heirs of King Abdallah demanding the questioning of al-Tuwayjiri?

ḥakawātī's narration in a café or public setting. Mujtahidd's tweets produce affective reactions operating in real time, as we have seen in the previous chapter, but also take shape through well-crafted and well-delivered narratives that need to capture, maintain, and multiply followers. Mujtahidd's storytelling, both as *ifshā'* (revelation) and *tafashshī* (proliferation), frames the leaking of *akhbār* and shape their aesthetics on Twitter.

Figure 9b. Mujtahidd's tweets and translation. Mujtahidd, https://twitter.com/mujtahidd.

April 29, 2015: Coming soon the names of the princes who didn't support the oath of allegiance

July 21, 2015: Tomorrow God willing details
The reason for Mashaal bin Abdel Aziz's (head of the Allegiance Council) eight-month absence from the kingdom
Ibiza is the next destination of Abdel Aziz bin Fahd

June 11, 2015: And we are expecting
How will Mohammad bin Salman manage to put Abdel Aziz bin Fahd under his control?
And what does he mean by revenge and humiliation?
And how will he fulfill his jealousy and satisfy his vanity?

July 19, 2015: The End
Frankly, Sabah came out stronger than I expected
He came across as strong and alert
He defended Qatar more than Tamim defended himself

MYSTERY OF KNOWLEDGE

Gathering and sustaining followers depend on Mujtahidd's construction of himself as both a mysterious yet trusted news source. He systematically quotes himself and refers to himself in the third person, as if he were a separate entity from the one tweeting. This process of doubling contributes to the perception of Mujtahidd as a mystery; Mujtahidd is tied to the Twitter account @mujtahidd yet exceeds it. This doubling takes yet another shape when Mujtahidd retweets one of his previous tweets in order to confirm what has been reported by conventional media sources or was made public by the government some time after he had divulged it. In this case the retweeting of "oneself" creates a process of self-legitimization. This self-*isnād* (authoritative transmission) produces a loop of *akhbār* cycling from Mujtahidd to Mujtahidd.

The tweets in figure 10 depict the structure of self-legitimization: Mujtahidd tweets a news report confirming what Mujtahidd had previously revealed. Self-legitimization is coextensive with a process of mystification, especially in the last tweet wherein Mujtahidd retweets an article about himself entitled "*Lughz mujtahidd*," "The Mystery of Mujtahidd" or "The Enigma of Mujtahidd." On the one hand, Mujtahidd certifies his claims and predictions, which has the effect of an appeal to truth, thereby countering the anxiety of Wayne Booth's "unreliable narrator."[41] On the other hand, Mujtahidd activates his own enigmatic status, which supports his position not only as a reliable news source but also as a mystery (*lughz*, which also means "riddle," "enigma," "conundrum"). Mujtahidd's enigmatic and mysterious "knowledge" (*ʿilm*) is not simply legitimized by traditional media sources (*iʿlām*) such as Reuters or the BBC, but also by the fact that the public doesn't know how Mujtahidd knows. This process moves us away from fiction/truth or fiction/objectivity as binaries of legitimization, as in the historical account of *akhbār* discussed earlier, introducing instead fiction and mystification as the miracle of knowing, as knowing through a process that shall remain mysterious, unseen, unexposed, and perhaps divine. It is its very mystery that makes Mujtahidd's knowledge *knowledge*. Breaking with the *kāshif/makshūf* model suggested by al-Ghadhdhami, Mujtahidd's ability to hide, veil, dissimulate, and in fact mystify others as to how he knows what he knows allows him to unveil and expose others, drawing thousands of avid followers. This process depends on a fictionalization that consists in the construction of Mujtahidd (by Mujtahidd) as riddle and enigma

Figure 10. Mujtahidd's tweets and translation. Mujtahidd, https://twitter.com/mujtahidd.

April 30, 2015: Mujtahidd's sources confirm that those opposed to giving allegiance and whose names we provided in yesterday's tweets have not changed their position much and reticence remains strong inside the family.

July 25, 2015: [News sources] *Al Eqtisadiah* and *Al Yaum* confirm Mujtahidd's [earlier] tweet regarding the submission to Russian demands [Mujtahidd's tweet:] MBS submitted to Russian demands (the dropping of the oil production rate and arms deals) and promised immediate implementation and he agreed with the Russians about a way of revealing this agreement to the public without exposing (*tafḍaḥ*) Saudi submissiveness.

May 1, 2015: The mystery of Mujtahidd

on Twitter. In this case the mystery and the inexplicable nature of knowledge structures the relation between followers, interpellating them as a community of believers in the mystery that comes from Mujtahidd and from somewhere else, from Twitter as formidable tool and from Twitter as a divine science akin to the telegraph at which Shidyaq marvels in the quotation at the beginning of this chapter. This mystification has direct implications on the kind of public or followership that is produced in the digital age through processes of hacking, leaking, and revealing, but also through the fictionalization involved in the production of avatars and online accounts tied to specific people (a Saudi dissident, a prince, etc.) yet exceeds them. Twitter puts in question notions of agency and ownership, individuality and the wholeness of the subject. Far from materializing online while preserving itself in accordance with the narrative of modernity (one person, one account, one text), the leaking subject theorized in this book offers the framework through which these radical transformations extend to notions of personhood, authorship, publics, and knowledge in the digital age.

Part of the process of constructing legitimacy for Mujtahidd's "knowledge" (*ʿilm*) or *khabar*/*akhbār* depends on his ability to create bewilderment and marvel (*ʿajab*) in his followers, as if pushing them to think or say: "Wow, Mujtahidd knew this before anyone else and revealed it a long time ago!" Receiving his information from "anonymous sources" and revealing them as stories and leaks bring to mind Julian Assange, who understands and practices this mystification of knowledge as well. In this sense Mujtahidd could be and has been compared to Assange, namely in terms of sharing and performing a particular kind of leaking that claims truth yet is shrouded in mystery. But while in Assange's case the mystery of knowing and leaking is tied to the work of whistleblowing, hacking, and mining secret information and revealing it through WikiLeaks, in the case of Mujtahidd the mystery of knowing is associated with an otherworldly power that sustains Mujtahidd's appeal—his own mystery.[42] Thus, the hacker and whistleblower in Assange becomes the jinn-like or the Sufi-like in Mujtahidd. In this context, Mujtahidd's mystery is no longer about who he is or where he's living (Saudi Arabia, England, etc.), but rather about how Mujtahidd knows what he knows, namely his function and practice as revealer of secrets and scene-maker on Twitter. Processes of self-erasure, and most importantly, mystification are fundamental to the power and proliferation of the leak revealed through long sessions or serialized episodes, from the Saudi Cables to @mujtahidd.

The *akhbār* that unfold through a narrative model on Twitter are always upholding both their fictionality and veracity, wherein the two properties are complementary, always erasing their source or any logic of causality that could be used to trace or locate the origin, i.e., the traditional route of *isnād* (authoritative transmission). The model of authenticity and legitimacy imagined in *akhbār* (as news in the contemporary sense) is unsettled in Mujtahidd's case, introducing instead a model of legitimacy through the mystery of knowing. It is the fascination with how what is known is known that drives forward the desire of the reader who cannot but tune in and follow, mesmerized and eager to know more, to hear the continuation of the story, and to take pleasure in Mujtahidd's interpretation of the text as he reveals secrets and scandals on his infinite scroll. In this sense the structure of revelation—its source—while it is constantly erased, fascinates and makes the desire for knowledge possible, generating affective reactions including awe and bewilderment (*ʿājab*), but also anger and outrage, transforming the leak into an affective fiction performed online. Mujtahidd's mystery of knowledge and literary virtuosity produce "followers" as a new public on Twitter.

Mystery and literary performance are fundamental to the production of the audience and to this audience's imagined bonds. Verifiable information and the trusted sources of *akhbār* depend on a reactivation of the mystery and the enigma as the bases of knowledge and community formation. The imagined community takes shape in the partaking in a literary aesthetic based on a digital performance on Twitter, and in the sharing of bewilderment and fascination generated affectively by the mystery that Mujtahidd's knowing and revealing produces. From Wael Abbas's "equality in insult" as the basis of the new community we move with Mujtahidd to the equality in bewilderment and the taste for the secret and the scandalous that rips through the teetering fiction of power. Thus, Mujtahidd is not doing away with that which is veiled altogether or revealing the inside in acts of affective transparency as in Wael's *faḍḥ*, but is rather reactivating the veiled and the mysterious in order to make a scene of the fiction of power, which is already exposed, unable to hide anything, with its dirty laundry hung for all to see and consume as news and scandal on Twitter. The imagined community emerging with Mujtahidd thus believes in the mystery and is attuned to the serialized scandals paraded online; it's an aesthetic community and a community of believers. The law of this community is that everything could be revealed and everything must be revealed. Such is the injunction of exposure.

CANONIZING EXPOSURE

Mujtahidd's revelations bring together exposure or unveiling as an obligation or practice with specific political effects, and as a miracle or a mystery that comes to him from somewhere else, namely "Mujtahidd's sources." In multiple interviews and comments, Mujtahidd identifies his work as an exposure (*faḍḥ*) of corruption. He states: "Exposing corruption contributes to accelerating political change. The more aware people are of what goes on, the more they will be ready to act."[43] According to Ibn Manzur, *faḍḥ* means, among other things, "to expose a misdeed."[44] Mujtahidd uses the term "expose" (*yafḍaḥ*) by linking it directly to an *acceleration of* rather than a *bringing about* of a political change. The notion of "acceleration" is tied to people's actions that arise from awareness, and, as I argued in chapter 2, from the awareness of the leaking subject who "knows" through a collective practice of reading and circulating videos, fragments, and *akhbār*. The proliferation of what is to be known and the collective acts of knowing thus embody the speed and the movement of the acceleration—Assange's "fast release of information." The notion of *tafashshī* (proliferation, virality) as the vehicle of *ifshāʾ* (revealing), and by association *tasrīb* (leak), gains a new meaning centered on the political effects of that which is leaked, released, or revealed. The acceleration of political change is linked to a new kind of consciousness that depends in Mujtahidd's case on the speed with which his revelations circulate and are retweeted and the speed with which his followers increase. Thus, we move away from the causal relation between awareness and change to a relation of speed through which awareness and change depend on tweeting in live time, retweeting, and accumulating more and more followers.

Complicating the modality of the political effects of his leaking, Mujtahidd appeals to duty and, more specifically, Islamic duty and ethics in order to justify his leaking practice—in fact, his *faḍḥ*. The relation between leaks and *faḍḥ* takes shape through a discourse on religious normativity and custom that overlaps with a class-based discourse that shames and busts those in power.

In the tweets in figure 11, exposing (*faḍḥ*) the deceitful ones (*al-munāfiqīn*) becomes part of *sunna* (orthodoxy), which is the custom or normative conduct associated with the Prophet and early Muslims.[45] Just as Wael Abbas's insulting (*shatm*) operates as a digital covenant of political subjectivity in Egypt, here *faḍḥ* as revelation is part of *sunna*, which is in practice the manifestation of divine will through people's acts for which the Prophet and his companions set

@mujtahidd مجتهد · Jun 5

ملحوظة
الاجتماعات جرت في فندق الحياة
لكن علوش يقيم في فندق كراون بلازا
طبعا كلها في عمان
نسأل الله أن يفضح كل المنافقين

↩   ⟲ 589   ★ 307   •••

@mujtahidd مجتهد · Jun 30

ولا يلومنا أحد على فضحه، فمن السنة فضح من يجاهر
بالمعصية، خاصة إذا كان يتسخدم أموال الأمة في فساده
وعربدته، ولو كان مستترا بها لسترنا عليه

↩   ⟲ 158   ★ 166   •••

Figure 11. Mujtahidd's tweets and translation. Mujtahidd, https://twitter
.com/mujtahidd.

> June 5, 2015: Observation:
> The meetings took place in the Hyatt Hotel
> But Alloush is staying in the Crown Plaza Hotel
> Of course, they are all in Amman
> We ask God to expose (yafḍaḥ) all the deceitful ones.
> June 30, 2015: Let no one blame us for exposing (faḍḥ) him,
> for it's religiously sanctioned (sunna) to expose him who flaunts
> his misdeeds, especially when he's spending public funds on his
> corruption and debauchery, for had he tried to hide it, we would
> have not exposed him.

the standard. Furthermore, the mystification of Mujtahidd is tied to what God already sees and knows, thereby putting those being exposed in the position of being always already exposed in God's eyes. The deceitful ones (munāfiqīn) are unable to hide, veil, or dissimulate their actions and intentions from the All-Seeing and All-Knowing God. Moreover, and according to the Sufi notion of kashf/mukāshafa discussed above, God can grant someone the power of unveiling and exposing others, namely someone whose motto is ḥārith wa-hammām, i.e., someone associated with truth-telling, who thus embodies God's sanctioned practice. Mujtahidd constructs himself like the Sufi who has been graced with the gift and power of *mukāshafa* (unveiling, revealing, collapse of the veil) and, more specifically, *faḍḥ*. In this way Mujtahidd relinquishes the agency of *faḍḥ*, or constructs his *faḍḥ* as a divine tool put in his hand to use in the tradition of early Muslims, thereby fully embodying and replicating the formidable tool that is Twitter and cyberspace more generally where nothing can be hidden or veiled anymore. *Faḍḥ* comes from him and from somewhere else, from what he sees through his perspective and what is seen from above or beyond, namely, from an otherworldly realm and from a previous time period associated with early Islam. His Twitter account, like that of Wael Abbas, is thus a receptacle of scandals (*faḍāʾiḥ*) coming from actual sources informing him about what happens behind the scene, like those sending Wael videos and stories about abuse and corruption or—and more importantly—coming from a mystical and mysterious insight and mode of seeing, thereby crossing space and time and unsettling definitions of reality, knowledge, and vision. This framework leads us to rethink Mujtahidd's doubling and quoting himself by saying: "Mujtahidd's sources have revealed." These "sources" are tied to this power of seeing, knowing, and exposing that comes to him and to his account from other realms. Twitter is no longer a platform for debate and political discussion, as in the Habermassian public sphere. A portal opens on Twitter through which an unveiled "knowledge" circulates and a Sufi form of seeing displaces ocularcentrism and the panoptical gaze. The new ethical code as "injunction to expose" or *faḍḥ* as *sunna* produces new "community guidelines" that require the kind of manual that al-Ghadhdhami sought to produce. These guidelines emerge from the practice of cyberexposure and leaks, and from the practice of *ijtihād*, thereby drawing on concepts such as *sitr* (veil, veiling), *jahr* (flaunting), and *maʿṣiya* (misdeed) in order to frame the collapse between the private and the public, and the sanctioned and the forbidden in cyberspace.

Mujtahidd's power and the mystery associated with his knowing what he knows lead us to reconsider the significance of Mujtahidd's name and function as a practice of *ijtihād*—the interpretation of God's intent through a reading of the text and other insights. In this setting Twitter, likened to a glass house, becomes the text of the *makshūf*, namely the text of the one whose veil has been lifted (*makshūf ʿanh al-hijāb*). Being in al-Ghadhdhami's glass house in the case of Mujtahidd thus means being in the position of having nothing to hide or, better, of not being there at all, or being purely *virtual*. In other words, for Mujtahidd the glass house is inhabited by a function of exposure, revelation, and unveiling that comes from beyond yet takes shape through specific insights, knowledge, narratives, *akhbār*, and a writing produced in a state of intoxication similar to that of a mystic. Thus, when Mujtahidd asks God to expose the deceitful ones (*munāfiqīn*), it is as if he is praying for the leaks to continue to flow through his account as if independent of his will and his ability to interrupt or stop them. Leaks and scandals form in this case a proliferating, non-ending text or "knowledge"—the infinite scroll—that continues to stream through the leaking subject, engulfing in its way follower and followed, exposer and exposed. Mujtahidd is the instrument, the "formidable tool," and portal of exposure and leaks rather than their author. The question of agency associated with the activist or the intellectual speaking truth to power is complicated in this case and, as we have seen, in the case of Wael Abbas, whose heart is directly linked to Twitter. These forms of revelation and contestation are tied to a digitial condition but also to models of beliefs and imagined communities that are no longer predicated on the enlightenment model or the public sphere populated by rational and ethical subjects whose reading practices produce secular time. Mystery, compulsion, literary performance, and affective transparency characterize the actions of these new figures inhabiting Arab cyberspace; they thus force us to rethink questions of public and community imagined from this perspective both in the Arab world and beyond. Practices of exposure are injunctions (*règles*) but also conditions for political engagement in the digital age.

Mujtahidd emphasizes *faḍḥ* as *sunna*, which operates as well in the context of those who are already *mafḍūḥūn* (exposed, shameless) through their blatant actions, i.e., those who are not trying to hide or veil (*yastatirū*), and even flaunting their vices ("flaunts his misdeeds," *yujāhir bi-l-maʿṣiya*).[46] This particular *faḍḥ* of the already-*mafḍūḥ* thus makes us think of *faḍḥ* not so much as a revelation of that which is unknown or unseen or "assumed to be true," but rather as an act of making a scene (*faḍḥ* as in *faḍīḥa*, scandal) of it on Twitter. This "scene-making" or scandalous knowledge is precisely the kind of knowledge I theorize throughout the book; it is integral to *faḍīḥa* in so far as it not only informs those who do not know, but makes that which is already known "scandalous"—a text that affectively draws in people and moves them to share and circulate. This acceleration and intensification of *faḍḥ*, coming from the exposer him/herself and from somewhere else through simultaneous and collective acts of "knowing" (reading or watching together, all at the same time), produces the scandalous effect that leads to awareness and action, according to Mujtahidd. "Making a scene" of the revelation as well as the revelation itself constitute the affective economy of leaks and scandals online. These scenes engulf the reader now mesmerized by the mystery of knowledge (how does Mujtahidd know?), and scandalized or perhaps titillated by that which is made a scene of. In this case the reader is drawn in as an avid consumer of scandals that gush out through an open faucet that continues to leak online.

SERIAL GUTTER

While the mystery associated with Mujtahidd is fundamental to his appeal and to the circulation and proliferation of his revelations, the narrative of scandal involving news and gossip about celebrities or public figures is essential to understanding the aesthetics of *faḍḥ* in his case. The unveiling and exposure that Mujtahidd practices involve both personal and political scandals as he weaves through his tweets instances of pleasure, excess, political abuse, and delinquency. The fiction of the leak is always tied to the fiction of scandal, especially in a context involving "celebrities."[47] Mujtahidd revels in revealing intimate details about those in power, turning his tweets into a portrait of private life, thereby linking it to the scene of political corruption and mismanagement. Illicit affairs and partying overseas are some of the *akhbār* that Mujtahidd reports that are intimately tied to the skirting of political duties.

> -It is expected that Mohammad bin Salman will stay in Paris until next Saturday or the one after to spend a swell time with his new wife who is also a granddaughter of Bandary bint Abdel Aziz.[48]
>
> -The country is at war and the secretary of defense is getting married in Paris and strolling down the Champs Elysée in order to prove that he is an even bigger spender than [Fahd bin] Abdel Aziz and Walid [bin Talal].
> What say you army officers?[49]

In response to his scandalous tweets, some readers gang up on Mujtahidd online, saying that he will die in London where he has been living for twenty years, and that he is rotten, a traitor, and a liar. Yet all these readers are commenting on his tweets, which means that they are all following him or at least reading his revelations. Thus, followers are not simply people who agree with him or share his views but rather constitute a public that wants to see what's "behind the scene" (*mastūr*) despite the fact that they feel repulsed and shocked by

Mujtahidd's revelations. This perverse consumption transforms Mujtahidd's tweets into a text that some readers would not want to read but cannot stop reading nonetheless. The fiction of scandal, though always tied to "exposing" some political abuse or squandering of public funds on lavish trips overseas by those in power while skirting their official duties, engulfs the scandalized and the exposed and the readers of scandal who cannot stop watching, reading, and consuming. The digital compulsion discussed in chapter 2 takes shape in the context of Mujtahidd through reading and following practices that hook viewers to their handheld devices, following the unfolding of the scandalous scroll, revealed in spurts and sarcastic narratives on Mujtahidd's account.

The steady flow of scandalous revelations is a readerly narcotic that needs to be consumed yet is often abhorred. This process is captured by the following characterization: "Mujtahiddd, an anonymous Twitter user from Saudi Arabia, has been called the 'gutter of the press.' A Saudi prince called him a 'slanderer' and a 'hired tool.' Some say the whistle-blower, who is now a household name among Saudis who use social media, is the Julian Assange of the nation."[50] The notion of "gutter" refers both to tabloid journalism and to the source of the text, giving a new meaning to the expression "Mujtahidd's sources," which leak and gush through his Twitter account. Thus, Mujtahidd writes the gutter and from the gutter that could not be contained. His tweets emerge from a mystical if not sacred knowledge and from the gutter.[51] Mired in dirt and salaciousness, the fiction of scandal involving the personal lives of "celebrities" thus coincides with exposing political corruption and abuse, a process that takes shape both voluntarily and involuntarily, arising from Mujtahidd and from somewhere else. These leaks burst out like fluids and excrement through the Twitter account now likened to overflowing sewage that proliferates and floods social media and those inhabiting it. The boundaries between the sacred and the profane discussed in chapter 1 as the framework for the event of leaking in *The Arabian Nights* are subverted once again in the case of Mujtahidd. *Faḍḥ* as *sunna*, which draws on a religious injunction mediated by the mystical unveiling with which Mujtahidd is graced, coincides with Mujtahidd the serial gutter and the king of tabloids on Saudi Twitter. The violation of this boundary as we have seen in the previous chapters points to a reconfiguration of the fundamental makeup of the law and of the community that abides (or ought to abide) by it. The fiction that legitimizes power and the symbolic, organizing *halal* and *haram*, the permissible and the forbidden, gender roles and sexual behavior, is fundamentally challenged and rethought in these instances of leaks and exposure. The collapse of the boundary necessary for the operation of the fiction of power makes leaking and scene-making from Wael Abbas to Mujtahidd no longer a marginal phenomenon reduced to a closed group of afficionados of scandal and politics online, but rather extends to a larger if not mainstream community and public moved by this affective exposure and brought into these leaks and revelations in the absence of an adequate public sphere that was and remains an ideal not only in the Arab world but also in the West, from eighteenth-century salons to cyberspace, and from Saudi Twitter as a glass house of exposure to the White House of the Tweeter-in-Chief.[52]

Mujtahidd the gutter "has become a household name." This association is key because the gutter has gone mainstream as it is recognizable to all and is consumed by all, even by those who view it as "gutter," "slander," or "salacious tabloid." Thus, the spewing of excrement and "discarded" fluids is no longer an isolated phenomenon, a breakdown in the system of containment and privacy, or a breach in the genre of news reporting or a political contestation. On the contrary, it is the gutter that captures the public's imagination, keeps them hooked and wanting more while being repulsed and shocked by that which gushes out. This fiction of scandal doubling as political exposure taking shape online conjures up new readerly practices and affective relations through which politics, fiction, and new media come together and get redefined—recoded—in the Arab digital age and beyond. The revelation of state secrets and the writing *from* and *of* the gutter unsettle the nature of revelation, intervening in the aesthetics of the text and in the audience's desire, consciousness, and disposition to act based on what is revealed and how and how often. The gutter thus consists in a steady flow of *akhbār* that mixes the personal and the political through a new literary and political genre that draws on the scandalous and the sensational but also on the mystical and otherworldly. This form of textuality is the stage for a new critique of power that has the effect of accelerating the process of "taking action" and confronting abuses, excesses, and violations. More dangerously, however, the leaks—those of Mujtahidd but also those of Assange and Abbas—run the risk of normalizing the abuse and the corruption by spinning them as consumable and titillating narratives and interactive scenes and scandals.

The gutter in Mujtahidd's case could be understood in relation to gossip and celebrity gossip more specifically. In *Publics and Counterpublics*, Michael Warner argues that gossip operates within strict rules as subversive public discourse. In the case of celebrity-gossip columnists or the "professionals," who could be themselves the object of gossip, this genre straddles a narrow line between gossip (among people who are familiar with each other) and scandal (among total strangers).[53] On Saudi Twitter and in the case of Mujtahidd, both gossip and scandal frame the nature and the unfolding of the leaks that target political deals and divulge personal information in order to paint a picture of excess, immorality, and political mismanagement, not unlike those that circulated in eighteenth-century France around Louis XVI and Marie-Antoinette.[54] Thus, celebrity gossip and scandal work in a complementary fashion in Mujtahidd's case, endowing his revelations with the power to unsettle and repulse yet always hooking and multiplying readers and followers. This gutter is no longer a marginal phenomenon or restricted to a particular public or, in Warner's terms, counterpublic but has gone mainstream.

The relation between leaks and gossip is best captured in al-Ghadhdhami's Twitter manual. Calling Twitter itself *al-nammām al-iliktrūnī* ("the electronic gossiper") or the gossip machine, he writes:

> **The Electronic Gossiper**
>
> Twitter plays the role of the gossiper (*nammām*) that has replaced the traditional gossiper. In the past, people used to indulge in all kinds of chatter in their salons, gossiping about others in their absence, and rarely did this gossip, which is socially and religiously abhorred, reach its victims. However, Twitter provided its own gossiper, with every tweet affecting a particular person, saying all kinds of things about him in his absence. It is sufficient to click on the search button on Twitter to find all that was said about a specific person. This makes digital gossip total and shameless for it unveils all comments and bites, enabling anyone to see what has become exposed (*mafḍūḥ*), and transforming a person's absence into a public discourse that is unveiling and unveiled (*kāshif wa-makshūf*) in accordance with the function of Twitter.[55]

In this description Twitter is a gossip machine, transforming the traditional gossip into a new model of broadcasting and circulation, where everything could be known simply by typing a person's name in the search box. In al-Ghadhdhami's description the notions of presence and absence become problematized and their binaries and distinctions unsettled. This unsettled presence/absence of the other makes Mujtahidd's role and function fundamental in this context. Mujtahidd is not a gossiper and scandal revealer on Twitter but is in fact reproducing and exposing the very function and characteristic of Twitter itself, the "unsafe" glass house and home of the leak that flows. To gossip and reveal information while at the same time addressing and confronting public figures removes Mujtahidd's work from that of traditional gossip, bringing it instead into cyberspace, where the other's absence and presence are inscribed in new ways, produced as fictional characters and as political players in the world. Gossip in this model intervenes in the orders of reality, contesting their opposition to fiction, and introducing a new relation between gossip and political scandal, the private and the public, and in the process endowing the scandalous revelations on Twitter with a political function that puts in question the political as such. The political is no longer separate from the fictional and specifically from the fiction of scandal—the family drama of the Saudi royals whose actions and tales have direct consequences on the public good and the country's future.

In his reading of Sonallah Ibrahim's novel *Dhāt*, intellectual historian Yoav Di-Capua discusses gossip as a symptom of a traumatized subjectivity, engaging it as "transmission" (*bathth*) that operates through a transfer of affects in and around Ibrahim's main protagonist, Dhat.[56] Dhat, in Di-Capua's model, is the leaking subject par excellence, wherein gossip and stories go through her body and into the body of others, pointing to a fundamentally intersubjective relation through which the narratives of the nation and of the self are constructed and propagated. Yet, Di-Capua's reading of the leaking subject emphasizes the mimetic function of the leak that proliferates and contaminates. *Akhbār*, just like Mujtahidd "the gutter," are no longer suspect texts or isolated phenomena or personal anecdotes and events that could be evaluated in relation to a normative model of truth, legitimacy, and political critique in an attempt to distinguish them from "fake news." Rather, *akhbār* as leaks and scandals become the mainstream—normative, *sunna*-like—form of transmission (*bathth*) and knowledge production. Likewise, Mujtahidd becomes intertwined and embodied in Twitter, incorporated into its networks and fibers, thereby reproducing its very function. *Baththth* in this context is both a body-to-body transmission and a "broadcasting," namely a radiation of *akhbār*.

The scandal and gossip machine that Mujtahidd embodies *on* and *as* Twitter occupies multiple sites and undergoes variations online. His *ifshā'* (revelation), coextensive with *tafashshī* (proliferation, contamination, virality), is not only restricted to the content of what he leaks, but also to the proliferation of the function of leaking as such. Just as Assange, to whom Mujtahidd is compared, proliferates as a brand and function of leaking, Mujtahidd himself starts to proliferate as a practice of exposure and as a fictional genre adopted by others. Mujtahidd spreads on Twitter as a function of scene-making, a narrative style, and a brand. As a literary tool or character he becomes a transferable model that gives rise most notably to other leakers and scandalizers adopting the same name and practice.

Dozens and dozens of "mujtahidds" have proliferated online such as Mujtahidd of Jordan[57] and Mujtahidd of the UAE,[58] to name a few. All these "mujtahidds" identify their accounts as specializing in exposing corruption in their respective countries. Of course, not all have the same following as the Saudi Mujtahidd, but they all claim to practice Mujtahidd's *ijtihād*. Openings such as "Expect the last revelations about . . ." or "Breaking: I just learned that . . ." are common features of these various accounts that seek to expose political corruption and financial scandals in their countries. The competition between these different practitioners of *ijtihād*, which is now a genre, thus mimics that of reporters, gossip columnists, and authors trying to outdo one another through access to information, style, virtuosity, and the number of followers they gather. Thus, the "mujtahidd" function becomes an aesthetic and critical machine embodied in Twitter—the *machine à scandale* and gossip machine as al-Ghadhdhami describes it. This machine produces political critique and processes of serialization, storytelling, suspense, and shock effect.

CONCLUSION

In early 2015 a series of leaked recordings of Egyptian President Abdel Fattah al-Sisi started to unfold online and in the news media.[59] The recordings allegedly expose private conversations from 2012 between then-chief-of-staff al-Sisi and his colleagues, debating the amount of aid money that they should request from Gulf monarchies and deriding the latter for their excessive wealth. Tied to the Saudi leaks with which I started this chapter, the leaked recordings revealed the extent to which certain monarchies (especially Saudi Arabia) were involved in propping up certain regimes and helping to stifle the Arab uprisings—a role that they were always accused of playing. These leaks, which foreground the relinquishing to Saudi Arabia of the Egyptian islands of Tiran and Sanafir in 2016 amid great public outcry, cast al-Sisi as the seller of Egyptian land in exchange for Gulf money.[60] The Sisi leaks captured a wide audience in Egypt and abroad, and were likened to a TV series:

> The fifth episode of the [TV] series of leaks from al-Sisi's office had a special taste. The drama ceiling was raised, speeding up the rhythm of events. . . . The series

> stars Brigadier Abbas Kamel, al-Sisi's office manager, as usual, General Mahmoud Hegazy, Chief of Staff of the Armed Forces ... and for the first time, the appearance of the awaited hero/star, the one with the soft voice and forgiving heart, protector of the lands, Field Marshal Abdel Fattah al-Sisi.
>
> This episode was entitled "Gulf Money." And every sentence that came out of Abbas Kamel and al-Sisi is worthy of being an epic statement, capturing this golden era of modern Egyptian history.... As the statement "If I weren't Egyptian I would want to be Egyptian" was immortalized by the leader Mustafa Kamel, many statements in this leak shall survive in our memory with *musique de film* playing in the background.[61]

As fiction of scandal, the Sisi leaks are announced and advertised like a TV series with actors, episode numbers, themes, and main developments that the audience should expect. Like the tales from the *Nights*, these leaks reveal secrets and promise developments and scandals to come, thereby gripping and arresting a public tuning in collectively either to attend a session on Twitter or to follow it on TV to find out whether Jon Snow will die in the next episode.[62] Theorizing this intertwinement of the fiction of the leak with practices of exposure and scene-making that are integral to social media platforms such as Twitter requires a critical engagement with the literary, the political, and media. Watching *akhbār* (as in a newscast) and following the *akhbār* (tales, anecdotes) of public figures who tweet or are cast as characters in an unending fiction of scandal produce new forms of political awareness, reading practices, and imagined communities.

Incorporating the personal and the political, Mujtahidd's fiction of scandal constitutes a flow of *akhbār* that moves outward and inward, circulating across cyberspace, but also a loop that relies on self-*isnād*—"Mujtahidd revealed to @Mujtahidd." Rather than producing growth or enlightenment, or a cumulative and progressive narrative (*bildung*) that leads to awareness in the liberal political sense, this fiction ends up repeating and mixing characters and violations. Like an infinite scroll, the revelations of the leaking subject shock and titillate, engulf and submerge, and operate through affective pathways and systems of pleasure that are often dismissed or considered as passing or marginal online phenomena. Yet, to dismiss them as marginal is to dismiss new technology and media platforms altogether. Leaks and scandals inhabit cyberspace and new media, thereby creating publics moved by systems of belief and systems of pleasure.

A structure of faith and belief is a fundamental constituent of a new public that has moved beyond truth and falsehood as the bases of decision making and participation in the Habermassian public sphere and the liberal democratic model. Current discussions of "fake news" thus need to take into account the kinds of transformation brought about by new media and cyberpractices, and social and political developments that are fundamentally reconfiguring and re-coding the constellation of modernity—the modern subject, the liberal state, political consciousness, the novel, etc. Only an interdisciplinary approach that investigates the intertwinement of mystery and certainty, faith and truth, fiction and news, and history and literature can reveal the kinds of transformation affecting cultural and epistemological models in the digital age. Literary virtuosity in writing and performance, as we saw with Mujtahidd, shapes the desire for the story and the desire to see those in power naked and touchable in the house of Twitter. This process, however, could turn into a perverse raiding and trolling ritual doubling as reading practice and canon formation when the objects of exposure and attack are the Arab woman author and her novel, as we will see in chapter 5.

This chapter showed that the leak is the nonreadable *readable* text that proliferates and unfolds *on* and *as* social media. Just like Wael Abbas's tongue, heart, and Twitter become body parts, the leaking subject and scene-maker (*faḍḍāḥ*) in Mujtahidd's case permanently enters the story, exposing Twitter itself as fiction and site of *akhbār*. He becomes a narrative function or practice of *faḍḥ*, which proliferates and sustains new media technology and the flow of the leak, comparatively tying in classical prose genres with new writing. Discussing the leaker, Geoffroy de La Gasnerie writes: "L'auteur des discours ou des actes s'efface. Il est inassignable. Il reste secret, caché, invisible, et, par conséquent, il n'entre pas en contact avec d'autres sujets. Il n'y a de visible, de public, que des actes et les effets de la mobilisation." [The producer of discourses and actions is erased. He is indeterminable. He remains in secret, hidden, invisible, and, ultimately, does not enter into a relation with other subjects except as a function and practice of leaking].[63] Like Mujtahidd who is "hidden" in and identified with Twitter itself, the self-effaced leaker with unknown whereabouts ushers in a new critical and readerly practice, and a digital aesthetic open to both classical and modern genres, from *akhbār* to the TV series. This complicates Assange's notion of the Platonic Cave as the site of knowledge that the leaker mines in order to enlighten and civilize others. The leaker enters the biopolitics of leaking; he/she disappears in solitary confinement, reduced to a leaking body or function, or becomes a virtual and ethereal presence inhabiting cyberspace rather than the traditional exilic capitals of Arab dissidents such as London where Mujtahidd is thought to be living.

The fiction of scandal that takes shape through leaks and revelations pierces the veil of those in power and power's fiction—from *adab* and *ta'dīb* in the Egyptian context, discussed in the previous chapter, to the stable and unified kingdom (and ruling family) in the Saudi one. The pleasure of the leak is not only about revealing information that everyone assumes to be true, but also about publicly exposing and busting those in power, which is a form of getting back, hitting back, shaming, making a scene, and getting revenge, as we saw with Wael. The pleasure associated with this fiction stems from the fact that celebrity scandals render the celebrities touchable, reachable, and violated. Exposing their misdeeds thus shapes a pleasure associated with retributive justice—or "Twitter justice" in this case—that counters the sadism and excesses of those in power through practices of *faḍḥ*. The pleasure of the text is thus linked to seeing the inside and the behind-the-scene, hearing muffled voices on recordings, and deciphering redacted text through which the celebrities are embodied, made tangible and legible. Thus, the narrative of the leak is the fiction of scandal that promises and performs the rupture. Like the tales from *The Arabian Nights* and Mujtahidd's tweets, and like Rajaa Alsanea's *Riyadh Girls*, as we will see in the next chapter, the promise of revealing more, of widening the gap, is precisely what unsettles and contests, and draws in the reader of the infinite scroll.

CHAPTER 4

Fiction of Scandal Redux

When Salman Rushdie decided to open a Twitter account in 2011, he realized that someone had already usurped his name and was tweeting in his stead. Feeling violated, he addressed the imposter directly: "Who are you?? Why are you pretending to be me? Release this username. You are a phony. All followers please note."[1] Rushdie "then faced the indignity of having to prove his identity, answering a barrage of obscure questions from would-be followers about, among other things, his late sister Nabeela's nickname, and the sometime hiding place of the Pakistani poet Faiz Ahmed Faiz."[2] Rushdie's reaction and the episode as a whole betray the anxiety of the author going on Twitter, and, to a larger extent, the anxiety of "literature" in the digital age. Notions of authenticity, property rights, personal identity, and the fundamental relation between fiction and reality all come into play in this telling event. Moreover, the relation between the private and the public collapses as Rushdie finds himself having to convince his "would-be followers" that he is who he is claiming to be by revealing family details and the secret location of Faiz. To reclaim his stolen identity on Twitter, Rushdie had to reveal "inside information" as the only mean of confirming his identity. The anxiety of literature in the digital age in Rushdie's case thus stems from a fascination with the digital and the attempt to harness it. The desire to reach a wider audience and tap "would-be followers" makes the author vulnerable, thereby recoding his role and function on Twitter. What Rushdie did not realize is that the very function of the author and the circulation of ideas and texts according to fixed and recognizable narratives of subjectivity are altered and recoded in cyberspace.

Going online makes authors vulnerable and subject to identity theft but also to a more sinister act of doubling and infiltration, namely hacking. In April 2012 Twitter witnessed a series of hackings targeting Saudi authors and intellectuals, including Abdo Khal. Khal's novel, *Tarmī bi-Sharar* (*Throwing Sparks*, 2009), which earned him the Arabic Booker prize in 2010, tells the story of a torturer in an unnamed Gulf kingdom.[3] Khal intervened to disown the hacked account, "@Abdokhal," which was spewing all kinds of vulgarities and indiscretions aimed at embarrassing the author and destroying his reputation. As a result of this hacking, Khal lost his 50,000 followers. As an act of tampering, hijacking, and infiltration, hacking delivers a blow that suddenly wipes out the author's identity and readership. The cyberattack knocked down the signifier itself—the award-winning author with thousands of followers. Hacking the author thus unsettles the economy of literary production and the public engagement (on Twitter) that complements and sustains it. Participatory debate and the critique of power, which imagine a public sphere online, collapsed in one blow.[4] The weakness of passwords and the instability of digital codes refigure the relation between Tweeting and writing, the author and the tweeter.

The cases of Rushdie and Khal, one involving an act of mimicry and the other an act of hacking, expose an interdependency between the fictional and the digital, wherein authorship and textuality, fiction and reality, become volatile and intertwined spheres with blurred boundaries and genres. Approaching Arabic writing as the stage for the anxiety of and the fascination with the digital, this chapter shows how new writing and genres, the bestseller and the fiction of scandal, paved the way for blogs, Twitter, and other social media platforms through which leaks flowed and became fictionalized as texts hooking avid readers and maximizing followers. These leaks have been framed in novels from the mid-2000s onward—a period that gave us Wael Abbas, WikiLeaks, and the Arab uprisings. In this light I analyze the works of Rajaa Alsanea (b. 1981) and Khaled Alkhamissi (b. 1962) as the fiction of the leaking subject who wants to reveal it all, mimicking e-mails about the private life of individuals turned characters and recording and circulating scenes of abuse and violation on the street through novelistic scenes. I argue that the author, who is traditionally understood as the function of discourse in Foucault or as the object of sacrifice in Barthes, emerges in this new fiction as the scandalous function of the leak that recodes the novel as medium. I explore how literature is reimagined and reaffirmed in instances of greed, exhibitionism, confrontation, and hacking that affectively grab and move readers, marking the emergence of a new literary culture and aesthetics tied to the bestseller and the pursuit of fame.

DIGITAL FASCINATION, LITERARY ANXIETY

Since the beginning of the new millenium, the Arab world has been witnessing a literary boom that has made being an author *cool* again. New voices have emerged from an array of presses such as Merit and Shorouk in Cairo, and Saqi, Jamal, and al-Ayn in Beirut, to name a few. This vibrancy has greatly benefited from various local and international writing festivals, awards (especially the International Prize for Arabic Fiction or Arabic Booker), and literary magazines and websites (*Akhbār al-Adab*, *Banipal*, *ArabLit*). New novels and short-story collections exhibit multiple forms of linguistic play and narrative structure, mixing techno-writing with *Jahili* poetry,[5] the diary genre with political critique. With varying aesthetic qualities, they include one-time hits and bestsellers, scandal literature, dystopian fiction, and graphic novels. While some are self-published and circulate within small communities of readers, others are marketed by larger presses and play into a new culture of "celebrity literature," with media limelight and big-budget translation deals. These works could be found in bookstores in Cairo and Beirut, or circulate online as PDFs, which allows them to reach a wider audience in countries where they might be censored or are simply unavailable. Given their modes of production and circulation, themes and narrative structures, these texts refigure notions of canon, authorship, readership, and the literary in a rapidly changing technological and political environment.

This new writing has often been dismissed as individualistic and self-centered, dealing with questions of desire and everyday life, a far cry from the concerns of *Nahda udabā'* (literati)[6] or the 1950s and 1960s practitioners of *iltizām* (political commitment).[7] Moreover, sensationalist, scandalous, and tell-all narratives have been cast in postcolonial criticism as mere enactments of a voyeuristic Western gaze onto Arab society and Islam. In dialogue with developments in world literature from Japanese manga to science fiction genres, and engaging digital technology, this new fiction arises from interactive spaces of literary production mediated by global culture, travel and displacement, and digital culture. Brian Edwards argues that "older models of comparative literature that imagine Egyptian fiction and other national literatures as cut off from the world—on the receiving end of literary influence—cannot hold sway when considering the give-and-take of the digital age."[8] He continues that "Egyptian fictions *of* the digital age" include "those by [Magdy] El Shafee, [Ahmed] Alaidy, Omar Taher, and others, those that produce an Egyptian public in the wake of the shock of multimedia and the digital revolution and were taken up by it, extending and expanding its lifeworld, in ways that defy translation."[9] Thus, the question of circulation and writing has captured the literary imagination at multiple levels.

Circulating online and purchased or illegally downloaded and read on tablets and handheld devices, new writing raises the question of the digital as both a legal and readerly framework as well as a theme in these works. Specifically, hacking and leaking have shaped this fascination *with* and all-presence *of* the digital in Arab literature and beyond. Iraqi author Hassan Blasim wrote and directed a play in 2016 (*The Digital Hats Game*) about hackers playing games but also trying to intervene in world events including drone manipulation and refugee crossings; G. Willow Wilson wrote a *New York Times* bestseller, *Alif the Unseen* (2013), representing hackers as jinn; and the award-winning cult TV show *Mr. Robot*, created by Sam Esmail in 2015, revolves around a young hacker who is recruited by a utopian collective and who hacks as a form of intimacy with others.[10] Jinn-like and threatening with doubling and erasure, as we saw in the case of Mujtahidd and as was experienced by Khal and Rushdie, hackers *in* and *of* literary spaces become representations of a changing political and security order but also reveal an anxiety about literature itself: the character as coherent subject, the novel as text with copyright, and the author as owner and source of the text. Literature as such is leaking in the digital age, requiring an investigation that takes into account new technologies but also classical genres and texts that blur the strict temporal and epistemological boundaries within which critics have operated. A new generation of authors comes across as hackers, infiltrating and altering systems of security and writing, thereby requiring new comparative approaches that engage multiple levels of transformation. These authors understand how "would-be followers" are multiplied, and they write novels that at times sell thousands of copies and attain global acclaim.

In 2011, author, blogger, and artist Youssef Rakha[11] captured this literary anxiety and sounded the alarm on the "hacking" of the literary field and the infiltration and mobbing of Cairo's writing scene by "engineers."[12] Akin to Khal's hackers or those who mimicked Rushdie and stole his identity on Twitter, the infiltrators and hackers according to Rakha are wannabe authors, seeking to displace and eliminate "true writers." As Rakha goes into a bookstore holding a creative-writing workshop, he notices a strange-looking crowd that seems out of place in the close-knit literary circle with which he is familiar. Rakha then points out that the unfamiliar faces are those of "engineers," aspiring to enter the literary field through mimetic desire and groupie behavior. "For a moment it seemed as though a mafia of those lever-wielding un-poets were ambushing the literary sphere, infiltrating writerly circles all across the city, befriending with a view to replacing true writers and eventually, well—eliminating them."[13] The crescendo in Rakha's narrative moves from terms such as "mafia" and "un-poets" to "ambushing," "infiltrating," "replacing," and "eliminating" authors. Rakha thus describes an attack or an aggressive takeover that threatens to erase "true writers." A flash mob that unexpectedly appears at the event stuns Rakha—the author—and takes him by surprise. The fear of elimination is the effect of a hacking that seeks to infiltrate like a virus the literary scene and reproduce itself in the guise of destroying it. Rakha's literary anxiety echoes the hacking of Khal's account and the theft of Rushdie's, which override yet replicate the author and his text, redirect his tweets, and reappropriate his function altogether. It also captures the proliferation of the Mujtahidd function of tweeting and exposure discussed in the previous chapter. The literary workshop, like the author's Twitter account, becomes a site of vulnerability that both empowers and undermines the author—the "true writer" of the literary text.

Having distinguished "un-poets" from "true writers," Rakha proceeds to name the latter. A new literary canon emerges from a liminal space of potential and possibility, which becomes exposed in the act of infiltration, contamination, and proliferation. The threat of elimination at the hand of an insidious mob of hackers/engineers sending a virus to crash the literary field leads Rakha to identify the representative figures of a new generation of Egyptian authors:

> [These authors] might be called the Twothousanders but not only because they started publishing after 2000. People like Nael El-Toukhy, Ahmad Nagui [Naji] and (to a lesser extent) Mohammad Kheir and Mohammad Abdelnaby also share something more profound. They are all internet-savvy, down-to-earth agents of subversion as interested in things as they are in people and as closely connected to pop culture, communications technology and the global media as they are to literary history. Kundera is their Balzac, Mahfouz their Greek tragedy. They are cynics and jokers and glorifiers of what they refer to (admittedly often with ignorance) as kitsch. By and large they eschew poetry; and until the Egyptian quasi-literary blogging craze fizzled out, many of them professed to eschew print publication. They may not always have as much access to non-Arabic culture as they claim or desire, but their position is truly postmodern in the sense that they own and disown many histories at once; they don't have a problem revolving

> around the commodity as a mode of being; they don't have a problem with commodification. In short, they live mentally in our times—and they try to do it unselfconsciously.[14]

In a Hegelian moment, which is experienced as a fear of death and erasure, Rakha embraces the position of the critic who assesses a literary work, identifies its main protagonists, and establishes its aesthetic values. This moment of consciousness calls attention to the vulnerability of the literary work—its compromised position at the workshop for new writers—yet simultaneously asserts its literary worth and significance. Just as Mujtahidd's "Trusted Book" or "best of" is a moment of canonization that both fixes the author and the text yet conditions their proliferation by imagining other "mujtahidds" practicing exposure on Twitter, the double movement in Rakha's case is key for understanding how this attack and infiltration threaten yet consolidate at the same time. In this light the attribute "truly postmodern"—as opposed to "phony" or "fake"—that Rakha employs does not announce the end of literature. Rather, it carves out a literary space for those authors threatened by mimicry and elimination yet who are able to survive the threat of mimesis and erasure in the digital age. Just like Mujtahidd's "best of," the moment of canonization coincides in Rakha's case with a recoding of the author/text function in the age of hacking, leaking, and proliferation.

Rakha presents the historical and technological context of new authors—playful "agents of subversion" in their own right. He identifies their position vis-à-vis world literature, new media, and political participation. Furthermore, he addresses their relation to the canon associated with Mahfouz, which he incorporates as "Greek tragedy" in a new literary setting. The reference to Mahfouz ties in to the "truly postmodern" framework that Rakha introduces as a direction, motif, and orientation in new—and noteworthy—works. As he situates new writing in relation to Mahfouz, he claims a literary trajectory that unsettles yet refigures—instead of breaking with—tradition. The politics of the canon in this context are complex; they operate across philosophical and literary models that position Arabic literature in a larger comparative context. Articulating the new author's relation to blogs and print, Mahfouz and Kundera, Rakha suggests that the new author, working across media and genre, is by no means a free-floating entity, lost and unhinged. Nor is he/she simply an innovator in the tradition of Arab and European modernism discussed by such scholars as Elisabeth Kendall or Stefan Meyer in their different studies of experimental literature and *jīl al-sittīnāt* (1960s generation).[15] The "true writer," though innovative and complex, lies at the intersection of a multiplicity of media and literary traditions and practices that are identified, if not produced, in a moment characterized by the fear of elimination and mimetic anxiety. This releases new writing in Rakha's characterization from a fixed and homogeneous literary model that could be clearly identified, such as *adab*. Instead, this characterization relegates new writing to a series of events, accidents, and scandals that shape and produce it in the digital age. These events include acts of hacking and mimicry, as in Rushdie and Khal's case, that render the relation to digital technology as the framework to think the canon, a site where new definitions and practices of literature are emerging.[16] The fiction of scandal, or the fiction of the leaking subject, needs to be read precisely within this framework that is both literary and technological, tied to continuity with the tradition of *akhbār* or the Mahfouzian novel yet also conversant *with* and conditioned *by* models of circulation, writing, and reception that make the author known, famous, with more and more readers and followers both online and off.

GIRLS OF RIYADH: HACKING THE BESTSELLER

The literary anxiety in the encounter with the digital expressed by Khal and Rushdie and captured in a wider literary framework by Rakha leads us to examine new writers performing a systematic infiltration and "knocking down" of literary spaces, threatening canons, author positions, and the work of translation yet also producing new versions of all these things. Rajaa Alsanea's *Banāt al-Riyāḍ* (*Girls of Riyadh*), a tell-all novel that allegedly sold over three million copies in Arabic, was published by Saqi Books in 2006 and subsequently translated, not without controversy, by renowned scholar and translator Marilyn Booth for Penguin, in 2009.[17] The controversy emerged when Alsanea and Penguin started revising Booth's translation to "domesticate" the text, packaging it for a world literary market that seeks to sanitize if not weed out cultural and linguistic specificities. "The revised *Girls of Riyadh* published by Penguin prefers an easy accessibility and monolingual anglicized tone to a rendering that emphasizes its rootedness in cosmopolitan Arabic language and culture. It gives play to similarity (the Arab *Sex and the City*) over cultural variance, 'equivalence' via smooth cliché over the more interesting bumpiness of stressing locality, over a 'resistant translation' that reminds readers that this text did not originate in English."[18] This domesticating act changed the translation without the translator's permission and eventually listed Booth as merely a cotranslator of the novel.

Booth, along with other critics, identifies in the production and translation of Alsanea's work the process of infiltrating or even hacking the literary scene by the "engineers" and "un-poets" that Rakha describes.[19] Booth engages the celebrity author of the literary hit by examining the way her work is produced through the manipulation of translation, marketing, and media. Whereas the hacking of Khal's Twitter account knocked down the literary signifier—the author—by eliminating his readership, hacking in Alsanea's context serves to consolidate if not construct the position of the author of a bestselling novel. Discussing *Girls of Riyadh*, Roger Allen argues that "this novel seemed to be symptomatic of the 'lid-off' category of writing by Middle Eastern women (i.e., a novel that Western publishers seem eager to snap up in order to cater to a market that is particularly interested in such apparent 'insights' into what is widely viewed as a closed world)."[20] Such novels also include "*Dhakirat al-Jasad* [*Memory in the Flesh*] by the Algerian writer, Ahlam Mustaghanimi, and *'Imarat Ya'qubiyan* [*The Yacoubian Building*] by the Egyptian writer (and also dentist!) 'Ala' al-Aswani."[21] Allen's "lid-off" points to sensationalist themes including sexuality and religious fundamentalism that offer "global readers" a window into Arab and Islamic culture in a tamed and sanitized prose.

Girls of Riyadh tells the story of four girlfriends from Riyadh as they go out, fall in love, get married, divorce, and travel.[22] The novel weaves in the role of the external narrator, Rajaa herself, who introduces every chapter as a weekly e-mail sent after Friday prayer to Saudi Internet subscribers. Alsanea starts each chapter by acknowledging the readers' responses to her e-mails. She claims that due to her revelations in an e-mail from the previous week some readers were angered. She also critiques Saudi authorities' alleged intention to shut her account and prevent her from sending the weekly revelations. Setting itself an imagined origin in cyberspace, the novel takes e-mail—an older technology compared to Twitter—as its narrative model.[23] This techno-fictionalization of the authorial position transforms the author into a character in her own text, revealing the details of her social circle and writing herself as a persecuted yet courageous young woman, armed with the fiction of scandal, and confronting political power and disgruntled readers online. This *mise en abîme* frames the production of the leaking subject as character and author performing *faḍḥ* while risking her life in the process. In this context the "author confronting power" is produced as a literary fiction in the narrative of the leak, thereby further eroding the distinction between leaking as fiction and leaking as exposure of abuse and oppression. In this way techno-writing and new literary genres represent activists as characters and avatars effecting real change yet accumulating more and more followers from e-mail to Twitter.

Alsanea's narrative about the exposure of the intimate and the social enacts a breakdown of the imagined boundary between private and public. Exposure, in this context, unveils the erasure of the very notion of the private. Alluding to Alsanea's framing of her task as that of a *faḍḍāḥa* (exposer, scandalizer, scene-maker), scholar Moneera al-Ghadeer argues that the author's play on the words *fataḥa* (to open) and *faḍaḥa* (to expose) is fundamental to the narrative. Specifically, Alsanea appropriates the register of *faḍḥ* from an Oprah-like TV show that aired via satellite on the Lebanese Broadcasting Corporation (LBC) station. Alsanea mimetically appropriates and recodes Zaven Kouyoumjian's "*sīreh w-infataḥit*" (open talk), transforming it into "*sīreh w-infaḍaḥit*" (scandal talk) to frame her revelations in *Girls of Riyadh*. Appropriating Kouyoumjian's title, Alsanea takes the act of writing on stage, into the studio, in front of the cameras, and under the projectors' lights. In *Lisān al-ʿArab*, Ibn Manzur defines *faḍīḥa* as the sudden exposure to light that awakens the sleeper in the morning (*faḍaḥah al-ṣabāḥ*), catching him or her off guard.[24] In this sense the stage (*scène* in French, as in "scene of writing") functions as a way of "shedding light" on a topic or a social or political practice, which is simultaneously exposed in the process of *faḍḥ* (exposition, exposure). Marilyn Booth notes: "The literal meaning of this cyber-transliteration is 'A life story and it has been exposed'; the verb *infaḍaḥ* implies exposure of something disgraceful or shameful."[25] In doing so, Alsanea "provokes the phantasm that ultimately intensifies the interest in gazing at *Girls of Riyadh*," thereby transforming the narrative into "a peephole into what a young woman sees in her society."[26] This "peephole" is also the conduit through which flow the revelations that leak and gush out through Alsanea's weekly e-mails—the novel's various chapters.

The serialized revelations that operate as "sessions" or tales, as discussed in the context of Mujtahidd, take shape here as scandalous e-mails that endanger their sender/author's life in Alsanea's case. Rajaa constructs herself, both diegetically and extradiegetically, as someone who is running great risk in fulfilling her task of exposure and scene-making. Her diegetic construction as the courageous woman leaker becomes intertwined with the mystification of the story within the book's narrative and the mystification of the Saudi woman author writing a daring, tell-all novel. The double construction both within the work and as a condition of its production shapes the success and celebrity of Rajaa, author and sender of e-mails—character-author. The chronicle of scandals and leaks in Alsanea's text (the weekly e-mails) is thus implicated in its process of production, blurring the distinction between subject and object, digital technology and literary writing. The desire to be on stage and acquire recognition as a courageous woman author from Arabia with translations in multiple languages coincides with the desire to expose the social and political context from which the work arises. The construction and manipulation of the author-narrator function operate as mimicry and hacking that produce the literary hit.

SCANDAL IN TRANSLATION

Alsanea's chronicle of scandals not only alters the role of the author and the novel, blurring the distinction between the digital and the literary, the author and the rapporteur online, but also recodes translation. The author's hacking of the process of translating her work into English sought to minimize if not altogether supplant the translator or the author as in the examples of Khal and Rushdie's hacking and identity theft discussed above. In a series of articles, Booth exposed (*faḍaḥat*) this intervention that aims at "effacing the translator" and "dismissing her reading of the text."[27] This dismissal, argues Booth, produces and consolidates the position of the Arab woman writer as "celebrity author."[28] The politics of translation and publication subject the translator to market forces, wherein the publisher sides with the author of the coveted work as she alters if not neutralizes—hacks—the expert's translation and the translator herself. The threat to the translator's role and the attempt to eliminate her operate as an attack, an infiltration, and a hacking of the economy of literary production (writing, reading, translating, and publishing). And just as Rakha distinguishes between "un-poets" and "true writers" when threatened by the hacking mob in Cairo, Booth explains what distinguishes the literary work from the ethnographic account when she experiences erasure herself. In her *faḍḥ* of Alsanea and of Penguin's practices in op-eds and academic articles, Booth identifies a genre of "Orientalist Ethnographicism," which packages and transforms the fictional text with an Arab female narrator and author into an authoritative testimony that provides a window into her culture.[29] In both Rakha's and Booth's cases, the threat of elimination through infiltration and mimesis produces a literary model or canon that reaffirms the aesthetic and the literary, asserting that despite the mobbing and hacking scenes, the "literary" survives if not thrives within a new model of production. The hacking/*faḍḥ* dialectics thus operate as a process of reading new writing along a trajectory that is new yet recognizable, innovative yet literary. More importantly, Rakha and Booth counter the act of hacking by upholding the literary without reverting to a traditional definition of literature as *adab*, but instead seeking to theorize a new aesthetic that is "truly literary" (Booth) or "truly postmodern" (Rakha). The act of hacking thus leads to the articulation and production of the canon of Arabic writing in the digital age.

As Alsanea exposes and leaks "secrets," as e-mails come into her inbox and go out as stories and book chapters, she becomes herself exposed in the process. The exposer/exposed dynamic explored in the previous chapters, from Wael Abbas's role on Twitter to al-Ghadhdhami's analysis of this "formidable tool," is reenacted in Alsanea's case. Exposing the economy integral to the work's circulation and notoriety, Booth "sheds light" on the scandalous author herself, the alleged *faḍḍāḥa* (exposer, scandalizer) of Saudi society, whose writing practice consists in revealing "the private." The scandal (*faḍīḥa*) that the translator enacts (op-eds, articles, etc.) is of the literary exposure (*faḍḥ*) itself as a quest for a stage (TV interviews, fame, limelight) and readership, namely the production of the author of the literary hit. In this context *faḍḥ* implicates, exposes, and takes over the act of writing, promotion, and translation. It also shifts the emphasis from the alleged object of scandal—Saudi society, the private, the hidden, and the veiled vis-à-vis "the Western gaze"—to the process of literary production that commodifies it. The translation scandal or scene thus engulfs the *faḍḍāḥa* and author of the literary hit who initiated it in the first place. *Faḍḥ* becomes a dangerous and wild writing, a set of practices that unfold beyond the text in order to shape its circulation, reception, and translation. Threatened with hacking and erasure, the translator comes out at the end as the true *faḍḍāḥa*. The hacking in Khal's case and with which Alsanea is allegedly threatened, which seeks to wipe out followers and interrupt the circulation of the text, is also part of the publicity that multiplies followers. The censuring and the attack are part of the celebrity/notoriety that produces both the author and the text that circulates and reaches thousands of readers and followers. Thus we move from the heroic author risking death to deliver her revelations and leaks through her weekly e-mails, to the translator who exposes and makes a scene of the fictional construction of the acts of leaking and exposure constitutive of this new writing.

The practice of exposure *in* and *as* Alsanea's text no longer reveals specific information about Saudi society or lifts the veil on particular practices, but rather leaks the manual if not the production codes of the text itself—a new fiction of scandal. In *A Most Masculine State: Gender, Politics, and Religion in Saudi Arabia*, Madawi Al-Rasheed relegates the Saudi woman novelist to a post–9/11 bourgeois phenomenon that she calls "cosmopolitan fantasy." According to Al-Rasheed, a new generation of Saudi women authors seeking fame, distinction, and worldwide notoriety fails to engage politically as did the older generation of authors and activists. Al-Rasheed writes: "Heroines are depicted as depoliticised and with no interest in the big picture in which women are enmeshed in a web encompassing society, politics, economics, and religion. They seek personal freedoms rather than social rights for themselves as a group. They launch into attacks on the rigid morality imposed in public places and aspire to free themselves from its prohibitions."[30] In this sense it is the translator, in the case of Alsanea's novel, who picks up the political engagement, focusing the power of exposure on the politics of translating Arabic fiction in the digital age. The production of the leaking subject as a "cosmopolitan" celebrity author is itself exposed by the translator of the work. This production mimics digital technology yet frames it at the same time. The one-time hit (meaning, the novel) transcends the intentions of the author or the specific "politics" of the author to become a phenomenon, a cache of leaks mined and circulated through the medium of the novel, producing the author in the process as famous, endangered, courageous, and scandalous. This cache of leaks or the compilation of *akhbār*, discussed in chapter 3, proliferates within the text as a series of scandalous e-mails, and as the compilation—a text to be bought or illegally downloaded as in Mujtahidd's "best of." The author is imagined in this context as a transcription machine that transforms e-mails into novelistic chapters, the digital into the literary, and revelations into suspenseful tales. Alsanea is constituted as author through her leaks and through her claiming of the leak (Assange, Mujtahidd) as someone on the inside who gains access to and exposes through weekly e-mails the private lives of the girls of Riyadh.

TAXI: LEAKING WHILE DRIVING

The "novel" as a gathering place of scandals and leaks akin to Wael Abbas's YouTube channel or to Mujtahidd's Twitter account is foregrounded in Khaled Alkhamissi's *Taxi: Ḥawādīt al-Mashāwīr* (*Taxi*, 2006), a compilation of *akhbār* that slap and knock out the author and draw him into his own text. *Taxi* presents a series of conversations with cabdrivers in Cairo that end up exposing the practices of the Mubarak regime and of the role of the intellectual and author in collecting and sharing these conversations and stories (*ḥawādīt*) as chapters in his text.[31] *Taxi* stages what Asef Bayat calls the "political street," which "denotes the collective sentiments, shared feelings, and public opinions of ordinary people in their day-to-day utterances and practices that are expressed broadly in public spaces—in taxis, buses, and shops, on street sidewalks, or in mass street demonstrations."[32] *Taxi*'s narrative is a crucible for the accumulation and proliferation of stories, mediated by the narrator's questions about the economy, the government, and daily life. From the TV stage of Zaven Kouyoumjian's show, "*sīreh w-infataḥit*" (open talk) and Alsanea's "*sīreh w-infaḍaḥit*" (scandal talk), we move with Alkhamissi to the cab as the fictional stage and inbox of scandalous stories. A journalist by training, Alkhamissi produced a diary of his interviews with drivers conducted over the course of one year. Fictionalized as a character in his own text, Alkhamissi relates conversations that take drivers back to their youth as moviegoers in the 1980s, soldiers in the 1970s, or foreign laborers in the Gulf States. Aligning the Nasser, Sadat, and Mubarak eras, and Egypt and the Gulf, these stories operate as a *faḍḥ* and *kashf* of the state of affairs in Egypt and of the historical trajectory underlying it.

Alkhamissi leaks out from the taxi, from the street, and from the daily violations that he observes and that Wael Abbas captured on his camera and uploaded online. In her review of the book, Omayma Abdelatif argues that "*Taxi's* brilliance is that it captures the point at which cabs cease to be just a means of transportation and instead become a space for debate and exchange, at a time when all other public spaces, including the street itself, had become inaccessible under the brutal force of the police state."[33] In this context the street has moved outside of the street in order to reclaim it through the literary work. The street–which has been emptied of its occupants, who moved into cabs and went on Twitter–was flooded with protesters, slogans, and signs during the 2011 uprising. However, while Abdelatif reads the taxi as a space of "debate and exchange," I read it as a stage for a literary and political performance that mediates the process of writing, circulation, and exposure. On this new stage the roles of journalist, author, and driver are unsettled, throwing into disarray both the text's narrative and language. It is from this space that stories and events are collected and recirculated in order to expose political corruption in Egypt. Circulating in the taxi while collecting stories and churning them out as chapters in the novel, Alkhamissi turns the cab into an inbox and outbox like Rajaa's e-mail, or a Twitter or YouTube account that receives and leaks out images, videos, and revelations.

With over twenty-six editions and translations into several languages, *Taxi* reproduces "street language," that is "special, raw, alive, real."[34] This language of new writing should thus be contrasted with the language of power and its multiple fictions (ideological, political, and literary).[35] The practice of exposure that arises from this new literary and material space—the cab—takes shape through a series of linguistic and narrative transformations. Whereas the conversations are in spoken Arabic (*ʿāmmiyya*), the author's reflections and narrative voice are in the formal Modern Standard Arabic (*fuṣḥā*). However, as the bulk of the text is devoted to conversations between driver and rider, *fuṣḥā* appears as the incongruous text, out of place, belonging to a different register, temporality, project, and space. As the conversations evolve over the course of the narrative, the street erupts, overcomes *Taxi*, and takes over its language. This accentuates the vulnerability of the narrator's voice and haughty language—that of *adab*—thereby making the latter unstable, prone to affective outbursts erupting in the cab and from the street. This back-and-forth between the taxi and the street transforms the text into a receptacle for stories in circulation and endows the work's language with an affective power that confronts the language and abuses of the regime. The conversation and its circulation enact a transfer of affects from the street to the taxi, and from the front seat to the back seat, thereby overwhelming and engulfing the discourse of the author.

In *Taxi* the author/narrator instigates the process of storytelling from a distance—from the back seat, both literally and figuratively—thereby turning the driver into an informer, storyteller, and leaker, reporting abuse to the narrator, who records it in the back. In one instance, a driver describes how a policeman in civilian clothes rode with him, only to extort money by threatening to take his papers and arrest him should he refuse to pay. Alkhamissi experiences this story about the disguise of the law as a "violent slap" in the face.[36] Exposing a model of abuse through multimedia processes of recording, storytelling, and circulation, the driver's language and account slap the narrator and violently unsettle his position in the text—his position as author. The slap, in this case, exposes the narrator who wants to locate exposure somewhere else, putting it in the mouth of the driver, while preserving his comfortable position of observer in the back. The slap in *Taxi*, reminiscent of the slap that ignited the Arab uprisings in the fall of 2010 with Bouazizi in Tunisia, reveals in this context the fictionalization of the author as intellectual who records and analyzes yet resists and avoids an affective confrontation with or indictment of the practices of the police state.[37] Just as Arab intellectuals experienced the uprisings as a violent and unsettling slap to their system of knowledge and political engagement, as discussed in the introduction, the slap in *Taxi* targets Alkhamissi's safe space and distance from his object of analysis, thereby fracturing the boundary between rider and driver, researcher and native informant, and intellectual and person of the street.

Modern Standard Arabic (*fuṣḥā*), *adab*'s handmaiden, was the vehicle of civilizing the "brute" and "wild" Arab masses. This process was integral to the *Nahda* project that consolidated *adab*'s civilizing and disciplining pretenses.[38] This "civilizing" process operates along various registers, including the primacy of *fuṣḥā* over *ʿāmmiyya*. Examining this dynamic in *Taxi*, one could claim that "affect," a force and duration, which binds space-time through an "impingement" on the body,[39] arises in the interstices of the *Nahda*-era disconnect between *fuṣḥā* and *ʿāmmiyya*, exposing their leaky boundaries. Emerging from linguistic registers, bodily postures, modes of circulation on the street and online, and arresting images and stories that slap and knock down, affects circulate from one linguistic register to another, from one mode of writing and storytelling to another, and from one subject position to another. The leaking subject in *Taxi* is thus both the driver and the rider, the person on the street and the one collecting and transmitting his/her stories through the medium of the novel, chronicle, or diary. The vulnerability of the activist in cyberspace who takes on a likeness to the street is reenacted in *Taxi* through similar forms of circulation, sharing, and proliferation that collectively constitute the literary work. This vulnerability is also the vulnerability of the regime itself, the system unable to contain its affects, *qillat adab* (incivility, misbehavior), and insecurities.

SHAKING THE REGIME

The story that slaps Alkhamissi violently in the face is aligned with the slapping of the government, which trembles and shakes due to a protest in 2005 by two hundred Kifaya activists surrounded by two thousand security officers. Describing this protest, which Wael Abbas filmed and put online as a video, one driver states that the government is so afraid that "its knees are shaking. I mean one puff and the government will fall, a government without knees."[40] The fragmentation of the regime and its proliferation as slapping hands and batons at various street corners and police stations, discussed in chapter 2, is reenacted in *Taxi* as shaky knees. The satirical yet powerful account of the shaking government prior to the Arab uprisings, for which Assange took credit ("shaking up power structures in the Middle East"), is associated in the driver's account with the government's fear of demonstration, foreshadowing the unrest starting in 2010 that was ignited by a slap in a souk in Tunisia. The police state counters this fear, suggests the cabbie, by raising prices and scaring people with the economic situation, thereby forcing them to think only of their livelihoods. The shaking of the knees and the demonstration cause an interruption in circulation. The ensuing traffic jam requires the rider to pay more for the story, ten pounds instead of three, in order to reach his final destination in downtown Cairo.[41] Slapping, shaking, and trembling thus describe the work of language, narrative, affective exposure, and political confrontation. This clockwork of driving, storytelling, and demonstrating is mediated through a register that calls attention to a new writing mode and critique of power, thereby refiguring the role of the author/intellectual staging and transmitting it.

In *Taxi*, the weakness and vulnerability of the government is exposed in the process of circulation and storytelling, and *ifshāʾ* (revelation) and *tafashshī* (proliferation). An affective language emerging from the distorted body of the driver in his shabby and claustrophobic cab exposes this vulnerability. Two hundred protesters managed to make a scene of the government's weakness, now reduced to legs and limbs that shake and tremble. Exposing the waning legitimacy of the fiction of power, a driver explains how the government makes up traffic regulations in order to extort money: "We live a lie and believe it. The government's only role is to check that we believe the lie, don't you think?"[42] The affective register of the driver expressed in a raw language exposes the official narrative as a lie, or an *old* fiction. The new literary work thus counters another fiction—the lie or "the same old story"—which is unable to veil its production, shakiness, and instability. The driver's discourse is "raw and real," not only because it employs street language or spoken Arabic, but also because it produces a new kind of narrative that affectively confronts and unsettles this lie. This is precisely the fiction of power that Wael confronts through *qillat adab* (lack of *adab,* incivility), further anchoring the state of collapse and the weakness and shakiness of the fiction of power unable to control its leaks, fantasies, and videos. *Taxi* and the literary works I examine in this chapter (including Alsanea's) anticipate and foreground Twitter culture and the kinds of activism that mediate and circulate videos and stories of abuse and violation.

Taxi reproduces the affects of riding: the crooked body posture and uncomfortable seats, the heat and stench in the cab, traffic sounds, and the radio tapes playing sermons, music, and news.[43] As the narrator rides, he accumulates stories that collectively expose political abuse, extortion, corruption, and the shaky and panicked government. Enticed, slapped, and overtaken by the chronicle of revelations and stories, the narrator, who was thus far collecting stories, instigating and recording them like a social scientist conducting an experiment, is both slapped and slaps back at the end. Through a transfer of affects—between the cabdriver and the rider, the street and the text—the narrative shifts to a direct and violent confrontation with power. Alkhamissi *takes his gloves off* to slap government practices and old fiction. Unlike the *fuṣḥā* (formal Arabic) framing each chapter, which captures the author/intellectual's voice, chapter 49 starts in *ʿāmmiyya* (spoken Arabic), employing the first-person pronoun. Alkhamissi relates that, having finished his tour of the booksellers in the Azbakiyya neighborhood, he decided to take the metro to Giza, only to discover that service was disrupted. Looking around in the station, he noticed a sign that read: "The Metro Underground: Mubarak's Gift to His People."[44] The author, continuing in *ʿāmmiyya*, launches a scathing attack against Mubarak, "Lord of the Universe and of Our Master Mohammed,"[45] making a scene of his shameless claim to public funds, which could be dispensed and offered as a gift from the ruler to his people. Shifting registers by appropriating the raw language of the street, Alkhamissi abandons the cautionary framing and language of his critique that had afforded him distance in order to confront political power head on.

In this satirical and violent diatribe, the identity of the narrator (Alkhamissi) is fused with the voice of the street and of the cab driver—the raw language of scene-making. The author finally embraces the position of *faḍḍāḥ* both by accumulating the drivers' micro-*faḍāʾiḥ* (stories, scandalous happenings) and publishing them in a book, and also by staging himself in another register through a direct confrontation with the police state. In this case the practice of *faḍḥ* links modes of circulation to confrontation, and demonstration to the uprising to come. Confrontation staged through literature thus moves from *iltizām* (commitment) and the prior *Nahda*-based critiques of social and political inequalities, colonialism, and imperialism, to *faḍḥ* as a mode of scandalizing and making a scene on the one hand, and recording and leaking abuses and violations that expose the regime as an assemblage of shaky knees on the other. This *faḍḥ* is staged in the cab, a place of physical distortion, leakage, decay, circulation, and storytelling. The critique of the regime associated with the author/intellectual conducting research and publishing a diary becomes consumed and engulfed by its object of research: the street, the taxi driver, and social and political corruption and abuse. The findings of Alkhamissi break with their neatly fictionalized frame in the shape of a published diary, taking over his narrative, language, and author function.

CONCLUSION

In Alkhamissi's text the author is unable to remain above the fray, safe in a public sphere where he interacts along fixed and recognizable rules of engagement, debating political issues, conducting experiments, and writing books. When authors go on Twitter or down to the street they are overwhelmed, slapped, and shaken as they try to gather information and leak it out to their reading public. The street as the scene of government abuse that Wael captured in his videos is captured by Alkhamissi in a text that exposes and unveils, records and circulates through thousands of copies of *Taxi* bought and downloaded online. The car's movement and stench generating bodily contortion and outrage unsettle the author's function and the literary space in which it prevails, yet simultaneously constructs the author as bestseller of the fiction of the street. The author, either on Twitter or in the cab, with his/her body bent over and crooked from typing or riding, succumbs to that which he/she seeks to describe, discuss, expose, and fictionalize. From that space of physical distortion and at times erasure, the stories proliferate and construct the leaking subject as celebrity author, tweeter, or whistleblower followed and read by thousands. We move in this context from models of critique and dialectical engagement to making a scene and exposure as new modes of confrontation and writing.

The interplay of language registers, the circulation of bodies and cars on the streets of Cairo, and the scandals revealed on this affective stage drag the authorial position into that which it sought to represent, analyze, and control from a distance (the backseat). The new authorial position, slapped and slapping, moving back and forth between "the scene of writing" and "making a scene," challenges our reading of the political in the context of *adab*. In this new setting the author is compelled to expose him/herself in the process of exposing the other, taking risks both as author and character as a way of exposing violations and abuse, leaking the inside, and selling more books and gathering more followers.

The economy of exposure, vulnerability, and confrontation identified in the texts discussed in this chapter breaks with previous conceptions of the literary, the author, and the relation between the intellectual and power. Replacing those "old fictions" are new genres and writing practices that embrace the street, the Internet, or rawness, marking the rise of the leaking subject. The "literary" characteristics of new texts are constituted and recognized in instances of hacking and attack that are unpredictable and threatening. That said, I'm not presenting here a comprehensive account of new writing in the digital age and identifying all the models of interplay and fascination and anxiety between the literary and the digital; that is impossible at this stage and will require several decades before we can begin to understand these texts' aesthetic and political significance in a larger historical context. All one can do at this moment is to expose the way new writing is being defined and produced by its practitioners (authors, tweeters, bloggers, translators) as they struggle with, dismiss, and reassert the question of literature. In this context new writing should be examined in instances and events, scandals and acts of hacking, wherein the literary and the author function specifically are both undermined and reaffirmed. These possibilities and dangers stage hacking and leaking as moments of subversion but also as threats both to political structures and to the agents of subversion themselves. In the next chapter I explore how this "subversion" operates in a dystopian setting by examining acts of cyber-raiding that recode the literary and the author function on Twitter.

CHAPTER 5

Cyber-Raiding

> Imagine if there was Twitter during the *Jahiliyya*, what would they write?
> —#twitterjahlih, a hashtag on Twitter for writing classical Arabic poetry

> Several news organizations and the Arabic Network for Human Rights Information reported on Wednesday that author Karam Saber had been sentenced, in absentia, by a court in Beni Suef to five years in prison on charges of insulting religion: The insult was allegedly made in a collection of short stories, *Ayn Allāh*?—"Where is God?" (2010). A suit was filed against Saber in April 2011 with the attorney general in Beni Suef, alleging that Saber's book contains statements insulting of religious beliefs. At the time, Saber said he'd been informed that his book would be referred to the Commission of Senior Scholars of Al-Azhar for content analysis to determine if it contains offensive words. Apparently some scholar felt it did, although Saber told *Aswat Misriyya* that the collection of short stories is a work of literature that shall not be measured using "religious standards." He also told *AM* that he will continue to defend his right of expression inside and outside of the court. Saber also said that he plans to appeal the verdict and plans to present the court with a legal challenge tomorrow. This comes with an apparent rise in blasphemy cases.
> —Arab Lit Blog

In the Arab digital age the definition of literature and the formation of the canon are emerging from prize culture and critical assessments, from acts of hacking and exposure as we have seen in the previous chapter, and from the kind of "content analysis" practiced by Al-Azhar's Commission of Senior Scholars in the news item quoted above.[1] Such "content analysis"—a form of literary criticism—issued by the highest center of Islamic jurisprudence and learning in Egypt (Al-Azhar) not only determines the book's success or failure but also the author's fate. This high-stakes assessment has direct implications for authors and bloggers as we have seen in the case of Ahmed Naji who went to jail for explicit passages in *Using Life*.[2] Many authors across the region are being subjected to persecution as a result of their writing and public engagement, and harassed or imprisoned for a poem or a tweet. Not even illustrious authors who are deceased are exempt from this violence. At the Riyadh Book Fair in March 2014, members of the Saudi religious police, *al-Hay'a* (Commission for the Prevention of Vice and Promotion of Virtue), stormed the booth of Palestinian poet Mahmoud Darwish's publisher, confiscating all his books due to a poem entitled "God, Why Have You Forsaken Me?" In a perverse literary performance, *Hay'a* members started reading aloud the "blasphemous passages" from Darwish's poem, decrying the publisher's willingness to subject "women and children" to such heresy.[3] In all these cases, acts of reading and literary reception are tied to practices that collapse fiction and reality, the author with her/his text. Literature becomes meaningful through perverse reading performances and the viral circulation of passages deemed heretical and threatening to social order.

Violent acts of recoding literature—a fight over reading and interpretation—are characteristic of religious and political repression that has gone on for centuries in various parts of the world. What is different today, however, is the way in which these acts not only prevent people from speaking but in fact redefine literature and introduce in the process models of performance, interpretation, and reading practices that are intertwined with digital models of circulation. The meaning of literature is no longer established based on a realist assessment of plot and narrative structure, but depends instead on quoting out of context and circulating passages or sentences marked for attack. An affective economy of circulation, proliferation, and performance online hacks the text and reproduces it as target and projectile. In this light when people are imprisoned, hacked, or persecuted for a poem or a tweet, it does not mean only that fiction (*khayāl*) has no place in a strict and intolerant realm, but rather that new forms of fiction, reception, interpretation, and reading practices are emerging instead.[4] In some cases these practices reveal the ways in which particular forms of fiction are completely taking over, thereby becoming a constitutive part of an overarching fantasmatic model that found its ideal home online, inhabiting the glass house of Twitter, and feeding off its leaks and affects.

Contesting traditional literature and pushing authors out of cyberspace and into prisons, new forms of fiction are immediate and all encompassing. Performed and practiced in real time on Twitter and coming from the present but also from a fantasized past, this new fiction is taking shape in the form of video games and tribal warfare erupting and leaking on social media platforms. Focusing on the Internet as a space of regression and harassment following the Arab uprisings, this chapter traces the violence perpetrated against Arab authors, activists, and intellectuals online to the emergence of fiction as hyperreality principle. Investigating the relation between reading practices and knowledge production, and continuing the examination of the function of the author as leaking subject in the digital age, I focus on the act of fragmenting the work itself through online campaigns and perverse literary performances. Specifically, I examine a hashtag campaign—in fact, a hashtag *ghazwa* (tribal raid)—launched on Twitter against a Saudi author, Badriah Albeshr [al-Beshr] (b. 1967), who was accused of apostasy for passages in her novel *Hend and the Soldiers* (2010). The attack and the literary performance that the hashtag enacted, I argue, recode the literary and open a portal to *Jahiliyya* ("heathen times" or the period predating the advent of Islam in Arabia, often perceived as a time of ignorance, violence, and excess) as the framework for a new hyperreal yet fictional and fantasmatic space framed as the culmination of "Arab Spring" emancipation.[5] The hashtag *ghazwa* directed against Albeshr establishes the meaning of the text, conditions its circulation and reading practice, and designates the action to be taken against its author all at the same time. This meaning-making hashtag *ghazwa* leads us to reconsider the meaning of literature emerging from acts of hacking and attacks that mediate and shape political activism, knowledge production, writing practices, and literary reception in the digital age. This chapter is about the "body fiction" of the Arab author leaking online as cropped text and limbs, marked and circulated, read and performed. It's also about *Jahiliyya* as a literary and political fantasy of revenge and lawless excess, erupting through a portal on Twitter, reactivated and fictionalized as concept and practice of hyperreality. This eruption puts in question literature's association with the novel as the genre most identified with Arab modernity and its civilizing fiction or *adab*, gauging the kind of community and publics that are produced through new writing and raiding practices online.

TWITTER: ALL THE RAGE!

The Internet ushered in utopian possibilities of communication and exchange meant to circumvent censorship and political and economic apparatuses, leading eventually to an open and free society. This utopian view of the Internet was cemented by the flourishing of social media and communication across borders. That said, within the promise of free communication lie forms of radicalism that unleash affective outbursts and conceptions of the other that eradicate difference. Cyberwriting and debating practices move beyond processes of editing and control, as I have argued previously and, more importantly, beyond conceptions of community and ethics grounded in models of intersubjectivity developed and theorized from the eighteenth century onward. Acts of hacking and attack, arrest and persecution, reinscribe notions of materiality often excluded from analyses of the transformations brought about by the culture of debate and nonhierarchical communication, as scholars like Henri Jenkins argue.[6] Material effects that eliminate the other, rather than simply contesting his/her views online and off, emerge from a context immediately following the Arab uprisings as in the case I examine in this chapter.

Twitter is most associated with this culture of exchange, yet also embodies its most dystopian transformation. Restricting participants to 140-character contributions or tweets (*wamḍa*, *taghrīda*, or *twīta* in Arabic), Twitter is one of the most notable and research-worthy social media platforms that is radically changing cultures of communication and systems of writing. Twitter has been theorized as a revolutionary public sphere, circumventing corporate forms of domination and enabling the production of counterpublics that horizontally intervene in the political through forms of e-mobilization and e-tactics.[7] This view, however, while it rightfully acknowledges this new media's potential to effect change, continues to consider Twitter as an expanded public sphere. My reading seeks to further problematize this framework by engaging the ways in which the "revolutionary" attribute of this new platform is produced through forms of mimicry and hacking that are grounded in archaic models of violence and suppression as well, both in the Arab context and beyond.

In a discussion of Twitter use in feminist debates in the United States, journalist Michelle Goldberg describes Twitter as "a machine for producing rage," wherein "anger spread like wildfire," thereby bringing to mind al-Ghadhdhami's description of Twitter as "gossip machine" and *machine à scandale* as discussed in chapter 3.[8] Goldberg presents this assessment in reference to a debate within a feminist group that soon degenerated into a self-cannibalizing process, radically transforming the platform that was meant to provide a forum for women to organize and discuss issues relevant to gender in the context of racial and sexual minorities in New York. "Katherine Cross, a Puerto Rican trans woman working on a PhD at the CUNY Graduate Center, wrote about how often she hesitates to publish articles or blog posts out of fear of inadvertently stepping on an ideological land mine and bringing down the wrath of the online enforcers. 'I fear being cast suddenly as one of the "bad guys" for being insufficiently radical, too nuanced or too forgiving.' "[9] In another instance feminist author Jo Freeman describes the reaction to a letter she published in *Ramparts* magazine from members of her own group: "'That was a public trashing,' she says. 'I was horrible, disloyal, a traitor.' It went beyond mere criticism: 'There's a difference between trashing someone and challenging them. You can challenge someone's idea. When you're trashing someone, you're essentially saying they're a bad person.' "[10]

THE BLASPHEMOUS AUTHOR

The fights and experiences of erasure by tweeters that Goldberg describes in an American context point to a model of interaction that is tied to a global phenomenon involving hacking users' accounts and forms of intimidation both verbal and physical. What was experienced as "trashing" in one context was experienced as *ghazwa* (raid or foray, which comes from *ghazū*, conquest, or *razia* in French) in another context involving a woman author from Saudi Arabia who became the target of a campaign on Twitter. This campaign of intimidation took the shape of a "tagging," which names an object in order to produce it discursively and to designate it as a target for attack in this case. The hashtag targeting Albeshr unfolded as a revenge campaign for a slighted deity, unleashing anger against an author whose work—passages from her novel, *Hend and the Soldiers*—was deemed blasphemous by a group of tweeters.

On May 29, 2012, Qatar University invited author, academic, journalist, and women's-rights activist Badriah Albeshr for a talk on women and culture in the Gulf. Albeshr is a well-known Saudi public intellectual who has been residing in Dubai since 2006. She is a columnist for *Al-Hayat* newspaper and an active participant in debates about women's rights, culture, and politics in the Gulf region. She is also the author of many novels including *Al-Urjūḥa* ("The Swing") (2010), *Hend wa-l-ʿAskar* (*Hend and the Soldiers*) (2006), and *Gharāmiyyāt Shāriʿ al-Aʿshā* ("Love Adventures in al-Aʿsha Street") (2014), which was longlisted for the 2014 International Prize for Arabic Fiction. In 2014 Albeshr got her own TV show titled, *Badriah*, which focuses on social issues in Saudi Arabia and the Gulf region and airs on the Dubai-based network MBC.[11]

In *Hend and the Soldiers*, Albeshr tells the story of Hend, who finds her voice through a series of social and familial struggles and through a literary map that extends from Arabian folktales to Nikos Kazantzakis's *Christ Recrucified.* In part, the novel fits into the "lid-off" genre that Roger Allen and Marilyn Booth identified in their assessment of Gulf women's writing. For instance, Albeshr depicts Hend's brother Ibrahim as ending up by joining al-Qaeda; she describes Hend's failed marriage with the controlling Mansur; and she tackles rape, both in folktales and as an integral reality of arranged marriages for underage girls. That said, Albeshr moves beyond these tropes to present Hend as a strong character who confronts these realities and is aware of her freedom and limitations in the process, ultimately managing to find her voice and become a writer against all odds. In particular, the relation between Hend and her mother, Heila, is a recurrent theme in the novel. Hend struggles with the mother's favoritism vis-à-vis her children, but also with her enforcing of the patriarchal codes against which Hend rebels.

Though *Hend and the Soldiers* was not banned in Saudi Arabia, it generated a wave of condemnation from religious conservative circles across the Gulf, leading for instance to Albeshr's being banned from entering Kuwait in 2013 and to the cancellation of her talk at Qatar University in 2012. When her talk was advertised, a Twitter hashtag, #La_LiBadriah (No to Badriah), was started by a handful of people seeking to pressure the university to cancel the talk.[12] These activists were protesting what they considered to be Albeshr's blasphemous novel, in which Hend as a little girl at one point compares her mother's constant anger to that which she imagines to be God's. Circulating the "injurious" passages online as "proof" of blasphemy, the attack soon degenerated into an attack against Albeshr herself, with some tweets describing her as an apostate, a liberal intellectual complicit in Western cultural and political hegemony and conquest (*ghazū*), a bad author, and a disobedient daughter (*'āqa*).

This attack, which highlighted questions of gender and the right of women to speak and take part in public culture in the Gulf, needs to be examined as a new form of literary reading and writing online, produced by a number of participants, including students and faculty members, each making various charges *against* the work and its author.[13] This collective performance doubling as an attack was seeking to discredit and exclude the author from the public forum, namely the university.

Albeshr's detractors cropped and circulated the passages shown in figure 12, tagging them "@liberalih" (liberal) and renumbering them in red (1, 2, 3), with the offending sentences bracketed as if to expose their blasphemy and to mark them for attack. Despite the fact that the novel is a work of fiction and that the

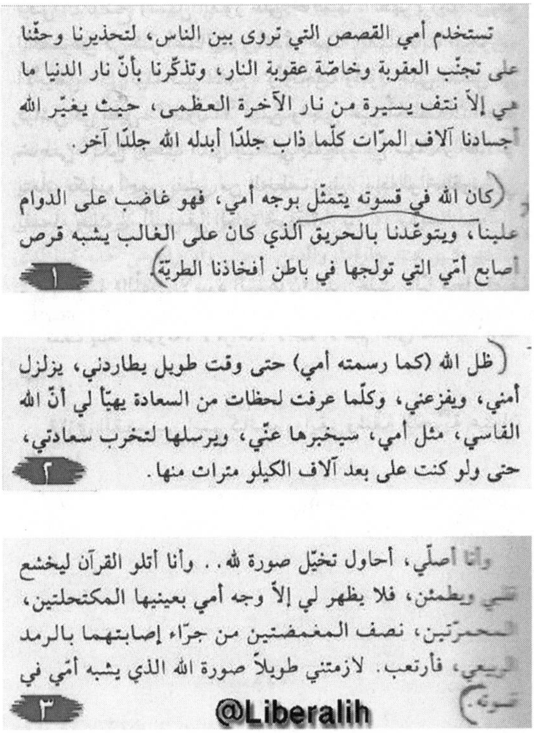

تستخدم أمي القصص التي تروى بين الناس، لتحذيرنا وحثّنا
على تجنّب العقوبة وخاصّة عقوبة النار، وتذكّرنا بأنّ نار الدنيا ما
هي إلاّ نتف يسيرة من نار الآخرة العظمى، حيث يغيّر الله
أجسادنا آلاف المرّات كلّما ذاب جلدًا أبدله الله جلدًا آخر.

(كان الله في قسوته يتمثّل بوجه أمي، فهو غاضب على الدوام
علينا، ويتوعّدنا بالحريق الذي كان على الغالب يشبه قرص
أصابع أمّي التي تولجها في باطن أفخاذنا الطريّة)

١

(ظل الله (كما رسمته أمي) حتى وقت طويل يطاردني، يزلزل
أمني، ويفزعني، وكلّما عرفت لحظات من السعادة يهيّأ لي أنّ الله
القاسي، مثل أمي، سيخبرها عنّي، ويرسلها لتخرب سعادتي،
حتى ولو كنت على بعد آلاف الكيلو مترات منها.

٢

وأنا أصلّي، أحاول تخيّل صورة لله.. وأنا أتلو القرآن ليخشع
قلبي ويطمئن، فلا يظهر لي إلاّ وجه أمي بعينيها المكتحلتين،
المحمرّتين، نصف المغمضتين من جرّاء إصابتهما بالرمد
الربيعي، فأرتعب. لازمتني طويلاً صورة الله الذي يشبه أمّي في
قسوته.)

٣

@Liberalih

Figure 12. Series of Arabic tweets tagged "liberal" and translations.

Mother used these stories, which other people also knew, to warn us about God's punishment, especially hellfire. She insisted that the flames of this world were nothing but tiny sparks of the colossal fire of hell, where God would melt our skin thousands of times, each time replacing the melted skin with a whole new one.

In my mind, God assumed my mother's face, always angry, always threatening; the fire he promised was, on the whole, not much different from the pinches that her fingers burned on the insides of our tender thighs. (Albeshr, *Hend and the Soldiers*, 13–14.)

God, as my mother portrayed him, continued to chase me for a long time, disturbing my peace and terrifying me. If I tasted a moment of pleasure, I couldn't help feeling that God, being cruel like my mother, would go tell on me and send her to wreck the happiness I had, even if I were thousands of miles away from her. (Ibid., 26.)

In my prayers I would try to envision God's image as I read verses from the Qur'an, to humble my heart and give it some peace; but all I could see was Mother's face, her kohl-lined eyes, reddish and half-closed, ridden with trachoma. I would shudder. For a long time, I carried with me this image of God, who resembled Mother in his cruelty. (Ibid.)

passages quoted above are words uttered by a little girl struggling with her mother's perceived cruelty, the cyber-raiders collapsed Albeshr with her text and launched their campaign online. Engaging in a different form of reading and consuming the literary text, the tweeters repaginated, cropped, and bounced the fragments back and forth along with images of Albeshr herself marked with a red circle across the face as if turning her into a shooting target. This economy of cyber-reading and circulation, protest and attack, reveals a new landscape from which suppression of women's rights and new definitions of literature are emerging.

Reading and bouncing back and forth the literary text, which is reduced to its "blasphemous" passages, needs to be framed in relation to women's activism in the Gulf region and in Saudi Arabia specifically. The campaign in 2011 advocating women's right to drive, which Albeshr supported, had been particularly acerbic, generating attacks against activists and resulting in prosecutions and arrests. A campaign on Facebook called "*ḥamlat al-ʿiqāl*" ("iqal campaign") showcased the black rope (*ʿiqāl* or *ʿagal*) adorning the headgear in traditional Gulf male dress as a brandished whip threatening physical violence against the "misbehaving" and "disobedient" women seeking the right to drive.[14] Manal al-Sharif, a women's-rights activist and organizer of the right-to-drive campaign, was arrested for filming herself driving and for posting the video on YouTube. She was forced to recant her actions before being released.[15] Therefore, the campaign against Albeshr should be read in relation to these campaigns playing out both online and off. Thus, the hashtag raid of Albeshr's talk in Qatar involves a new reading and writing performance on the one hand, and an attack and a condemnation that lead to charges ranging from treason to blasphemy, with concrete material effects, the least of which is imprisonment.

Though the campaign against Albeshr was eventually countered by a #Naʿam _LiBadriah ("Yes to Badriah") campaign advocating for her right to speak, the #La-LiBadriah hashtag succeeded in intimidating university officials and pressuring them into canceling the talk.[16] In the days following the incident, Albeshr raised the issue in an *Al-Hayat* op-ed, describing the campaign as *ghazwat al-hashtag* (hashtag raid) and bemoaning the university's decision to cave in to extremists.[17] In other interviews Albeshr claimed that this hashtag raid, led by "the forces of darkness" (*qiwā ẓalāmiyya*), was a testimony to the inability to distinguish fiction from reality: "those who condemned my novel as usual did not read it but adopted instead this juvenile belief that makes one condemn an actor because he played the role of a killer."[18] Albeshr explained that the intended meaning (*maghzā*) of her text was already established by the raiders who felt no need to read and engage the actual novel.[19] The hashtag campaign thus generates a debate about free speech and gender in the Gulf but also about the meaning of literature in the context of new writing genres, cyberattacks, trolling, and online harassment.

Albeshr's experience of the campaign as a raid or foray (*ghazwa*) led by "forces of darkness" or obscurantism conjures up the collapse of the university as a public space for debate and simultaneously betrays a powerful anxiety in the Arab imaginary about the tribal raid. A raid or a night raid unfolding under the cover of darkness (*ẓalām*, as in *ẓalāmiyya*) involves slaying the men and taking the women as slaves. Cyberspace thus transforms into the desert of tribal warfare, which coincides with the demise of a public culture associated with the *Nahda* ideals of debate and communication, and civilization and civility. The category of "liberal" in the Gulf region especially, which was integral to discrediting Albeshr (*al-librāliyya*, the liberal one), is associated with this *Nahda* framework.[20]

Moreover, the hashtag *ghazwa* to which she was subjected determined the meaning (*maghzā*) of her text in an a priori fashion. In this way the connection between *ghazwa* (raid) and *maghzā* (meaning) allows us to identify acts of suppression, silencing, and cyberattack as a new framework that shapes the meaning of texts and articulates a new relation between fiction and reality, and author and the novel. The reading and sharing of fragments of Albeshr's work by the Twitter activists take shape as acts of cyber-reading—and -raiding—that hack and recode the author and her text. What remain are cropped passages marked in red, circulating online and generating calls for revenge.

Albeshr's experience of the attack as *ghazwa* also brings to mind a very powerful discourse in the modern Arab context, namely that of the Western *ghazū*: the perceived cultural and political onslaught on the Arab-Islamic world by the West. In the case of Qatar, this *ghazū* is associated with the American military base near Doha and the presence of foreign commercial interests in the country, as well as the establishment of an educational complex in Doha containing campuses of prestigious American universities.[21] Attacking Albeshr, one activist says, "our voice against all distortion and *ghazū*," thereby identifying Albeshr's visit as an extension of a Western hegemonic project or *ghazū* (conquest) that needs to be countered.[22] The attackers, in this context, occupy the role of the outnumbered group resisting foreign conquest by defending the faith: "May God forgive us for what the misguided ones at Qatar University have done by inviting the liberal thinker and Masonic agent 'Badriah Albeshr' who dared to disrespect God Almighty."[23]

Some activists took this collapsing of Badriah with an invading West a step further by comparing her to the Israeli ambassador whose talk at a university in the United States was successfully disrupted by a group of Arab students.[24] Israel, the most concrete embodiment of Western *ghazū* of Arab land, is conjured up in order to legitimize the group's attempt to sabotage Albeshr's talk. Unfolding as a Twitter campaign, the *ghazwa* of Badriah's talk is thus a consorted and well-planned act of sabotage against a hegemonic and colonial project embodied in liberal values, American military presence in the Gulf, Israeli occupation of Arab land, freemasonry, and women's rights. Though centered on one event, the campaign exposes a series of struggles, anxieties, and fantasies that converge and recode the literary text. The campaign thus reveals a new political and cultural economy playing out in the Gulf. Examining this *ghazwa* requires an investigation of the interconnection between aesthetics and politics in a local and global context and an explanation of the ways in which ideological conflicts and historical positions connect Gulf culture to the *Nahda* tradition, and pan-Arab struggles to the American presence in the Gulf. As in the hacking of the Lebanese ministry discussed in the introduction, cyber-raiding in Albeshr's case conjures up histories and conflicts that shape reading practices and public formation in the Arab digital age.

The hashtag *ghazwa* against Albeshr imagines a new community online, which is produced through reading practices with strict binaries of East and West, *dār al-Islām* (Land of Islam)[25] and *dār al-ḥarb* (Land of War)[26]—binaries with which *Nahda* thinkers had to contend and overcome, starting with Rifaʿa Rafiʿ al-Tahtawi in the 1830s. While Mujtahidd's revelations imagine a public tied by mystery, literary virtuosity, and affective justice, the public emerging from the hashtag *ghazwa* examined in this chapter puts in question the liberal—ideal—framework of the *Nahda* project and of *adab* when it moves to the Gulf. Thus, in addition to the discourse of Western military and ideological *ghazū* in pan-Arab and Islamist discourse (the two Gulf wars, Israel, etc.), we have to contend here with what could be an anxiety about a literary *ghazū* as well, mediated by global literary systems that have suppressed and excluded the Arab arche—poetry. This *ghazū* is experienced as perhaps extending as well to encompass Gulf-based prizes centered on the novel as the most "modern" and most valued literary genre, and on women's writing from the region especially.

GHAZWA: A HASHTAG RAID

The term *ghazwa* used in Albeshr's reaction to the cancellation of her talk is tied to a form of tribal warfare predating Islam. In the Islamic context *ghazwat Badr* marks one of the first decisive victories of the Prophet and his outnumbered followers against the Quraysh tribe at the wells of Badr near Medina. In this light the attack on Albeshr began with a mobilization through repeated calls to join the hashtag:

> -I urge you to follow this hashtag . . . Qatari youth are waging a campaign against the hosting of the liberal Badriah Albeshr at Qatar University for insulting God.
>
> -The issue does not only concern Qatari youth but the entire nation (*umma*) as well for we have to avenge God from misdeeds, the Glorified Lord of Honor and Power.[27]

The rhetoric of these tweets captures the reaction to a slighted deity that will not accept any other power or authority other than his. Cyberactivists gather as if in a tribal setting to wage religious war, thereby collapsing e-mobilization with tribal mobilization. The notion of "waging" (*shann*) as in "waging war" (*shann ḥarb*) is deployed to incite but also to describe the ways in which the youth (*shabāb*) ought to launch this campaign in order to avenge God. The campaign against Albeshr operates in this case as an exacting of revenge (*ḥamlat tha'r*) that involves a re-enactment of tribal mobilization and warfare. The hashtag and the calls for revenge thus operate as a form of *taḥrīḍ* ("inciting the menfolk to battle") against a woman they consider to be associated with Western ideological and political hegemony but also with *Jahiliyya*.[28] Represented as immoral and impure, Albeshr is thus drawn into a *Jahili* dialectic that erupts fantasmatically online. The campaign performs the unleashing of the desire for blood vengeance that the advent of Islam as *ḥilm* (patience, restraint) was meant to contain. Pan-Arab discourses on resistance and anticolonial struggles converge in the hashtag campaign with tribal mobilization that could be traced to *Jahiliyya*.

Nadia el-Cheikh argues that the "narrative that the Muslims gradually constructed was that the rise of Islam, that original moment of purity, brought about the elimination of the impurity and corruption of the pre-Islamic 'time of ignorance' (*jahiliyya*). The accepted features of life in *jahiliyya* that we find in the traditional texts were tribal feuds, lawlessness, sexual immorality, lax marital practices, killing by burial of infant girls [*wa'd*], the absence of food taboos and rules of purity, and idolatry."[29] In this light drawing on *Jahiliyya* in the name of combatting it, the hashtag campaign exposes the collapse of an Arab centralized authority and symbolic order. Confronting the allegedly lawless and decadent *Jahiliyya* associated with a conquering West requires deploying and reproducing that same violence and lawlessness associated with this powerful framework. Thus, the digital needs to be explored in light of the current political state of the Arab world and the nature of the Internet. Staging the unraveling of forms of authority, this new landscape gives rise to both freedom of expression but also *Jahiliyya*-like acts of vengeance as violent rituals of subjectivity online and off-. Whereas Foucault and Althusser have located subjectivation in discourse, power, and the state, subjectivity in this context—the leaking subjectivity—could be traced to digital practices and the return of *Jahili* rituals that seek to undo and contain (as Alan Nadel argues) the leak in all its "fluid" manifestations—the feminine, unbelief, decadence, and the West.[30] *Jahiliyya* is activated as a fantasized narrative of violence, blood vengeance, and tribal warfare that returns through online portals, assigning roles and performances—casting out Albeshr from the university and casting her as a leaking subject and a character from *Jahiliyya* that needs to be contained, eliminated, erased, buried (*wa'd*). In the name of fighting a modern *Jahiliyya* generally associated with an invading West and its cultural *ghazū* (Hollywood's sex and violence, liberal values, the *Nahda* narrative of the subject) as embodied in Albeshr's work and practices and in women's right to drive, the youth are called upon and incited (*taḥrīḍ*) in this hashtag to combat *Jahiliyya* and avenge the slighted deity by performing a *ghazwa*.

Just as the digitizing of medieval manuscripts by scholars and practitioners of digital humanities brings something of these manuscripts' genre and order into the contemporary setting, rather than simply subjecting them to our genres and ordering mechanisms, the treatment of Badriah as a *Jahili* disobedient woman in need of *ghazwa* (raid) by dissecting and consuming her modern novel brings something from the *Jahili* context into Twitter as such. The portal into *Jahiliyya* that opens up on Twitter is shaped by the interplay between the contemporary context, including the social and political environment, new genres, and technologies on the one hand, and classical genres and histories on the other. This movement codes both the present and the past, Twitter and *Jahiliyya*, juxtaposing and interwining new Arabic writing and contemporary practices on the one hand with classical genres and practices from Mujtahidd as the intrepid knight defending his beleaguered tribe to the *ghazwa* campaign against Albeshr on the other. Fiction and the study of fiction reveal the ways in which the archaic erupts and is experienced on Twitter. A close attention to the rhetoric and deployment of Twitter raids doubling as reading practices with a close examination of their justifications and registers uncover this interplay, which collapses space/time understood in light of modern epistemological and historical frameworks.

Scrutinizing the rhetoric of the campaign targeting Albeshr on Twitter reveals an attempt to triumph over the deity and beliefs of the other—the idolaters.

> This is not an attack against a liberal intellectual or a defense of Salafism but a vindication of the Divine Being for our Qur'an does not teach us to respect base sects but rather to regard as Holy the creator of the universe.[31]

In this tweet the revenge campaign, which disavows yet exposes its violent nature ("this is not an attack") takes shape as an act of *nuṣra* (championing, vindicating) that requires mobilization and war so that God, demanding vengeance according to the tweet, triumphs over those who belong to "base sects."[32] Albeshr's experience of the Twitter campaign as a "hashtag raid led by the forces of obscurantism" (*ghazwat hāshtāg li-quwā ẓalāmiyya*) thus fully captures the campaign's language and intents. In this context the raid or foray is the outcome of a campaign (*ḥamla*) wherein the raiders (*ghuzāt*) march and reach their destination in ethereal time in cyberspace. Reaching the encampment of the enemy is no longer a matter of days and weeks of desert riding, but rather hours of virtual time. The *ghazwa* also stages a particular deployment of literature (poetry) to express loss, pride, and triumph. This leads us to reconsider *ghazwa* and examine its resurgence in cyberspace either as the failure of the literary or as its complete and absolute triumph. The *nuṣra* campaign is deployed in this cyber-raid (*ghazwa*) as an intervention in and production of the literary text of the Arab woman author and public speaker. The language and practices of war drawn from the pre-Islamic and early Islamic contexts become the language of aesthetic normativity practiced by a new generation of trolls and cyber-raiders. The quest for *nuṣra* (revenge, triumph) is thus cast as a resistance against a larger onslaught targeting the Muslim *umma*, from dictatorial Arab regimes associated with the West and its decadent culture to colonial and imperialist practices targeting Muslim lands.

Ghazū is a term that has taken many meanings from pre-Islamic *ghazū* to *ghazū al-ʿIrāq*—the American invasion of Iraq in 2003. Tied to this political onslaught is *ghazū al-thaqāfa al-gharbiyya* ("Western culture's conquest"), which is a fundamental framework in Islamist discourses especially. A series of works and frameworks that engage the West as conqueror (*ghāzī*) emphasize the war against the East and Islam militarily, ideologically, and culturally. An iconic book from the 1960s about this topic is Muhammad Jalal Kishk's *Al-Ghazū al-Fikrī* (Ideological *Ghazū*) (1964).[33] Western *ghazū* in Kishk's model extends from the Crusades onward as it consistently and permanently targets Islam. In this perceived metaphysical assault, which is captured by someone like Sayyid Qutb as well, Arab nationalism and Arab modernity are viewed as complicit with if not an extension of Western *ghazū* that brought down the Islamic caliphate after World War I and eventually led to the emergence of Arab dictators from Nasser onward. According to Kishk, Arab thinkers such as Salama Mousa, Muhammad al-Sharqawi, Shukri Ghali, and Louis Awad are either apologists for or victims of this unfolding *ghazū*. The project of Arab modernity or *Nahda*, which could be traced to the nineteenth century, is cast in this light as an instrument of Western conquest and invasion, engendering *al-librāliyya* and a distorted discourse on women's rights and the subject, and which needs to be countered by the campaign on Twitter in a *ghazwa*, or counter-*ghazū*. Acts of counter-*ghazū* as acts of resistance seeking *nuṣra* (triumph, revenge) both on the ground and online are cast in emancipatory terms militarily, culturally, and oedipally. It's no coincidence that the Arab *adīb* and *Nahda* intellectual par excellence, Taha Hussein, is none other than Sayyid Qutb's teacher. The emancipatory fantasies of the sons/students reminiscent of Freud's *Totem and Taboo* need to be mentioned insofar as they inform a particular kind of gender politics that ties in the Freudian primal horde with *Jahiliyya* as structure and fantasy erupting in cyberspace.

A Marxist-turned-Islamist like many members of his generation who underwent this conversion all the way through the 1980s and 1990s,[34] Kishk presents *ghazū* in similar ways to the Leninist permanent revolution.[35] Starting with the Crusades and continuing into modern times, *ghazū* is thus an ongoing process that seeks to dismantle political and social structures and derail a civilizational trajectory, redirecting it along a different path already charted by the *ghāzī* from the West. Though the *ghazwa* in Albeshr's case could be a response to what is perceived as a Western *ghazū*, one could also argue that *ghazwa* is a flash attack and an incursion tied to a campaign that unfolds as an ongoing march transcending temporal and spatial frameworks. While *ghazū* is ongoing, *ghazwa* is its sudden manifestation through incursion, battle, and foray. The *ghazū* thus manifests itself in both military and epistemological outbursts. *Ghazwa* reveals the true meaning (*maghzā*) of *ghazū* and concretizes it, makes it legible, known. *Ghazwa* is the violent and rapid process through which the derailment, the shift in meaning, and the military defeat take place simultaneously. Thus, acts of war and acts of reading are integral to the *ghazwa* that determines the meaning of Badriah's text and recodes her position as author and speaker given the hashtag campaign.

In a 2013 article in *Al-Hayat*, penned while Mohamed Morsi was still president of Egypt, a columnist critical of the Muslim Brotherhood's interference in the judiciary wrote the following:

> The Purging Raid [*ghazwat al-taṭhīr*]!
>
> The *maghzā* [intended meaning] of the Muslim Brotherhood campaign against the judiciary and the statements of president Mohamed Morsi to *Al-Jazeera* regarding this issue are clear and don't require deep analysis. The *ghazwa* [raid] seeking to purge the judiciary proved that the Brotherhood believes that they are always right, marching forward with all their *āliyya* [machinery, mechanism] on the path they chose for themselves since the revolution without any consideration to the groups rejecting their authority or opposing their policies. This is not only due to the fact that the Brotherhood, the party, and the president consider all opponents to be either foreign agents, old regime supporters, counter-revolutionaries, or religion haters, but also because they consider that this opposition will have little effect on the development of events in the long term.[36]

In this contemporary use of *ghazwa*, one can identify a campaign that involves a march toward achieving a meaningful aim (*maghzā*). The march follows a steady path from which no veering is allowed. It is also likened to both a religious and a political mandate excluding opposition, divergence, and difference. This march proceeds through an *āliyya*, which refers to machinery and mechanism, but keeping Heidegger and the question of technology in mind, the *āliyya* here is a divine process that will purge the judiciary from opposition and drive through the intended goal (*maghzā*) unfolding on a path to a future devised by the group in power (the Muslim Brotherhood). *Ghazwa* is thus an instance of an ongoing *ghazū*, namely the purging of the judiciary and the control of all state institutions by the Brotherhood. This *ghazū* thus involves a *maghzā*, an intended meaning that becomes manifest in the *ghazwa* itself. While the meaning of *ghazū* is confirmed by speech and opinion (what Morsi said), its real truth is revealed and made legible in the *ghazwa* as purging (*taṭhīr*), which involves an act of violence that marks the advent of subjectivity, the moment of entering the community, and recodes it through a violent ritual. Purging thus exposes (*yafḍaḥ*) the ongoing *ghazū* and makes meaning possible by the same token.

DISPLACEMENT OF KNOWLEDGE

Turning to *Lisān al-ʿArab*, the medieval lexicon by Ibn Manzur, *ghazā/yaghzū* is to want something; to attain what one seeks to express and what one means and intends; and to reach one's intention and express it fully.[37] *Ghazū* is spatial and trajectorial: reaching a destination, going in a direction, walking towards, "marching to fight the enemy and dispossessing it."[38] *Ghazū* is thus a violent act and a process of obtaining the spoils (*ghanm*): "the raider fails unless he carries the spoils of war."[39] In *ghazū*, it is in the act of violence that knowledge and its true meaning are revealed, making the acquisition (the spoils) both material and epistemological. *Ghazū* is about reaching the enemy camp and destroying the enemy as a process of meaning-making and knowledge production. Meaning, however, is not produced externally but is rather a priori, yet only revealed in the act of violence against the other. Purging, in this framework, is true violence that involves winning and carrying the other as spoils.

Elaborating on its nuances, Ibn Manzur suggests that *ghazū* is a knowledge that relies on a particular interpretation with specific effects: "I understood what is intended (*yughzā*) by this speech, i.e., what is meant by it."[40] *Maghzā* is thus the moral of the story, what is to be learned, retained, taken away, and kept. *Maghzā* is the true and intended aim of learning, conquest, and attack. It is the point and the real issue, which needs to be understood, taught as a lesson, permanently inscribed and tagged (as in tagging, hashtagging, *waṣm*) in the mind and on the body of the "learner" and the "learned from." *Maghzā* is also the message ("you got the message?") that is acquired, received, but also delivered as a blow. It is in the process of delivery—the blow—that this meaning is manifested, highlighted, made legible, and exposed; it's the message that one *delivers* and that one *takes* at the same time through the raid or the act of hacking. The *maghzā* is thus dual: a lesson for the raider and for the raided. *Maghzā* collapses the logic of communication and the binary of sender/sendee and teacher/student associated with the university setting and public-sphere context. In *ghazū*, which is manifested in a singular *ghazwa* or multiple *ghazwāt*, meaning is no longer based on a model of exchange and dialectics that allows opposition but is precisely the moment of simultaneity, violence, and affectivity, which *ushers in* and *is ushered in by* a new form of knowing, displacing knowledge altogether and revealing a new text.

Ghazū embodies an act of violence but also one that displaces learning in the *Nahda* epistemological context. The *ṭālib* (student, seeker of knowledge) in *ghazū* is the mobilized warrior attacking the other camp, the believer in the right path regardless of opposition, and most of all, the one who ushers in a different epistemology that has broken fundamentally with the ideal of Arab modernity and its offshoot, *librāliyya*. In the case of the Twitter campaign against Albeshr, the attack is not merely an incursion to silence a woman speaker but rather a manifestation of a different kind of learning that is enacted and performed in the very act of violence that determines the *maghzā* (meaning) of Albeshr's text and unsettles the university as a space of learning and exchange. The *ghāzī* in this case is the mobilized student (*ṭālib*) and seeker of knowledge (*ṭālib al-ʿilm*), trying to fulfill that which is already intended, attempting to reach a designated spot and concretize meaning (*maghzā*) in the act of violence. The *ṭālib*, in this case, transforms the object of knowledge into a target. At the historical level, we move from Rifaʿa al-Tahtawi as seeker of knowledge (*ṭālib al-ʿilm*) in France in the 1820s and 1830s and the discourse of the Arab renaissance (*Nahda*) that ought to produce the modern subject, to the *ṭālib* (student) mobilized on Twitter as tribal warrior and raider in cyberspace, advocating opposition (*munāhaḍa*, which shares the same root as the word *nahḍa*) to a novel and an academic lecture in the case of Albeshr.

Reading *ghazū/ghazwa* as a cyberintervention that recodes the literary text requires a close examination of hashtagging (*hashtaga*, *waṣm*) as a form of knowledge production online. Naming the object of knowledge and constituting it as target, or hashtagging in Albeshr's case, involves a mobilization through a process of circulation and proliferation. Hashtagging determines the conditions of knowledge and anchors its *maghzā* (meaning). The interaction that follows is tied to that which has been named and sought after. Hashtagging thus operates as tagging or branding a ganging up on the object of knowledge, which is exposed in the act of violence in Albeshr's case. Hashtagging as branding consists in calling people to a scene online (making a scene, staging a scandal) as a way of revealing the object of knowledge through a mobilization that designates the site of attack as both action and information.[41] Moreover, tweeting operates as the mode appropriated in the violent raid and literary performance that led to determining Albeshr's blasphemy and to the cancellation of her talk, shifting meaning and writing practices in this new model of knowledge production and textual analysis. Moving from Mujtahidd's fiction of scandal on Twitter, the hashtag campaign against Albeshr reveals a poetic of violence, ushering in online reading and writing practices as *āliyya*, a mechanism of war (*āliyyat al-ḥarb*) and writing (*āliyyat al-kitāba*) integral to the tagging process. In this context education becomes a branding of knowledge no longer in the mind of the *ṭālib* as in the *Nahda* narrative of *adab* but rather on the skin. Like the branding of cattle that burns on a claim of ownership, a new knowledge is branded on the skin of the student, the author, and the text.

CAN THE *MAW'ŪDA* SPEAK?

With *ghazwa* operating as a form of derailment of the educational model and of the reading practice associated with a *Nahda* project, and hashtagging as a form of mobilization integral to the act of knowledge, a fantasized *Jahiliyya* returns through cyberspace as a mode of warfare and practice of writing and reading.[42] *Jahiliyya* is embodied in calls of mobilization doubling as poetic code that sets the possibility of circulation, sharing, retweeting, and expanding (the language of Twitter). Cyberspace has opened a portal through which *Jahiliyya* leaks out, both in its political (tribal warfare, revenge, *ghazū*) and literary (adopting Twitter to write classical poetry) forms. In the context of literature, we move from acts of reading as involving processes of identification and interpretation to reading as a violent extraction of true meaning by "getting the message" and "getting to the point" through a knock-out blow. The *ghazū*/*ghazwa* dynamic thus designates an economy of reading and meaning-making that operates as a new literary critical tool deployed *against* the text and the author, branding and collapsing them in cyberspace. Specifically, we move from *ghazwa* as attack and raid to *ghazū* as an act of reaching a destination online, the aim of which is displacing and repositioning the object of knowledge from literary reading to blasphemy, and from the modern novel as a coherent work of literature available in bookstores to cropped and branded fragments circulating online.

In literary analysis it has been the rule since Barthes that the author has sacrificed him/herself for the text to live. The death of the author implies in this now-traditional literary critical framework that meaning (*maghzā*) is no longer reduced to the intentions of the author nor fully contained within the text's aesthetic and cultural context. Just as Assange cannot control the proliferation and the effects of the leak, literary critical models can no longer control the text reduced to fragments bouncing back and forth like "wildfire" on Twitter. The activists in #La_LiBadriah's campaign usher in a new meaning of authorship and textuality, fundamentally recoding if not reversing the Barthesian and more traditional models.

> Because we have principles we refused to welcome Badriah Albeshr as we are able to distinguish good thought and literature [*adab*] from rubbish and nonsense.[43]

Following the aesthetic logic of this tweet, true literature or the literature that elevates as in *adab* ought to adhere to superior aesthetic and intellectual standards.[44] Certainly this conception of literature becomes embodied not only through an act of violence but also through an aesthetic model in terms of which Albeshr's work falls short according to the raiders. The "rubbish" and "nonsense" she utters and writes are associated with her *librāliyya*, literary production, and women's-rights activism. The assessment that mounts a defense of "good literature" or "high literature" reminiscent of *adab* emanating from solid principles of reception and engagement fragments and breaks down the text to be consumed online. This *adab*-like practice adopts the rhetoric of revenge and *ghazwa* as a form of confronting a *ghazū fikrī* embodied in Western ideas but also in "bad literature" produced by an Arab female author from the Gulf. *Adab* here is exposed as a prohibitive category that ties in the archaic violence of the hashtag campaign, and *adab* as a fiction of power involving a "civilizing" and "disciplinary" fiction, behavior, and morality. The hashtag raiders appropriate *adab* from authoritarian Arab states and their ministries of culture to deploy it in an archaic defense of a slighted deity. The discourse of *adab* here is thus Islamist and Arab nationalist, *Jahili* and digital at the same time.

The Twitter campaign, which has taken as its object of conquest Albeshr's text, Albeshr's lecture, and Albeshr herself, is tied to a politics of silencing the Arab woman. The charge of *ʿuqūq* (disobeying the parents) leveled against Albeshr, which is an accusation deployed against women and is punishable by law in some Gulf countries, accentuates the *taṭāwul* (daring to speak up) that Albeshr practices in the eyes of her detractors. "How dare Albeshr speak" is the ultimate shape that the campaign takes, targeting simultaneously her talk, her work, and her gender identity. As I mentioned earlier, this is complemented in the attack by references to another Saudi woman who dared to demand the right to drive, Manal al-Sharif. The #La-liBadriah Twitter feed mentions al-Sharif's actions as bringing about an unnecessary disturbance when al-Sharif decided to drive her car, film herself doing it, and put the video on YouTube. Denying their right to speak or drive, the campaign produces in this context a discourse on disobedient women (*ʿāqāt*), outlaws and rejects that need to be disciplined as in the *ʿiqāl* (rope-like head gear) campaign against women drivers, and the #La-LiBadriah hashtag in this case. Disciplining in this context means *taʾdīb*, another category tied to the economy of *adab* and the disciplining project associated with it. In practice, *taʾdīb* has come to mean torture (*taʿdhīb*), thus the *ʿiqāl* campaign threatens physical violence against women outlaws who are practicing *qillat adab* (lack of civility, lack of *adab*) by uttering and writing "nonsense" and "rubbish."

The recognizable fundamentalist rhetoric targeting women activists in the Gulf and beyond informs not only the campaign that led to the cancellation of Albeshr's talk but extends as well to the way her text was cropped, circulated, read, and interpreted as blasphemous.[45] More specifically, the anxiety that the little girl expresses in the novel is reproduced in the hashtag *ghazwa* against Albeshr as just punishment, namely "hellfire." Quoting Albeshr's text again:

> Mother used these stories, which other people also knew, to warn us about God's punishment, especially hellfire. She insisted that the flames of this world were nothing but tiny sparks of the colossal fire of hell, where God would melt our skin thousands of times, each time replacing the melted skin with a whole new one.
>
> In my mind, God assumed my mother's face, always angry, always threatening; the fire he promised was, on the whole, not much different from the pinches that her fingers burned on the insides of our tender thighs.[46]

These words were enough to earn Albeshr the burning (in the form of branding, tagging, and hashtagging) that the little Hend feared most. The raiders perversely deploy the literary anxiety in the text against its author. From a literary critical standpoint, it is impossible to separate these words from their context, but it is precisely the context that makes them even more "abominable." Not only are these words deemed blasphemous in the absolute sense, but the fact that it is a little girl who utters them exacerbates their infraction. How dare a little girl say this about her mother, let alone God?[47] The charge of *ʿuqūq* (disobedience) emerges more clearly from these lines and the meaning produced through their sharing and circulation as a cropped and mutilated text online. The circulation of Albeshr's passages like "wildfire" on Twitter reproduces the fire that the little girl fears most in the novel. The archaic image of hell guarded by a cruel and unflinching deity that arises from the mind and mouth of a terrified little girl becomes materialized, taking the shape of a hashtag campaign that seeks to consume Albeshr, the public intellectual, woman author, and guest lecturer.

The fact that it is a little girl speaking and speaking up, risking the fires of hell both in her recollection of her relation to the mother and online, resuscitates the discourse of the *maw'ūda* (the infant girl buried alive in pre-Islamic Arabia) as the framework for interdiction and prohibition.[48] The attack against Albeshr, which collapses her with the little girl in the story and subjects her to the threat of fire as ultimate punishment, is not only warranted by what the girl had to say but also by the fact that it is a little girl speaking in the first place. In this context it's important to read this text's cropping and circulation as a retrieval of the *maw'ūda*'s buried and mutilated body. The *maghzā* (intended meaning) of the attack against Albeshr emerges from the activation of the discourse on the *maw'ūda* and the practice of *wa'd* that ties in the *Jahili* practice of burying newborn girls alive. This discourse aligns *wa'd* with *ghazū*, cropping and mutilating the text with the enslavement of women practiced online and on the battlefield (ISIS). Albeshr's text is reduced in this new fictional and epistemological model to *al-kitāba al-maw'ūda* (the writing of the infant girl buried alive) that is mutilated and consumed by raiders in a fantasmatic setting online. The Twitter raiders' message is: How dare Albeshr speak while she was buried alive, with sand in her mouth? By speaking and writing Albeshr defies the act of burial that the Twitter campaign reenacts. The Arab woman here is not free from the curse of *al-maw'ūda*, especially when she speaks. The fact that she was resurrected after they had buried her constitutes the true infraction that warrants the blasphemous charges and that sets in motion the act of reading and the "literary" performance of the text online.

In the *ghazwa* of Albeshr's talk, we move from the inability to read literature to a determination of its *maghzā* through a violent campaign that produces meaning in the act of raiding and suppressing women. The collapse of the author with the cropped passages circulating online fragments the authorial position and body, burns it through hashtagging as branding, and crops it so that it can be consumed as limbs and body parts. Like Wael's tongue, heart, and mouth discussed in chapter 2, the novel's cropping and circulation is no longer complementary in this new model with a coherent subject-author but rather opens up the possibility of transforming the author into a fictional character; Badriah is cast as the *maw'ūda* of ancient Arabia both in her own novel (the little girl) and in a dark (as in "power of darkness" or "power of obscurantism," *qiwā ẓalāmiyya*) and perverse fantasy unfolding on Twitter. In this perverse literary reading the author inhabits his/her text, which is reduced to fragments and tweets—titillating body parts that are exchanged and consumed by cyber-raiders in a ritual of archaic violence. In this sense the failure to read literature—its reduction to *maghzā*—ushers in a literary practice that consumes the reader and the author, the tweeter and the reader of tweets. In this way we move to another definition of the death of the author that reintroduces a model of fiction as a mode of interaction governing online relations at multiple levels.

When authors go online, they permanently enter their text. The intertwinement of author and text, literature and the digital, exposed in the hashtag *ghazwa* against Albeshr heralds the establishment of fiction as new reality principle. In this environment the quest for self becomes displaced onto compulsive models of externalization that further blur the distinction between self and other, subject and object. While at the political level this is symptomatic of the erosion of the *Nahda* project as an ideal at the basis of modern Arab subjectivity, at the epistemological one it reveals modes of knowing akin to *mukāshafa* (unveiling) and *faḍḥ* (exposure, scandal), *tasrīb* (leaking) and *tafashshī* (proliferation) arising from the ashes of causality and duality. In this setting the act of reading literature is subsumed into an act of becoming—inhabiting a text unbound, constantly reproducing itself in fragments circulating through viral forwarding and retweeting. Thus we move from the literary Bovary-esque fantasy and identification to literary dystopia as the organizing principle of a new hyperreality. Online raiders become characters, engaging in tribal warfare, avenging a slighted deity, cutting and burning the raided and her text. These characters, however, are able to effect real change with recognizable material effects—like forcing the university to cancel the talk, censoring books, imprisoning and killing authors. In this sense the triumph of the campaign is also the triumph of a new fictional model that succeeds in mobilizing Twitter activists as tribal warriors from Arabia. In this new fiction, which is bound by archaic fantasies through a portal to *Jahiliyya*, the collapse of past and present in the ethereal space-time of Twitter, as we saw with Mujtahidd, produces new forms of reading and writing practices. In Albeshr's case, perverse literary performances are tied to sadomasochistic porn fantasies and the harassment of women in which "blasphemous passages" operate as limbs and body parts to be exchanged and consumed online.

IN THE NAME OF THE YOUTH

The end of literature as the fiction we associate with the novels of Flaubert and Mahfouz is attributed to a new generation effecting change in the Arab world. Hailed as the hope for a bright future, the youth (*shabāb*) mentioned in the tweets are reduced to the economy of avatars, video games, and archaic fantasies.

> In order to combat (*munāhaḍa*) liberal thought, in the name of the youth, our voice against all distortion and *ghazū*, and no blowing things and individuals out of proportion, because liberalism and its followers do not deserve our attention.[49]

In this tweet the notion of *ghazū* deployed by Twitter activists in reference to the West and liberalism moves from *nahḍa* (Arab Renaissance or *Nahda*) to *mu-nāhaḍa* (opposition, anti-*nahḍa*), all in the name of the youth (*bi-lisān al-shabāb*) and *adab*. Thus the youth are co-opted as a constituency and a vulnerable group in whose name and for whose protection attacks, raids, and "anti-liberal" positions need to be deployed and good literature (*adab*) needs to be upheld and defended. They are mobilized as characters performing the roles of students, activists, warriors, and literary critics all at the same time. In this mobilization the youth are reduced to a digital horde that mutilates the other's text, tags it, and marks it for attack and consumption through different modalities of reading and circulation. So when the decision by the university finally came through on the morning of the ill-fated talk, the cyber-raiders were quick to hail it as a triumph of a new generation that is finally coming to itself and recognizing its own power to effect change.

> I just heard from the university: Badriah Albeshr's lecture was cancelled due to powerful student pressure decrying hosting her at the university! For the first time the university listens to its students![50]

The cancellation of the talk—the fulfillment of the promise of revenge and the literary denouement—is presented as the triumph and advent of *true* democracy. This new generation is mobilized at the literary, epistemological, military, and technological levels, recoding texts, authority, activism, knowledge production, and revolution. What is hailed as an uprising against antiquated systems of authority appears here as that which will strengthen and perpetuate them in the name of *true* democracy, going through the portal of a fantasized *Jahiliyya* that opened online. The *true* democracy and *true* freedom that Wael Abbas enacted through his scene-making and confrontations, thereby shattering democracy and freedom as liberal fictions of the post-revolutionary healed state, expose a radical transformation in the social and political makeup of the community and its moral, cultural, and aesthetic ideals. This radical act of undoing the political produces an untamable text, contract, and code, thereby requiring new "manuals" such as the one al-Ghadhdhami sought to provide for Twitter. In this opening lie the potential and the danger of a *true* revolutionary unfolding with which the Arab uprisings were associated, or from which they were excluded and thus dismissed.

Ultimately, the Arab uprisings have been employed discursively to justify various political and social projects that will continue to grip the region for the forseeable future, breaking with certain models of confrontation and *adab* and sustaining yet speaking the language of democratic change.

> -The Western Madonna's concert was banned in the UAE and now the Madonna of the East is banned from Qatar . . . remarkable mobilization by a promising generation God willing.[51]

> -A glorious position on the part of our Qatari people who prevented the thug (*shabbīḥa*) Badriah Albeshr from giving her talk here, she should learn good manners (*adab*) before coming here to teach them to us.[52]

In these tweets the vengeful tribe is presented as being "democratic" while the author and the university are cast in the position of regime thugs (*shabbīḥa*, or *balṭagiyya* in the Egyptian dialect) that Arab dictators let loose on protestors during the uprisings. In this context the youth are meant to lead this campaign and put an end to this blasphemy, teaching the author a lesson (*taʾdīb*) and a new *adab*—"good literature" but also "proper manners"—by invoking yet multiplying the disciplinary framework of *adab* discussed in previous chapters. In this context *taʾdīb* as lesson no longer designates a disciplinary model à la Foucault but rather an act of pure violence, erasure, and burning reminiscent of Damiens's torturing with which Foucault opens *Discipline and Punish* as the event to be sublated for the modernity-to-come (*à venir*). This lesson is inscribed on the author's work and on her skin through acts of material violence. From the *adab* of the *Nahda* appropriated to justify autocratic rule to *adab* as a lesson mediated by a Twitter campaign, the recoding of the disciplinary as a tribal war of elimination is fundamental to the return of *Jahiliyya* through a portal on Twitter both as a fictionalized culture of violence and as a code of behavior and reading. The *adab* being taught appropriates and recodes its idealized *Nahda* origins in a *Jahili* setting of tribal warfare unfolding in cyberspace.

By the same token the act of reading is also an aesthetic and violent process that reduces the novel to textual fragments and the Arab woman author to the buried infant girl of pre-Islamic Arabia. While the cancellation of the talk is represented as an act of democratic triumph in the "civilized" Western sense, involving both male and female students, it is in fact the outcome of a tribal warfare unleashed in the fictional model of belonging and group identity proliferating online and off. However, the tribe in this context is not the tribe studied by anthropologists but emerges instead from the intersection of cyberspace, authoritarian structures, and a fantasized tradition that conjures up *Jahiliyya* as archaic and video game–like. The effects of this hyperreality are not reduced to cyberfantasy but reflect and are reflected by material forms of violence against authors, activists, and books, containing and suppressing their leaking mouths and texts, thereby purging them and cleansing them (*taṭhīr*) from the social and from cyberspace. The fiction emerging in this case could not be theorized or identified except in the moment of collapse, or the life-and-death encounter that is producing the canon, as we saw in the case of Rakha in chapter 4. In fact, the act of violence seeks to protect and engender a new fictional reality that needs to be maintained at all times and at all costs, blurring the distinction between author, reader, and text. Violence in this case is directed against those who insist on the distinction between reality and fiction, and between the author and the character like Albeshr, and thus against authors and poets who are getting arrested or killed for their literary works and tweets.

CONCLUSION

While in chapter 2 I theorized notions of scene-making and *qillat adab* (lack of *adab*, incivility) as modes of confronting the fiction of power, in this chapter I examined how similar processes become appropriated in the name of civility and a newfound democracy and *adab* (true literature, good manners) in order to censure and persecute authors and activists. The analysis provided above situates *ghazū/ghazwa* (conquest, raiding) as practices of writing, knowledge production, and literary performance made possible by digital culture. Forms of knowledge acquisition and writing practices stage the collapse of object/subject relations through new models of violence. And just as the meaning and affects of exposure involve and consume both *fādiḥ* (exposer) and *mafḍūḥ* (exposed), so do *ghazū* and *ghazwa* discussed above. It is in the interstices of these new meaning-making processes that we find the framework for the emergence of *maghzā* (meaning)—the new codes of literature in the digital age. This highlights cyberspace not as a forum of exchange or a revolutionary public sphere but as a space of harassment, regression, perverse pleasure, literary production, and mobilization. In this framework we know through leaks (Assange) or we know because knowledge is available (Snowden), as discussed in chapter 1. Compulsive browsing and tweeting at night and visceral reactions to images and words usher in models of fiction and simultaneity that require further investigation. The attempt to bring back true literature by the *balṭagiyya* (thugs) online unleashes the worst form of violation and acts of erasure from which the speaking subject who contests and exposes is completely eradicated, kicked out, and knocked down. While the leaking subject I have been theorizing throughout the book crosses and unsettles gender codification, the attack I analyzed in this chapter seeks to re-entrench and consolidate gender codification in the most brutal form: reducing the Arab woman author to the position of the *maw'ūda* (infant girl buried alive in pre-Islamic Arabia).

The ISIS terror attacks in Brussels in 2016 have been framed by ISIS as *ghazwat Bruksell*.[53] This is not meant to draw a direct link between the cancellation of a talk in Qatar and ISIS practices, but rather to show how the premodern and the archaic are part of a contemporary reality that recodes and deploys them in their various shapes and forms. The *ghazwa* (raid) discussed in this chapter reveals the leaking and fragmentation of a particular constellation of subjectivity that is tied to the *Nahda* as liberal fantasy countered by a *Jahili* one. The act of violence as a form of hacking and raiding juxtaposes these narratives of subjectivity, recoding what it means to be Arab, Muslim, woman, intellectual, and author in the digital age. The fiction of *Jahiliyya* shatters and leaks through the fiction of the *Nahda* online, revealing the nature and operation of the ideological struggles playing out in the Arab world today that have come to the surface in a state of war and confrontation, both online and on the battlefield, targeting rivals, institutions, authors, books, and women.

The portal that opened up in cyberspace into the archaic as ideological and literary fantasy captures this back-and-forth between the contemporary context, including the social and political environment, genres, and technologies, and the classical ones as well. This movement codes both the present and the past, Twitter and *Jahiliyya* as new but old fictions that require a comparative analysis. Engaging this recoding and fantasmatic return to *Jahiliyya* and the early days of Islam (which exposes a "leaky" demarcation between what is Islamic and what is pre-Islamic) is fundamental to understanding how the aesthetic and the political are being redefined in the digital age. Moving from the modern Arab state imagined by *Nahda* thinkers and coopted by authoritarian regimes to define *adab* and impose its own cultural standards and *taʾdīb* (as disciplining), we are confronted today with more decentralized models of identity and community formation that are proliferating online and throughout the Arab world and its diaspora. The engagement with a hashtag raid is an attempt to identify the processes and registers through which the questions of writing, gender, and politics are being defined and practiced in such ways that require the critic to return to the classical tradition, to excavate the *ghazū* and the *mawʾūda*, and comparatively engage the trials of the leaking subject.

CONCLUSION

> I have a taste for the secret, it clearly has to do with not-belonging; I have an impulse of fear or terror in the face of a political space, for example, a public space that makes no room for the secret. For me, the demand that everything be paraded in the public square and that there be no internal forum is a glaring sign of the totalitarianization of democracy.
>
> —Jacques Derrida, *A Taste for the Secret*

When looking at the Arab world since 2010, observers experience both exhilaration and complete despair. Whereas the Arab uprisings initially brought about the fall of dictators, they also led to foreign military interventions, civil wars, refugee crises, the return of authoritarianism, and tribalism and fundamentalism in ways that leave the spectator baffled and mute. This social and political collapse coincides with a breakdown in systems of knowledge, disciplines and genres, and cultural models that were shaped by the legacy of modernity and centered on the nation-state, secularism/religiosity, individual/community, tradition/modernity, classical/modern, and the novel. Specifically, when the relation between the novel and the postcolonial nation can no longer account for the complexity of the technological and political state of the Arab world following the uprisings, new models of critique and conceptual tools are needed. However incomplete these tools might be, they chart a trajectory for reflecting on Arab culture at a time of momentous political and epistemological transformations.

Examining literature and social media, activism and politics, I identified in this book a techno-archaic portal, breaching the narrative of modernity. The role of the Internet as "public sphere"—a utopian framework that promised an open and nonhierarchal encounter with the other—has given way to pre-Islamic raids and sophisticated hacks, trolling and attack that come from the present and a fantasized past, and jinn-like seers and narrators of *akhbār*. I argued that both the Internet and the subject of modernity are leaking, unable to contain their enlightenment and liberal narratives, or to control the gushing from a dimension that lies beyond. This leaking, thus, is not a techno-salvation, as Assange described the role of WikiLeaks in fostering the Arab uprisings. Instead, leaking creates the possibility of change but also involves dangerous processes and openings that risk engulfing authors and activists. The leak, I argued, is a wild text that could be put in motion or identified, but its meaning and effects could never be governed by the author of the leak, by the hacker trying to infiltrate secure systems, or by the activist aiming to reclaim the liberal state, literature, or *adab*.

Theorizing the leaking subject required an engagement with questions of scandal and scene-making, materiality and digital compulsion, and authorial and political functions from the activist to the gossiper. Leaking characterizes subversive practices and bodily conditions that are involuntary yet political, well-planned yet exceeding the intents and ideologies of the agents engaging in them. The leak is an untamed text that needs to be read and interpreted, deciphered and translated. It perforates bodies and mimics bodily performances of scene-making or *faḍḥ*, tying together the Internet and the street, the Arab digital age and the age of uprisings. The critique of ideology had to give way in this investigation to conceptual tools that venture to explain the relation between affect and activism, mobilization online and on the street. These two levels are not connected by causal relations or Cartesian models of truth and reality wherein one is more true than the other, as Descartes explains the difference between God and the idea of God in his famous *Discourse on Method* while trying to ground modern epistemology. The digital and the material coexist, inform and shape one another, and operate through the logic of simultaneity. "Vulgar" *faḍḥ* and scene-making are fundamental components of a culture of contestation and dissent that doesn't simply seek to fix a broken system but to completely dismantle it. The outcome is full of potential for radical transformation, both in terms of literary genres and artistic practices, but also in terms of "real" social and political change. Yet this outcome is full of danger and uncertainty, sometimes erupting in archaic violence that seems to consume with no end authors and critics of power.

Engaging digital humanities and new experiences and models of knowledge online, I deployed comparative and philosophical approaches focusing on the Arab world in a transnational context. I examined how new writing and the critique of power are produced, reworked, and interrogated in instances of exposure, hacking, leaking, and contestation. Literature is fundamentally intertwined with the fiction of the leak and the fiction of scandal, thereby entering into a mimetic relation with the digital, reproducing its rhythm and affect, flow of information and release of data. Approaching the literary through leaks and exposure, I investigated what constitutes the literary and what frames the novel. Moving beyond Anderson's model of circulation and print culture, nation-state and language, I explored the kinds of consciousness and imagined community arising from reading practices in the digital age. This led me to engage what constitutes knowledge and how the leaking subject knows, writes, and becomes conscious and politically aware. The knowledge could not be reduced to the control and mastery associated with the Foucauldian knowledge/power model or to the knowledge of the Enlightenment produced in colonial and academic labs. I drew a map of scandalous knowledge that affectively interpellates new readers and viewers, preventing them from looking away and from not knowing, titillating and bewildering them, and hooking them through salacious revelations and fabulous tales. This interpellation confronts silence and political apathy yet, in its most extreme form, turns spectators into interactive participants in sadomasochistic scenes and consumers of celebrity gossip.

I theorized the consciousness of the leaking subject, who is bound to take account of and uphold the fragment, the limbs, and the slapping hands in Cairo's police stations and streets that Wael Abbas and Khaled Alkhamissi exposed. When the relation between the inside and the outside, and the heart and Twitter, collapses, transparency becomes an affective exposure of body parts such as the heart and the tongue. In chapter 1, I discussed how Zizek reads the leaking subject as the one who cannot cede his/her desire. Drawing on Lacan's ethics of psychoanalysis, Zizek presents a framework for reading leaks as compulsive and involuntary actions that confront and transcend models of legality and authority. However, Zizek does not fully explain the constitution of the leaking subject who intervenes in the political and becomes shaped by his/her interventions. I engaged leaks by tying them to incivility (*qillat adab*) and the involuntary discussed in chapter 2, examining how the leaker of videos and online scene-maker cannot hold his tongue or turn off his camera, or refrain from uploading to his YouTube account. I looked specifically at the making of the leaker in the event of the leak and examined how it is then framed, deciphered, and claimed as the redeemed subject of the "excessive" and "exceptional" liberal state in need of fixing, as was the case with Snowden, or the autocratic state and its *adab*, as was the case with Wael Abbas. The leaking subject reveals and exposes the monster both as a literary and informational fiction (the NSA's "collect it all"), and as a deployment of brute force.

At the philosophical and literary levels, I traced leaking (*tasrīb*) to an aesthetic and culture of revelation (*ifshāʾ*), exposing, and scene-making (*faḍḥ*) that shapes both local and global models of contestation and literary and artistic production. I investigated the ethics and biopolitics of leaking scandals in between the United States and the Arab world. I argued that what makes the narrative of the leak so powerful is not its revelation of information—"presumed to be true" or "already known"—but rather the promise and anticipation it offers to further disrobe and humiliate those in power. This anticipation and unveiling of the inside of the other—and of oneself—unfolds as an affective narrative that exposes insecurity, the failure of the containment of data and of the fantasmatic. Thus, the leak breaks with the Orientalist discourse of the enlightening and civilizing information to which Assange and Zizek refer. Instead, the leak operates affectively as "concrete data" in a "felt present," and in so doing it takes public figures down to the street to face mob justice (Abbas, Alkhamissi) or online to face Twitter justice (Mujtahidd) through a crowd-gathering performance involving scene-making (*lam al-nās*) but also hashtagging (Albeshr). Leaks, hacks, and scandals, I argued, disrupt the containment of information, thereby producing a sudden rupture of controlled spaces.

The author and the activist encounter the eruption of the fantasmatic and stage it through embodied confrontation and critical assessment. Albeshr recognized the fantasmatic economy of the Twitter activists who attacked her when she called their hashtag a *ghazwa*—a tribal raid unfolding in ethereal time. Snowden also recognized the fantasy of Keith Alexander, the "cowboy trekky" and NSA chief who cannot cede his desire not to collect it all, no matter what is being collected. The leaker and whistleblower's encounter with the effects of this fantasy incurs material consequences such as exile, torture, and incarceration. Therefore, the acts of exposure and leaking are not just "critiques" but rather a coming in touch with the material effects of the fantasy of the other. This encounter brings the fantasmatic onto one's own body and into one's own text, making the fantasmatic legible yet risking being engulfed by it. This process of staging and embodiment produces a new genre and set of codes, what Youssef Rakha identifies and what the Mujtahidd clones all reproduce and practice as fiction of scandal and as exposure of political corruption and abuse in their respective countries.

The confrontation with the fantasmatic comes at a price; it takes a toll on the body, endangers it, and marks it, causing Wael Abbas bruises and fragmenting Albeshr's text. The scene-making and exposure (*faḍḥ, faḍīḥa*) are not the voyeuristic scandals performed for the Western gaze but rather capture the breakdown of subject/object relation in a new digital landscape. Exposure thus consists in *being in* the scene as a way of *seeing* it. The denouncer of abuse is him/herself tied to this logic as online activist or author of fiction. There is no escape from the text that arrests, unsettles, and submerges. Booth, Rakha, and Albeshr all confronted and theorized the threat of erasure and engaged in the exposure that strips naked both hacker and hacked. "Putting oneself out there," "going out on a limb," and "turning up one's nose at" are not simply metaphors in the digital age but rather material processes and acts that entail risks of hacking, abuse, incarceration, and death.

This scene of violent confrontation, of radical *faḍḥ* that stages a breakdown and risks submerging the author or activist, is also productive. It generates fear and anxiety that lead the author to reclaim and redefine *adab* (Booth, Rakha, Albeshr), democracy (Snowden, Assange), and freedom (Abbas). The leaking subject insists on the "true" meaning of democracy and literature, or points to a democracy and literature to come, *à venir*, as Derrida would put it. Leaking and exposure, which might appear as a destructive unraveling of the structure or system in place, also offer ways to restore it to its proper functioning, to insist that it adheres to its fundamental values. Leaking and whistleblowing, and hacking and exposure thus could arise from a disappointment and a betrayal that need to be addressed, rectified, reversed. We saw this process at work with Wael Abbas's insistence on "real democracy," Assange and Snowden's return to the founding fathers, and Rakha, Booth, and Albeshr's defense and defining of "true" literature. However, these events do not only reveal an attachment to an idealized model of literature and politics but also produce new definitions and practices that uphold the literary and the political in a new age. Rakha defines the "truly postmodern" in his defense of new writing, while Booth confronts the ethnographic de-aestheticization of the literary in a global market place. Though the subversive processes I examined arise from an anxiety about the loss of the familiar and the stable (privacy, transparency, the novel), they also designate moments where the meaning of the literary and the political is taking shape, adjusting and adapting in a new landscape. I examined moments of vulnerability and identified what they reveal and generate epistemologically and aesthetically in order to understand new relations between the political and the literary in the digital age. Acts of whistleblowing, hacking, and raiding force literature to rethink itself, to reclaim itself as literature in new words and new codes, requiring manuals like al-Ghadhdhami's *Twitter Culture* or Ahmed Naji's *Using Life.*

My return to the classical tradition was not an etymological pursuit of a trace in writing but rather an exposure of a portal that opened on Twitter from which emerge past and future, ancient Arabian warriors and genres. Twitter and digital media more generally are sites of operation of the tribal, of the classical poetic tradition and prose genres, including *akhbār*, and of the narratives at the origin of systems of codification (gender, nationality, genre). When online, we encounter writing systems and heroic fantasies that come from the past but also from the future, as Snowden describes the trekky fantasy of the NSA chief. Classical genres and the fantasies governing historical and cultural imaginaries are activated online through digitizing projects and searchable engines, video games and linguistic registers that shape and are shaped by new technologies. The past is not fixed and static but codes in its turn the very tools that access it, intervening in systems of knowledge and data collection. "To know" and "to access," I argued, are also forays and raids that leave both the raider and the raided altered and bruised. Digital humanities and the infinite portals and points of access they provide are full of possibilities only when we have acknowledged the interplay and the dynamic rhythm of access and entry. The leak as data is not only damaging numerical information but also operates as a poetics that triggers associations with specific publics, opening up and reconstituting cultural imaginaries and activating them online. In this new landscape memory, like the Lacanian unconscious, is never a storage unit from which emerges symptomatically the drama of the past, but is rather an interface through which the past, the present, and the future are perpetually being reconstituted by acts of hacking, leaking, and storytelling.

Leaking and hacking characterize a model of knowledge production that arises through different circuits, adopts different means, and exposes insecurity in order to crash the system or make it more secure. The leaking subject is also the fixer, not in the engineer sense that Rakha warned against, but rather in the sense of the bricoleur (Levi-Strauss, Derrida) who amplifies the leak. This is precisely what Edward Said sought to achieve in his critique of Orientalism: hacking it and leaking out its manuals and codes, and making a scene of its fantasies. Said busted the underlying racism and prejudices of those texts and authors he admired, such as Flaubert and Nerval. Thus, focusing on leaks, hacks, and scene-making practices was not only a way to engage Arab scandals in the digital age but also to develop critical tools that allow us to read leaking and scene-making in other theoretical interventions that make legible and name that which was always there but never acknowledged, turning that which we always knew to be true into "concrete data" that moves readers and publics affectively. Leaking and exposure bring the violation and the fantasmatic to light in ways that permanently inscribe them in discourse, on the body of the leaking subject, forcing it to contort in the act of riding in cabs or writing, and forcing the pupils to dilate and contract to access more light as in the hacking scene discussed in the introduction.

Though this book is fully in the affective turn, it did not adopt a singular theoretical framework (Deleuze, Massumi, etc.) but rather drew on and read comparatively "affect" in the Arabic and the digital, in the leak and the fiction of scandal. In this context my work resisted giving up the subject in favor of the body. The body is ever present in my analysis, part of a leaking subjectivity and a narrative that is being undone and reconstituted in the digital age. The body is cut up and circulated online or reduced to slapping hands and shaky knees associated with the security systems of Arab regimes. In this sense my work arose from the theoretical intersection of the subject and the body, at the porous or leaky boundary that connects and separates them. My reading of leaks as body function and contestatory movement that unsettle boundaries and expose their porousness entered into dialogue with psychoanalysis, deconstruction, and feminist theory yet resisted the treatment of leak as lack or symptom, and materiality as effect of discourse.

But now that the subject is leaking, at what point do we move beyond the notion of the subject altogether? This book engaged the subject as fragments and leaks, both bodily and textual, but is there a moment when the very notion of subject no longer applies? At what point do we read from the perspective of the monster, the machine, the non-I, no matter how disjointed and shattered this non-I might be? Pushing the epistemological boundaries of knowledge, literature, and critique requires abandoning the subject-centered investigation to fully engage monsters and cyborgs, the animal, the non-human, and the machine. This investigation requires a different philosophical trajectory. In order to embark on it one must enter fully into the portal to the archaic that I began theorizing in this book. It is through these portals that the investigation of what comes after the subject will continue.

NOTES

INTRODUCTION

1. Oliver Holmes, "Hackers Take Down 15 Lebanese Government Websites," *Reuters,* April 17, 2012, http://www.reuters.com/article/2012/04/17/net-us-lebanon-hackers-idUSBRE83G0IQ20120417. This organization's video manifesto portrays an individual wearing the mask featured in the film *V for Vendetta* (dir. James McTeigue, 2005), an iconic symbol associated with protest movements in the Arab world and elsewhere after 2010. See "Anonymous #OpLebanon Announcement," YouTube, uploaded March 3, 2012, http://youtu.be/3YyWvZP1QcQ.

2. *Fiʿl fāḍiḥ* means "public indecency" or "indecent exposure." For its use as a legal term in Egypt for instance, see http://www.youm7.com/Tags/Index?id=34972&tag=-%D9%81%D8%B9%D9%84-%D9%81%D8%A7%D8%B6%D8%AD.

3. The screenshot text reads "bare"; I have corrected the word to "bear" when quoting.

4. I'm thinking of *Al-Jazeera*'s advent in 1996 and its iconic talkshows such as "*Al-Ittijah al-Muʿakis*" ("The Opposite Direction"). See Zayani, *Al-Jazeera Phenomenon.*

5. The typical expression for this type of embodied *faḍḥ* is *ḥafḍaḥkom ya wlād l-kalb* (I will expose you, you SOBs).

6. The "Kullena Khaled Said" ("We Are All Khaled Said") Facebook page helped support online organizing and communication before and during the uprising. See https://www.facebook.com/elshaheeed.co.uk. In this context, see *#Chicago Girl: The Social Network Takes on a Dictator* (dir. Joe Piscatella, USA, 2013), a documentary about a teenage Syrian girl coordinating protests in Syria on social media while in the United States.

7. Rasha Azb, *Jarīmat Jīl Bahaa Taher* ("The Crime of Bahaa Taher's Generation"), *Huna Sotak*, June 20, 2014, https://hunasotak.com/article/8896.

8. See Rasha Azb, September 22, 2016, https://twitter.com/RashaPress.

9. The notion of *iltizām*, which echoes the Sartrean model of *littérature engagée*, takes shape in the Arab context of anticolonial struggle, class struggle, and pan-Arabism from the 1950s onward. Though it is Taha Hussein who first coins the word *iltizām* in 1947, it is Suhayl Idris (b. 1923), author of *Al-Ḥayy al-Lātīnī* (*The Latin Quarter*), who becomes its most recognizable advocate. Idris's journal, *al-Ādāb*, founded in Beirut in 1953, became the crucible for *iltizām*'s leftist and nationalist articulations through literary criticism and philosophy from across the Arab world. For more on this application in a number of postcolonial novels, see al-Musawi, *Postcolonial Arabic Novel.* Given its various articulations by Arab intellectuals in the 1950s and 1960s, *iltizām* calls for a literature that socially and ethically engages Arab reality within a larger nationalist narrative of progress and emancipation, thereby critiquing modernist aesthetics as bourgeois and regressive. *Iltizām* thus became a vehicle of social and political transformation through writing and cultural production. Discussions in Arabic are many, especially in the writings of members of the 1960s generation, such as Aziz al-Sayyid Jasim, Sabry Hafiz, Ghali Shukri, Iliyya Hawi, and others in *al-Ādāb*. See Badawi, "Commitment in Contemporary Arabic Literature"; Klemm, "Different Notions of Commitment"; Khaldi,

"Multiple Intellectual Engagements?." On the reverberations and the situation in the 1950s across the region in poetry and criticism, see al-Musawi, *Arabic Poetry*.

10. Armstrong, *How Novels Think*, 1.

11. Ibid., 3.

12. Anderson, *Imagined Communities*, 25.

13. Naji, *Using Life*, 117.

14. For information about Naji's case, see https://pen.org/defending-writers/ahmed-naji.

15. See Berry, *Critical Theory*.

16. Abdo Khal, *Tarmī bi-Sharar*. The book was translated by Maïa Tabet and Michael K. Scott as *Throwing Sparks*.

17. See al-Musawi, *Simāt Riwāyat al-Jawā'iz* ("Features of Prize Novels"), *Al-Hayat*, July 24, 2014, http://www.alhayat.com/Articles/3755351.

18. The *Nahda* is the Arab project of modernity most associated with universalism and secularism from the mid-nineteenth to the early twentieth century.

19. Here I'm thinking of Sonallah Ibrahim, for instance.

20. On this topic, see Ziajka Stanton, "Labor of Love."

21. Apter, *Against World Literature*, 41.

22. See Allan, *Shadow of World Literature*; Tageldin, *Disarming Words*; and McLarney, "Freedom, Justice."

23. I also think of "disciplining" as *tahdhīb* and *indibāt*, both *Nahda* processes pertaining to language, culture, law, and behavior.

24. Deleuze, "Societies of Control."

25. Ibid., 5.

26. See the notion of "expository power" and "expository society" in Harcourt, *Exposed*. Harcourt, however, relies on a notion of exhibitionism that renders Internet users complicit in, if not precipitators of, their relinquishing of control and privacy vis-à-vis models of surveillance.

27. See Mitchell, *Colonizing Egypt*. The prevalent *Nahda* narrative starting with the work of Albert Hourani has approached Arab modernity through the colonial gaze and the epistemic break brought about by Napoleon's invasion of Egypt in 1798. More contemporary studies have moved away from this narrative, challenging this epistemic break. See al-Musawi, *Medieval Islamic Republic*.

28. For readings of "Arab-Islamic affects" (soundscapes, public emotions, rituals) that could not be incorporated dialectically within the economy of the Western gaze and its ocularcentric model, see Hirschkind, *Ethical Soundscape*, and Mahmood, *Politics of Piety*.

29. The reference here is to the gruesome and public scene of the torture of Damiens the regicide that Foucault reads as the last gasp of the premodern regime of punishment in eighteenth-century France. See Foucault, *Discipline and Punish*, 3.

30. For a discussion of Egyptian street festivals, see Fahmy, *Ordinary Egyptians*, 134–66.

31. See Habermas, *Structural Transformation*.

32. See Le Bon, *Psychologie des foules*.

33. See Fraser, "Rethinking the Public Sphere."

34. Warner, *Publics and Counterpublics*, 46.

35. Ibid., 146–47.

36. Ibid., 56.

37. Doueihi, *Digital Cultures*, 6.

38. Ibid., 63.

39. Edwards, *After the American Century*, 41.

40. Ibid., 37.

41. Ibid., 24–25.

42. Of course, this interdisciplinary approach is already present in McLuhan's *Understanding Media*, which features his famous essay "The Medium Is the Message." McLuhan's work is in dialogue with literature and philosophy from Greek mythology to Shakespeare and Beckett.

43. Jenkins, *Convergence Culture*, 208–9.

44. Jenkins, Ford, and Green, *Spreadable Media*, 27.

45. Ibid., 4.

46. Ibid., 30.

47. Ibid., 29.

48. Ibid., 20.

49. Ibid., 44.

50. Hayani, "Arab Media."

51. Kraidy, *Naked Blogger*.

52. Papacharissi, *Affective Publics*, 126.

53. Ibid., 125–26.

54. Ibid., 15.

55. Mark Poster critiqued Foucault on this point in *The Information Subject*, as well as in his subsequent engagement with Deleuze's work and its application to new technologies.

56. See Dabashi's critique, which deals with this model as well. Dabashi, *Can Non-Europeans Think?*

57. For a discussion of the advent of neoliberalism in the Middle East and the eventual "deradicalization" of revolutionary movements based in cohesive ideological and intellectual projects, both secular and Islamic, see Bayat, *Revolution without Revolutionaries*.

58. Hastings, "Julian Assange."

59. Zizek, *Trouble in Paradise*, 122. In her discussion of the *Dictionary of Untranslatables*, Emily Apter argues that while the "encyclopédie" frames the rise of cybernetics, as Roland Barthes has observed, it also veils in its "civilizing" mission a French-centric model that suppresses origins and languages—its own untranslatables. See Apter, *Against World Literature*, 124–25.

60. Zizek, *Trouble in Paradise*, 128–29.

61. Chun and Friedland, "Habits of Leaking," 4. Wendy Chun's book *Updating to Remain the Same: Habitual New Media* (Cambridge: MIT Press, 2017) came out after my book was completed, and I add the reference here to acknowledge its publication without being able to fully engage its elaborate argument beyond the essay quoted above.

62. Marks, *Hanan al-Cinema*, 4.

63. Hourani, *Arabic Thought*.

64. See Arnold, *Culture and Anarchy*. Also see Sonallah Ibrahim's critique of Guy de Maupassant's theory of literature as that which elevates the soul in his novella *The Smell of It* (1966). See Ibrahim, *Tilk al-Rāʾiḥa wa-Qiṣaṣ Ukhra*.

65. El-Ariss, *Trials of Arab Modernity*, 155.

66. Ibid., 165.

67. For example, see "Announcements and Anecdotes (1870)" from *al-Jinan* and *al-Zahra*, in *Arab Renaissance,* ed. El-Ariss, 241–52.

68. For an engagement with Egyptian literary blogs as an "autofiction" that recodes *adab*, see Pepe, "When Writers Activate Readers."

69. I find Rita Raley's notion of "tactical media" very useful in this context, as she draws on Deleuze's notion of the "event" and Paolo Virno and Hannah Arendt's "virtuosity" to identify a micropolitics of disturbance that takes shape through performances and interventions that unsettle the "dominant semiotic regime" by relying on the participation of an interactive audience attending and partaking in the event. Raley, *Tactical Media*, 6.

70. See Rancière, *Lost Thread.*

71. For debates and discussions of the field of digital humanities, see Burdick, Drucker, and Lunenfeld, *Digital Humanities*, and Gold, *Debates in Digital Humanities.*

72. Sakr, "Digital Humanities Approach," 249.

73. Muhanna, *Digital Humanities*, 8.

74. Papacharissi, *Affective Publics*, 50.

75. Sakr, "Tweet World."

76. Al-Ghadhdhami, *Thaqāfat Twitter.*

77. Karl Sharro, editor of the blog, "Karl reMarks," www.karlremarks.com, revealed to me in a private conversation in 2015 how tweeting and social media use generally is compulsive, done almost exclusively on mobile devices. Updating, checking, and responding emerge from a desire to share real-time experiences with followers.

CHAPTER 1

1. Arendt, *Origins of Totalitarianism*, 267–304. For a more recent engagement with subject and citizenship, see Balibar, *Citoyen sujet.*

2. Though not all leakers are whistleblowers, all whistleblowers are leakers. I use these two interchangeably, especially in the context of Chelsea Manning and Edward Snowden, who are both at the same time.

3. Wolfgang Ischinger, "The End of Diplomacy as We Know It?," *New York Times*, December 3, 2010, http://www.nytimes.com/2010/12/04/opinion/04iht-edischinger.html?_r=0.

4. We can also consider the Abu Ghraib torture images as a spectacle of the leak. See al-Ghadeer, "Cannibalizing Iraq."

5. Jim Sciutto, "OPM Government Data Breach Impacted 21.5 Million," CNN, July 10, 2015, http://www.cnn.com/2015/07/09/politics/office-of-personnel-management-data-breach-20-million/index.html.

6. Ibid.

7. Ibid.

8. Some leaks are edited and interpreted or made "textual" and "readable" by newspapers and traditional media.

9. For background on the Panama Papers, see the reporting of the International Consortium of International Journalists, https://panamapapers.icij.org/. Also see Scott

Shane and Eric Lupton, "Panama Papers Source Offers to Aid Inquiries If Exempt from Punishment," *New York Times*, May 6, 2016, http://nyti.ms/1ryhR2L.

10. See https://www.theguardian.com/news/series/panama-papers and http://www.lemonde.fr/panama-papers/.

11. "*Muḥākama 'Askariyya wa-Ghaḍab fī-Lubnān*" ("Military Trial and Anger in Lebanon"), *Al-Jazeera*, June 21, 2015, http://www.aljazeera.net/home/Getpage/f6451603-4dff-4ca1-9c10-122741d17432/9fef04b2-e8ed-42ea-90fa-4b6c7376684c.

12. For an article on Assange's role in the 2016 US presidential elections, see Robert Mackey, "Julian Assange's Hatred of Hillary Clinton Was No Secret. His Advice to Donald Trump Was," *Intercept*, November 15, 2017, https://interc.pt/2iWVv94.

13. I'm thinking here of films such as *Snowden* (dir. Oliver Stone, USA, 2016).

14. Of course, one can think of Mme. de Sévigné's multi-volume *Correspondances* or the letters she started writing primarily to her daughter Françoise when the latter left Paris in 1671, revealing court gossip, intrigues, and scandals. For the English translation, see Madame de Sévigné, *Selected Letters*.

15. "The Lady and Her Five Suitors," in *Thousand Nights and a Night*, trans. Richard Francis Burton, 5: 89–90. This tale is from the Bulaq Arabic edition of the *Nights*.

16. Mahdy, *Arabian Nights*, "Night 126," 281. For the Arabic, see Mahdi, *Thousand and One Nights (Alf Layla wa-Layla)*, 1: 309–10.

17. For essays on Hagar's expulsion, see Sherwood, "Hagar and Ishmael." Also see Poorthuis, "Hagar's Wanderings." Zizek reads the pilgrimage ritual of walking back and forth between Safa and Marwa near Mecca on the Hajj to reenact Hagar's search for water in the desert—a "search which resists sublation"—as the suppression of Hagar's story, which haunts Muslim tradition. See Zizek, *Absolute Recoil*, 264.

18. See al-Ghadeer, *Desert Voices*.

19. In contemporary literature the fragmented body, torn apart by war, is a leaking body, as seen in Anton's *Corpse Washer* and Saadawi's *Frankenstein in Baghdad*, works that I take up in a future project.

20. See Maggi, *Our Women Are Free*.

21. Katz, "Scholarly versus Women's Authority," 73. Also see Reinhardt, "Impurity/No Danger."

22. "Niddah," in *Encyclopaedia Judaica*, 15: 253.

23. Ibid., 15: 254.

24. Fonrobert, *Menstrual Purity*, 17.

25. Ibid.

26. Irigaray, *Speculum*, 164. See in this context the seminal work of Douglas, *Purity and Danger*. Also, Julia Kristeva's theorization of the "abject" is very important in staging the threat to the boundaries of the ego in the encounter with the leak. She writes: "Urine, blood, sperm, excrement then show up in order to reassure a subject that is lacking its 'own and clean self'" (*Powers of Horror*, 53).

27. FEMEN is a feminist group originally from Ukraine known for guerilla activism.

28. See Rupi Kaur's Instagram, https://instagram.com/p/0ovWwJHA6f/.

29. Ibid.

30. Purvi Thacker, "Instagram Apologizes to Woman for Censoring Her Photo," *New York Times*, March 27, 2015, http://nytlive.nytimes.com/womenintheworld/2015/03/27/instagram-apologizes-to-woman-for-censoring-her-photo/.

31. See Elmahdy, *Mudhakkarāt Thāʾira.*

32. See Maya Mikdashi, "Waiting for Alia," *Jadaliyya*, November 20, 2011, http://www.jadaliyya.com/pages/index/3208/waiting-for-alia. For scholarly analyses of gender and the revolution that problematize the exclusion of women from the narrative of political struggle prior to and following the events of the Arab uprisings, thereby reintroducing questions of the female body as site of coercion and resistance to state power, see El Said, Meari, and Pratt, *Rethinking Gender*; Khalil, *Gender, Women*; and Amar, *Security Archipelago.*

33. Mourad, "Naked Body of Alia," 67–68.

34. See "Egypt's Nude Protester Alia al-Mahdy to Be Stripped of Citizenship," *Al-Arabiyya*, January 1, 2013, http://english.alarabiya.net/en/News/2013/01/01/Egypts-nude-protester-Alia-al-Mahdy-to-be-stripped-of-citizenship.html. The same calls were made with regard to Wael Abbas in the mainstream media in Egypt. Murtada Mansour, anchor at the Egyptian TV network Al-Faraʿīn, demonized Wael as a Qatari agent and called for stripping him of his Egyptian citizenship. Reading Wael's tweets on the air and insulting him, he called Wael "*min al-jins al-tālit*" (of the third gender), which means trans/queer/hermaphrodite. See https://www.youtube.com/watch?v=uUKgfas5OE4.

35. See "Video Alia Mahdy Undress in Protest at the Egyptian Constitution," https://www.youtube.com/watch?v=vlsD0Be_40s.

36. Kraidy, *Naked Blogger*, 183. Also, drawing on the work of Giorgio Agamben, Hamid Dabashi compares Elmahdy's naked protesting to self-immolation and other protest gestures reduced to the body as the last site of confronting tyranny. For Dabashi, these are not obscene images because obscenity is the torture images of Abu Ghraib and the like. See Dabashi, "La Vita Nuda: Baring Bodies, Bearing Witness," *Al-Jazeera English*, January 23, 2012, http://www.aljazeera.com/indepth/opinion/2012/01/20121211123868 8792.html.

37. Elmahdy, *Mudhakkarāt Thāʾira.*

38. Kraidy, *Naked Blogger*, 215.

39. Elmahdy, *Mudhakkarāt Thāʾira.*

40. Jon Jensen and Tim Hume, "Who Will Win Battle for the New Tunisia?," CNN, January 11, 2013, http://www.cnn.com/2013/01/11/world/meast/tunisia-salafists-artists-battle/.

41. Lacan, *Le séminaire*, 368–70.

42. Mitchell and Rose, *Feminine Sexuality*, 29.

43. Ibid., 30.

44. Ibid., 36.

45. The "règles" of the leaking subject consist in moving from the Freudian structure and the Oedipal model of desire and subjectivity into affect and into a radical critique such as that we find in Deleuze and Guattari, for instance. See Deleuze and Guattari, *Anti-Œdipe*, 17.

46. De Lagasnerie, *L'art de la révolte*, 165. While "thug" means something very specific in the context of Wael Abbas and in Egypt after 2011, in this case "voyou" is being reappropriated to mean rogue or unlawful, closer to the term *futuwwa* than *balṭagī.*

47. Zizek, *Trouble in Paradise*, 122.

48. The leaks included "a classified, explosive video of an American helicopter attack in Baghdad that left 12 people dead, including two employees of the Reuters news agency," which WikiLeaks titled "Collateral Murder" (akin to the military's use of "collateral

damage"). See Elisabeth Bumiller, "Army Leak Suspect Is Turned in by Ex-Hacker," *New York Times*, June 7, 2010, http://www.nytimes.com/2010/06/08/world/08leaks.html.

49. Bumiller, "Army Leak Suspect."

50. Ibid. In *Risk* (dir. Laura Poitras, USA, 2016), the documentary about Julian Assange, there is an interview of Assange by artist Lady Gaga at the Ecuadorian embassy from 2012 in which he is seen explaining to her structures of surveillance.

51. See in this context Halberstam, *Gaga Feminism*.

52. Greenwald, "Inhumane Conditions."

53. See Greenwald's interview with Amy Goodman, "Glenn Greenwald on Bradley Manning: Prosecutor Overreach Could Turn All Whistleblowing into Treason," *Democracy Now*, March 5, 2013, http://www.democracynow.org/2013/3/5/glenn_greenwald_on_bradley_manning_prosecutor. Manning ended up receiving a thirty-five-year prison sentence, only to be pardoned by Barack Obama in 2017.

54. Aaron Swartz, the young man who hacked the academic publishing platform JSTOR, committed suicide in 2013 after being convicted. His trial is described repeatedly as a "vindictive act." See John Naugton, "Aaron Swartz Stood Up for Freedom and Fairness—And Was Hounded to His Death," *Guardian*, February 7, 2015, http://www.theguardian.com/commentisfree/2015/feb/07/aaron-swartz-suicide-internets-own-boy.

55. Hastings, "Julian Assange."

56. The "hacker" in Ahmed Alaidy's *Being Abbas el Abd*, examined in chapter 1 and in my first book, *Trials of Arab Modernity*, is none other than Julian Assange. See Alaidy, *Being Abbas el Abd*, 96. Also see El-Ariss, *Trials of Arab Modernity*, 165.

57. Zizek, *Trouble in Paradise*, 120.

58. Derrida writes: "Democracy is what it is only in the différence by which it defers itself and differs from itself. It is what it is only by spacing itself beyond being and even beyond ontological difference; it is (without being) equal and proper to itself only insofar as it is inadequate and improper, at the same time behind and ahead of itself, behind and ahead of the Sameness and Oneness of itself; it is thus interminable in its incompletion beyond all determinate forms of incompletion, beyond all the limitations in areas as different as the right to vote (for example in its extension to women—but starting when?—to minors—but starting at what age?—or to foreigners—but which ones and on what lands?" (Derrida, *Rogues*, 38–39).

59. Ibid., 20–21.

60. De Lagasnerie, *L'art*, 48–49.

61. Ibid., 43.

62. As Barbara Harlow (1948–2017) was demonstrating in what would have been her forthcoming book, *The Drone Imprint*.

63. James Bamford, "The Most Wanted Man in the World," *Wired Magazine*, August 2014, https://www.wired.com/2014/08/edward-snowden/.

64. Glenn Greenwald, "Inside the Mind of NSA Chief Gen Keith Alexander," *Guardian*, September 15, 2013, http://www.theguardian.com/commentisfree/2013/sep/15/nsa-mind-keith-alexander-star-trek.

65. Greenwald, "Inside the Mind."

66. Bamford, "The Most Wanted."

67. Nadel, *Containment Culture*, 14.

68. Ibid., 4.

69. Ibid., 16.

70. Ibid., 17.

71. Ibid., 29.

72. Hastings, "Julian Assange."

73. Assange, *When WikiLeaks Met Google*, 124.

74. See Judith Butler's engagement with "governmentality" and "indefinite detention" as using the laws selectively in *Precarious Life*.

75. "Glenn Greenwald on Bradley Manning," *Democracy Now*.

76. Ibid.

77. Assange states that "it is WikiLeaks' mission to receive information from whistleblowers and censored journalists, release it to the public, and then defend against the inevitable legal and political attacks. It is a routine occurrence for powerful states and organizations to attempt to suppress WikiLeaks publications, and as *the publisher of last resort* this is one of the hardships that WikiLeaks was built to endure" (my emphasis) (Assange, *When WikiLeaks Met Google*, 213).

78. Zizek, *Trouble in Paradise*, 122. Also, see Dabashi's critique of Zizek in *Can Non-Europeans Think?*

79. Zizek, *Trouble in Paradise*, 128–29.

80. Greenwald, *No Place to Hide*, 18.

81. Ibid., 19.

82. Ibid., 20.

83. Ibid., 21.

84. Ibid., 75.

CHAPTER 2

1. The video title, "the scruff" (*al-qafā*), is tied to the vernacular expression *yākhud ʿalā qafāh*, which literally means "to be beaten on one's scruff," and metaphorically "to get roughed up," "mistreated," or "to have one's rights trampled." This expression encapsulates the conditions of Egyptians under Mubarak and his security apparatus.

2. Naji, *Al-Mudawannāt*, 33.

3. See Rasha Azb speaking on how the revolution started and critiquing Wael Ghonim as its symbol in the eyes of Western media, https://www.frontlinedefenders.org/en/profile/rasha-azab. The Mahalla Riots in 2005 are often cited as an antecedent to the January 25, 2011, uprising. For an assessment of the labor history of Mahalla, see Hammad, *Industrial Sexuality*.

4. See Gregory, "Tahrir."

5. For Wael Abbas's blog, see http://misrdigital.blogspirit.com/, and for his YouTube, see https://www.youtube.com/user/waelabbas. Abbas eventually started other media outlets as well, including an account on *ask.fm* and a news site entitled "The Wael Abbas Daily," http://paper.li/waelabbas. He also has a self-published book, entitled *Al-Hurūb min al-Ṭāṣa* ("Escape from the Pot"), a collection of articles he wrote following the Tahrir uprising.

6. In Modern Standard Arabic, the word is *qillat* (less of, lack of), but in colloquial Egyptian the "q" is dropped and the "a" sound becomes an "i" sound. So although I will be using it as "*qillat*" throughout, it is pronounced "*illit*."

7. I'm thinking here of activist and blogger Rasha Azb, discussed in the introduction, and of Khorm—his real name is Islam al-Rafei—who was arrested for allegedly insulting President Sisi in November 2017; see https://twitter.com/5orm. For a work engaging political blogging and digital activism in the region, see Lenze, Schriwer, and Jalil, *Media in the Middle East*.

8. Kefaya is the Egyptian political movement opposed to the succession of Hosni Mubarak by his son Gamal, a succession that was thwarted by the January 25, 2011, revolution. See Christian Junge, "On Affect and Emotion as Dissent: The Kifaya Rhetoric in Pre-Revolutionary Egyptian Literature," in *Commitment and Beyond*, eds. Pannewick and Khalil, with Albers, 253–72.

9. Mark Zuckerberg, founder of Facebook, announced in April 2017 that his company was developing software that would allow users to "type with their brains and hear with their skin." See http://www.wired.co.uk/article/facebook-messenger-bots-developer-conference-2017.

10. For a discussion of transparency as "neoliberal dispositive," see Han, *Transparency Society*. I thank Dani Nassif for this reference.

11. Though this notion has seen many articulations from Zola to Foucault, I'm thinking here of Said's "lonely intellectual" speaking truth to power while upholding humanist and universal ideals. See Said, *Representations of the Intellectual*, 84–102. For a representation of Egyptian intellectuals in the context of the uprisings, see Youssef Rakha's novel *Al-Tamāsīḥ* ("The Crocodiles"). For an analysis of Sartrian *engagement* in the Arab context, namely 1950s and 1960s *iltizām*, see Klemm, "Different Notions of Commitment," 54.

12. For an engagement with the bloggers and Wael's contribution specifically from this perspective, see Mohamed, "Political Discourse of Egyptian Blogs."

13. Amar, *Security Archipelago*, 6.

14. *Adab* has generated renewed interest in literary studies, revisited and deconstructed as the ordering mechanism of the discourse on civilization (*tamaddun*) and as world literature by scholars such as Shaden Tageldin, Michael Allan, Samah Selim, and Ellen McLarney. In a previous work I have analyzed *adab* as a site of affective and somatic breakdown (*Trials of Arab Modernity*). On *adab* in the classical context, see Kennedy, *On Fiction*.

15. Al-Bustani, "Lecture on the Culture of the Arabs," in *Arab Renaissance*, ed. El-Ariss, 3–19.

16. Elshakry, *Reading Darwin in Arabic*, 19.

17. Ibid., 197.

18. See Di-Capua, "The Intellectual Revolt of the 1950s and the 'Fall of the *Udabā*,'" in *Commitment and Beyond*, ed. Pannewick and Khalil, with Albers, 89–104. Also see Di-Capua, *No Exit*.

19. See Elias, *Civilizing Process*. For a discussion of incivility as a practice to confront and speak truth to power, see Salaita, *Uncivil Rites*. For an engagement with Elias's "civilization/civility" in Salaita's case, see Joan Scott, "The New Thought Police," *Nation*, April 15, 2015, http://www.thenation.com/article/new-thought-police/.

20. The novella was published in Cairo in 1966 but withdrawn by the authorities immediately afterwards. It did not reappear in its entirety until 1986.

21. See Mehrez, *Egypt's Culture Wars*, 14–22 and 58–88.

22. For a deconstructive critique of *khadsh al-ḥayāʾ* and the ways in which regimes and cultural institutions use *ḥayāʾ* to oppress and persecute musicians and oher cultural producers, see *Ma3azef*'s special issue edited by Zeina G. Halabi on the notion of *khadsh* in Arabic music. The issue features a collection of essays and testimonies prompted by Ahmed Naji's sentencing. See *Ma3azef*, May 16, 2016, http://ma3azef.com/category/%D8%A7%D9%84%D9%85%D9%84%D9%81/%D8%AE%D8%AF%D8%B4-%D8%A7%D9%84%D8%AD%D9%8A%D8%A7%D8%A1/.

23. *Al-ādāb*, the collectivity of *adab*, became synonymous with vice and specifically the "vice squad," which is called *bulīṣ al-ādāb*.

24. Apter, "Fictions politiques/démarches impolitiques."

25. This is to be compared and contrasted to the Arabic poetics of *hijāʾ* (invective poetry), which was essential to the tribal economy for the activation of symbolic power against the other. See van Gelder, *Bad and Ugly*. For an engagement with "flyting" and invective sparring in the famous case of poets Jarir and Farazdaq, see Farrin, *Abundance from the Desert*, 115–29. For invective use in the medieval Egyptian context and the origin of the infamous *aḥḥā* (fuck that!) used by bloggers and others today, see Stewart, "Popular Shiism."

26. Said, introduction to Halim Barakat's 1969 novel *ʿAwdat al-Ṭāʾir ilā al-Baḥr* (*Days of Dust*), ix–xxxiv, xxvi.

27. Elliott Colla engages contemporary protestor slogans through a comparative dialogue with the classical poetic tradition of *hijāʾ* (invective) and *ḥamāsa* (zeal). See Colla, "In Praise of Insult."

28. Naguib Surur's 1969 poem *Kussummiyat* was never published, and circulates only on tapes and in manuscripts. For a recording of the poem, see https://soundcloud.com/cairolondonnyc/sets/naguib-sorours-koss-ummiat/. For a discussion of the poem and Egyptian popular culture, see Koerber, *Conspiracy*, chapter 2, "Naguib Surur: The Poetics and Politics of *Niyaka*." See also Atef Botros, "Rewriting Resistance: The Revival of Poetry of Dissent in Egypt after January 2011 (Surūr, Najm, and Dunqul)," in *Commitment and Beyond*, ed. Pannewick and Khalil, with Albers, 45–62.

29. For an analysis of processes of orientalization in this context, see El-Ariss, "Future Fiction."

30. See Jacquemond, *Conscience of the Nation* and "Satiric Literature."

31. Halabi examines the ambivalence of contemporary writers about politically committed Arab intellectuals. See Halabi, *Unmaking of the Arab Intellectual*.

32. Ibid.

33. Though this hashtag started in 2013, the examples quoted here were added in July 2015. https://twitter.com/hashtag/%D9%85%D8%A7%D8%B0%D8%A7_%D8%AA%D8%B9%D8%B1%D9%81_%D8%B9%D9%86_%D9%88%D8%A7%D8%A6%D9%84_%D8%B9%D8%A8%D8%A7%D8%B3?src=hash.

34. "To give (or get) satisfaction" could be understood in the European aristocratic sense, i.e., dueling to restore honor and dignity.

35. This brings to mind Gates, *Signifying Monkey*.

36. See Paul Amar's notion of "thug state" in "Turning Gender Politics?"

37. I'm thinking of Kirsha's wife in Mahfouz's *Zuqāq al-Midaq* (Midaq Alley), 1:660. Also, the power of shaming and the relation to affect theory could be thought through

in Eve Sedgwick's sense and that of Silvan Tomkins. See Sedgwick and Frank, *Shame and Its Sisters.*

38. Wael Abbas, December 2, 2011, https://twitter.com/waelabbas.

39. See Murtada Mansour, https://www.youtube.com/watch?v=PDGBMIiv3Zg.

40. "Exposure, n." OED Online, June 2017, http://www.oed.com.dartmouth.idm.oclc.org/view/Entry/66730?redirectedFrom=exposure.

41. Ibn Manzur, *Lisān*, 11–12: 190–91.

42. Ibid.

43. See *Miramār* (dir. Kamal El Sheikh, Egypt, 1969).

44. Lebanese political scientist and journalist Samer Franjieh describes *faḍḥ* as a dangerous weapon in the face of political corruption. See "*Al-Faḍīḥa fī Wajh Ibtizāz al-Ḥad al-Adnā*" ("Scandal in the Face of Minimum-Wage Blackmail"), *Al-Hayat*, June 21, 2015, http://alhayat.com/Opinion/Writers/9593380.

45. See Mina Naji, "*An Takūn Mithliyyan Miṣriyyan*" ("Being an Egyptian Homosexual"), *Al-Mudun*, September 12, 2014, http://www.almodon.com/society/68dffd98-d2d6-4f00-93d1-616f5bdc8b3e.

46. Ahmed Gharbeia's blog (http://zamakan.gharbeia.org/) was the first to appear. See Naji, *Al-Mudawannāt*, 9.

47. Naji is here referring to Malik Mustafa's blog "Malcom X"; see http://today.almasryalyoum.com/article2.aspx?ArticleID=108398.

48. Ibid., 43. For an article on political blogging in Egypt with an emphasis on the Muslim Brotherhood, see Lynch, "Young Brothers in Cyberspace."

49. Naji, *Al-Mudawannāt*, 33–34.

50. *Fiʿl* as in *fiʿl fāḍiḥ*, which means "indecent exposure."

51. For a discussion of the place of the "heart" in the narrative of subjectivity, see Doueihi, *Perverse History*.

52. Butler, *Excitable Speech*, 15.

53. Sonallah Ibrahim claims that the uprising in Egypt in 2011 "certainly was not a revolution. A revolution has a program and goal—a complete change of reality or the removal of one class by another. What happened was a popular uprising." See Ibrahim interviewed by Elliot Colla, "The Imagination as Transitive Act," *Jadaliyya*, June 12, 2011, http://www.jadaliyya.com/pages/index/1811/the-imagination-as-transitive-act_an-interview-wit. Uprising as *intifāḍah* is a shedding event (*nafḍ*, from the verb *nafaḍa*, which means "to shake off" or "to shed"), a stripping naked (*taʿriya*) of oneself and the other, a moment of deterritorialization, which needs to be compared to but also distinguished from *nahaḍa/nuhūḍ/nahḍa*, rising and awakening as that which leads to a new realization and a new *waʿī*.

54. See "Wael Abbas interviewed by *The Hub*," uploaded on August 7, 2008, http://www.youtube.com/watch?v=VShnSpsYcQE&feature=channel_page. For an article on the use of the camera as tool for exposing abuse and civic engagement, see Andén-Papadopoulos, "Citizen Camera-Witnessing."

55. See http://misrdigital.blogspirit.com/archive/2009/04/index.html.

56. Ibid.

57. Here I'm thinking of the notion of "assemblage" in Deleuze and Guattari's sense articulated in *Anti-Œdipe*.

58. Doueihi, *Digital Cultures*, 2.

59. Clough and Puar, "Introduction," 15.

60. Wael Abbas, "Video Blogging and the Egyptian Uprisings," talk at the University of Michigan, November 14, 2013, https://www.youtube.com/watch?v=aAwaWhg-eX8.

61. Reminiscent of the famous Amadou Dialo case in New York City in the 1990s, the video of *'Imād al-Kibīr* was published a month after Wael posted *Al-Qafā* in 2006. The video earned Wael great recognition for his fight against torture. For an interview with the bus driver tortured in the video, describing how the officers filmed him as they tortured him, see Wael's YouTube upload from December 13, 2006, https://www.youtube.com/watch?v=Dcxttwg1-vo.

62. For a reporting of this incident that describes the reason provided by YouTube as "inappropriate material," see "YouTube Shuts Down Egyptian Anti-Torture Activist's Account, "CNN, November 29, 2007, http://www.cnn.com/2007/WORLD/meast/11/29/youtube.activist/. For an interview with Wael discussing this issue, see "Inside Story—The Impact of Twitter's Censorship Plan," *Al-Jazeera English*, January 28, 2012, https://www.youtube.com/watch?v=BBkXp89rJWM.

63. Smolin, *Moroccan Noir*, 10.

64. I'm thinking here of the "woman with the blue bra," a protestor in Tahrir Square, who was dragged and exposed by the police. This incident became iconic. See Ahdaf Soueif, "Image of Unknown Woman Beaten by Egypt's Military Echoes around World," *Guardian*, December 18, 2011, https://www.theguardian.com/commentisfree/2011/dec/18/egypt-military-beating-female-protester-tahrir-square?CMP=share_btn_tw.

65. Here I'm thinking of Ahmed Saadawi's *Frankenstein in Baghdad*.

66. Harcourt takes up this question in *Exposed*.

67. Abbas, "Video Blogging."

68. For a critique of the "democratization" thesis, see Achcar, *Morbid Symptoms*, 1–14.

69. Tawfiq al-Hakim, *'Awdat;* for the English translation, see *Return of Consciousness*, trans. Winder.

70. For an engagement with al-Hakim's work, see El-Ariss, " Future Fiction."

71. Al-Hakim, *'Awdat* 42.

72. Hegel states that the demand for recognition that produces subjectivity entails a violent confrontation with the other. This constant demand is what fuels the movement of history. In Marx, the demand for recognition is class struggle, which moves toward the end of history as the fulfillment of this recognition. So the negation of the other, his enslavement by the master, continuously moves through thesis and antithesis to a moment of total recognition and the end of dialectics.

73. I'm thinking here of Rachid Ghannoushi's "*Al-Nahda* party" in Tunis that briefly came to power after the ouster of Ben Ali in 2010.

74. Bamyeh, "Arab Revolutions."

75. Ibid., 9–10 (emphasis added).

76. See El-Ariss, *Trials of Arab Modernity*, 145–71.

77. See Naji, *Using Life*, which engages with this model of blocking circulation.

78. Brown, *Walled States*, 26.

79. Warner, *Publics and Counterpublics*, 143–44.

80. For an essay assessing the transformations pertaining to activists now behind bars from 2011 to 2016, see Lauren Bohn, "A Revolution Devours Its Children," *Atlantic*, January 23, 2016, http://www.theatlantic.com/international/archive/2016/01/egypt-revolution-arab-spring/426609/, and Joshua Hammer, "How Egypt's Activists Became 'Generation Jail,'" *New York Times Magazine*, March 14, 2017, https://nyti.ms/2nj74vZ.

81. State actors tried to hack a number of dissident accounts in March 2016, including Wael's. See Ramy Raoof, "Two-Step Verification in Egypt: Strength or Weakness for Online Security," *Advox*, April 7, 2016, https://advox.globalvoices.org/2016/04/07/two-step-verification-in-egypt-strength-or-weakness-for-online-security/.

CHAPTER 3

1. "The Saudi Cables," *WikiLeaks* June 19, 2015, https://wikileaks.org/saudi-cables/press.

2. Ibid.

3. Marc Lynch, "How Leaked Saudi Cables Might Really Matter," *Washington Post*, June 21, 2015, http://wpo.st/Sqn12. Italics are my emphasis.

4. See https://twitter.com/Mujtahidd. The 2015 "Arab Social Media Report" states that 55 percent of the Arab world use social media; 83 percent of users access social media on smartphones or handheld devices; and 39 percent use Twitter daily. In Saudi Arabia, over half of all social media users have Twitter subscriptions. Many of these users turn to Twitter for news and information, but also for gossip and entertainment. See https://www.wpp.com/govtpractice/~/media/wppgov/files/arabsocialmediareport-2015.pdf. The most-followed account on Saudi Twitter is that of Islamic preacher Mohamad Alarefe, who draws on followers from across the Islamic world, https://twitter.com/MohamadAlarefe. Madawi Al-Rasheed, the London-based scholar and opposition figure, is very active on Twitter as well with 184 thousand followers. See https://twitter.com/MadawiDr.

5. For instance, see Maxim Romanov's essay on al-Dhahabī's *Ta'rīkh al-Islām* in "Toward Abstract Models for Islamic History," in *Digital Humanities*, ed. Muhanna, 117–49. Also see Romanov's website, "Al-Raqmiyyāt: Digital Islamic History," https://alraqmiyyat.github.io/.

6. Leder and Kilpatrick, "Classical Arabic Prose Literature," 11.

7. De Blois, et al., "Ta'rīkh."

8. Ibid.

9. Engaging al-Asfahani's *Kitāb al-Aghānī* as a curated work of literature, Kirsten Beck argues: "Scholars have tended to seek to tame the foreignness of *akhbār*-based genres through questions about the authenticity of *isnād* and through historical approaches. Such approaches ignore the literary value of the form and content and view literary concerns to be at odds with historical concerns, which they take to involve a preoccupation with fact-based accuracy." See Beck, "Destabilizing Knowledge."

10. Leder and Kilpatrick, "Classical Arabic Prose Literature."

11. Ibid., 14.

12. Al-Musawi, "Abbasid Popular Narrative," 274.

13. Ibid.

14. Referring to Manning's leaks to Assange in 2010, an *Al-Jazeera* article headlined: "*Ifshāʾ Bayānāt Siriyya*" ("Revelation of Secret Documents"). See "*Malaffāt WikiLeaks ʿAzzazat al-Tajnīd li-Qāʿida*" ("WikiLeaks Files Helped al-Qaida Recruiting"), *Al-Jazeera*, August 9, 2013, http://www.aljazeera.net/home/Getpage/f6451603-4dff-4ca1-9c10-122741d17432/1a9d60cc-5d47-44bd-bf4c-1eedfb2922d4.

15. Al-Musawi, *Mujtamaʿ Alf Layla wa Layla*, 191.

16. Al-Musawi, "Abbasid Popular Narrative," 274.

17. See Ayalon, "Historian al-Jabartī."

18. De Blois et al., "Taʾrīkh."

19. Al-Ghadhdhami, *Thaqāfat Twitter*, 6.

20. Ibid., 43.

21. Adonis, *Sufism and Surrealism*, 97.

22. For the somatic function of *kashf* in the context of the Arab encounter with modernity, see El-Ariss, *Trials of Arab Modernity*, 63.

23. Gardet, L., "Kashf."

24. *ʿIrāq: Kashf al-Mastūr* ("Iraq: Revealing the Hidden"), *Al-Jazeera*, http://www.aljazeera.net/home/Getpage/466530fd-e741-4721-acd2-a85c1ce6092a/02aa2cf1-2e4e-47c0-9727-7416288781a4.

25. Most media sources and experts speculate that he is either the Saudi dissident Saad al-Faqih, who lives in London, or Prince Sultan bin Turki bin Abdulaziz ("*Man huwa 'Mujtahid' fī-Twitter al-Saʿūdiyya*?" ["Who is Mujtahidd on Saudi Twitter?"], *Al-Jazeera*, July 14, 2012, http://www.aljazeera.net/home/print/f6451603-4dff-4ca1-9c10-122741d17432/53eda36c-0868-4157-8d06-91918554cf44). When Mujtahidd's account was hacked and his almost two million followers at the time were completely wiped out in September 2015, the hackers claimed that they were able to trace him to Saad al-Faqih, but this has not been confirmed. See *Al-Madina*, September 29, 2015, http://www.al-madina.com/node/633292, and *747 News*, October 9, 2015, http://www.747news.com/politique/18399.html.

26. Laura Secorun Palet, "Saudi Arabia's Twitter Whistleblower," *OZY*, September 3, 2014, http://www.ozy.com/provocateurs/saudi-arabias-twitter-whistleblower/33635.

27. Conspiracy theory is rampant around Mujtahidd's identity and backers, including one theory that considers Mujtahidd to be a CIA/WikiLeaks project at the service of a "brotherly" Gulf state, implying Qatar. See Ziad al-Salih, "*Man huwa al-Mugharrid 'Mujtahid*?' " ("Who is the tweeter 'Mujtahidd' "), July 21, 2012, http://alhaqaeq.blogspot.co.uk/2012/07/blog-post_7647.html.

28. Since his move to Russia, Edward Snowden has been regularly appearing as speaker at various events in the United States via video. For example, he gave a TED talk via video, see TED, March 2014, https://www.ted.com/talks/edward_snowden_here_s_how_we_take_back_the_internet?language=en.

29. I'm thinking of Munif's representation of the oasis culture in *Cities of Salt*, an idyllic space preceding the advent of oil in Arabia.

30. Wensinck, A. J., et al., *Concordance et indices*, 3:297b. Moreover, both contemporary dictionaries and classical lexicons mention a meaning for *hammām* as *nammām*, tying it to *hamhama*, which refers to the unclear speech. This is also tied to the notion of *ahammiyya/muhim* (importance/important), which points to a level of meaning that

connects the important and true speech to the unclear speech. See Ibn Manzur, *Lisān*, 15–16: 94–96. Also see Wehr, *Modern Written Arabic*, 1033 and 1035.

31. Roula Khalaf, "Daring Saudi Tweets Fuel Political Debate: Mujtahidd Phenomenon Triggers War of Words Online," *Financial Times*, March 16, 2012, https://www.ft.com/content/1749888e-6f5e-11e1-b368-00144feab49a.

32. Mark Lombardi (1951–2000) was an American librarian turned artist who drew diagrams of corporate and political scandals. His work is exhibited at the Museum of Modern Art in New York; see http://www.moma.org/artists/22980?locale=en.

33. Mujtahidd, *Al-Kitāb al-Muʿtamad fī Taghrīdāt Mujtahidd* ("The Reliable Book of Mujtahidd's Tweets"), see https://docs.google.com/file/d/0ByFCK2y8C52aSklYRmg4dmRyajA/edit.

34. For instance, he lists this *New York Times* article about him, see Robert F. Worth, "Twitter Gives Saudi Arabia a Revolution of Its Own," October 20, 2012, http://nyti.ms/T7oSTy.

35. Mujtahidd, "Reliable Book," 34.

36. This incident was reported in the media when Sultan bin Turki decided to sue Abdulaziz bin Fahd in Swiss courts over the abduction. See Hugh Miles, "Senior Saudi Prince Accuses Cousin over Alleged Drugging and Abduction," *Guardian*, July 17, 2015, https://www.theguardian.com/world/2015/jul/17/senior-saudi-prince-accuses-cousin-over-alleged-drugging-and-abduction?CMP=share_btn_tw.

37. See Peter Waldman, "The $2 Trillion Project to Get Saudi Arabia's Economy off Oil: Eight Unprecedented Hours with 'Mr. Everything,' Mohammed bin Salman," *Bloomberg*, April 21, 2016, http://bloom.bg/1r1ukvY.

38. See https://www.hrw.org/news/2017/11/23/saudi-arabia-new-counterterrorism-law-enables-abuse.

39. For instance, see Raif Badawi, https://www.amnesty.org.uk/issues/Raif-Badawi. For a report prepared by Human Rights Watch in 2015 on the arrests of Twitter activists in the Gulf, see https://features.hrw.org/features/HRW_2016_reports/140_Characters/index.html#.

40. *Qāṣṣ* simply means storyteller, while *ḥakawātī* is both storyteller and performer, derived from the word *ḥaka/yaḥkī* (speak, talk).

41. Wayne Booth, *Rhetoric of Fiction*.

42. In his play *The Digital Hats Game* (2016), Hassan Blasim has made the connection between jinn and hackers, http://www.teatteritelakka.fi/?page_id=4818&lang=en, as did G. Willow Wilson's novel, *Alif the Unseen*. In the case of Mujtahidd, the emphasis is on the miracle or the mystery of knowledge that should not be explained or divulged.

43. Secorun Palet, "Saudi Arabia's Twitter."

44. Ibn Manzur, *Lisān*, 11–12: 190–91.

45. Juynboll and Brown, "Sunna."

46. Mujtahidd is playing on the expression, *izā btulītum bi-l-maʿāṣī fa-statirū*, which means "if you are bound to sin, don't flaunt it." These sins or misdeeds refer to acts involving sex, drugs, and rock and roll.

47. For an interesting analysis of celebrity gossip and discussion of celebrity drug use specifically, see Tiger, "Celebrity Gossip Blogs."

48. Mujtahidd, May 19, 2015, https://twitter.com/mujtahidd.

49. Ibid., May 21, 2015.

50. Joshua Berlinger, "An Anonymous Twitter Account May Be Starting a Quiet Revolution in Saudi Arabia," *Business Insider*, October 22, 2012, http://www.business insider.com/mujtahidd-saudi-arabias-rebel-tweeter-2012-10.

51. In *Being Abbas el Abd*, Ahmed Alaidy describes Abbas's anger as exploding like "the sewer pipe that can't hold the shit anymore," 34. See also El-Ariss, *Trials of Arab Modernity*, 153.

52. Tweeter-in-Chief is the sarcastic expression used by some media sources to refer to US President Donald Trump, who uses Twitter "gratuitously" according to these sources. For example, see http://www.cnn.com/2017/01/18/politics/twitter-primer-donald-trump-trnd/index.html.

53. Warner, *Publics and Counterpublics*, 78–79.

54. Ibid., 79.

55. Al-Ghadhdhami, *Thaqāfat Twitter*, 50–51.

56. Di-Capua, "Traumatic Subjectivity," 88.

57. Mujtahidjo, https://twitter.com/mujtahidjo.

58. Mujtahiduae, https://twitter.com/mujtahiduae.

59. Patrick Kingsley, "Will #SisiLeaks be Egypt's Watergate for Abdel Fatah al-Sisi?," *Guardian*, March 5, 2015, http://www.theguardian.com/world/2015/mar/05/sisileaks-egypt-watergate-abdel-fatah-al-sisi.

60. Declan Walsh, "Egypt Gives Saudi Arabia 2 Islands in a Show of Gratitude," *New York Times*, April 10, 2016, http://nyti.ms/25TEWx4.

61. Ahmed Nada, "*Tasrībāt 'Alī Bābā' al-Miṣrī*" ("The Leaks of the Egyptian 'Ali Baba'"), *Al-Modon*, February 9, 2015, http://www.almodon.com/media/a3410e03-c9f5-4e04-bbe0-c34af8e56c78.

62. I'm thinking of the cliff-hangers of *Game of Thrones*.

63. De Lagasnerie, *L'art de la révolte*, 115.

CHAPTER 4

1. Jon Henley, "Salman Rushdie's Twitter Debut," *Guardian*, September 20, 2011, https://www.theguardian.com/books/2011/sep/20/salman-rushdie-twitter-debut.

2. Ibid.

3. *Throwing Sparks* operates as scandal fiction in its own right, exposing the violence that both constitutes and breaks down the subject in an "unnamed kingdom." The leaking subject in Khal's text is the recanting torturer at the service of a sadistic master, spewing horror stories about his childhood, daily life, and the nature of his work.

4. Egyptian writer and journalist Ibrahim Farghali claims that online interactions often involve a certain tone and mode of expression that break with "the propriety of bourgeois and middle-class conventions." See Ibrahim Farghali, "*Al-Internet … ka-Fāḍā' li-l-Thawra*" ("The Internet … as the Space of Revolution"), March 19, 2012, http://ifargh ali.blogspot.de/2012/03/avatar.html.

5. *Jahili* is in reference to the classical poetic tradition predating Islam. See Robyn Creswell and Bernard Haykal, "Battle Lines: Want to Understand the Jihadis? Read Their Poetry," *New Yorker*, June 8 & 15, 2015, http://www.newyorker.com/magazine/2015/06/08/battle-lines-jihad-creswell-and-haykel.

6. *Nahda* authors and intellectuals such as Taha Hussein (b. 1889), Tawfiq al-Haqim (b. 1898), and Yahya Haqqi (b. 1905).

7. See note 9 to the introduction.

8. Edwards, *After the American Century*, 76.

9. Ibid., 112.

10. See *Mr. Robot*, http://www.usanetwork.com/mrrobot/videos/mr-robotdec0d3ddoc.

11. Rakha is the author of *Kitāb al-Ṭughra* ("Sultan's Seal"). He keeps a blog entitled *The Arabophile*, https://yrakha.com/tag/youssef-rakha/.

12. Associated with infiltration, scandal, and leaks, hacking is the instrument of activists, conscientious objectors, government agents, disgruntled fans, and random saboteurs (*kharābkārī*, in Farsi). Hacking is a bricolage with wide-ranging aesthetic, social, and political repercussions. *The Jargon File*, an online resource for hacker subculture, defines the "cracker" (a type of hacker) as someone who "stretches the capabilities of programmable system"; "delights in having an intimate understanding of the internal workings of a system"; "programs enthusiastically (even obsessively)"; or is a "malicious meddler who tries to discover sensitive information by poking around" ("Hacker"). These various characterizations involve systematic acts of writing, knowing, and revealing. Hacking a website could involve writing a malicious program that infiltrates and infects it. It could also occur by overloading the site with requests that it cannot handle; this process depends on a consorted attack by a group of individuals who all send requests simultaneously in order to crash the site, as in the people who sent requests to the university and hacked Badriah's talk through a DOS request, as we will see in the next chapter. In this sense hacking exposes the inability of the *secure* system to handle the overwhelming requests, thereby stretching its limits and forcing it to recant its protected status. See Coleman, "Hacker Politics and Publics," and *Hacker, Hoaxer*.

13. Rakha, "E-cards for Mohammed Rabie."

14. Ibid.

15. While Meyer reads modernist innovation in the sixties in the works of Sonallah Ibrahim and Edward Kharrat in relation to European authors such as Camus (*Experimental Arabic Novel*), Elizabeth Kendall maintains that the avant-garde work of the sixties published in the journal *Gallery 68* should be "judged by its distinctiveness and specific concerns rather than its provenance in or ability to match to European or American culture" (*Literature, Journalism*, 145).

16. On the affectivity of the new literary canon examined through the perspective of prize culture in the Gulf, see Ziajka Stanton, "Labor of Love."

17. This controversy became public when Marilyn Booth first wrote a letter to the editor in the *Times Literary Supplement*, September 27, 2007, which she eventually developed into a series of articles.

18. Marilyn Booth, "Muslim Woman," 171–72.

19. Alsanea is a dentist by profession.

20. Allen, "Fiction and Publics," 9.

21. Ibid.

22. For an ethnographic study of young women in Saudi Arabia that moves beyond the binary of liberation and oppression, see Le Renard, *Society of Young Women*.

23. For a recent epistolary novel structured as e-mails, see al-Qamhawi (b. 1961), *Kitāb al-Ghiwāya* ("Book of Seduction").

24. Ibn Manzur, *Lisān*, 11–12: 190–91.
25. Marilyn Booth, "Translator v. Author," 204.
26. Al-Ghadeer, "*Girls of Riyadh*," 299.
27. Marilyn Booth, "The Muslim Woman," 153.
28. Ibid.
29. Ibid., 151.
30. Al-Rasheed, *Most Masculine State*, 214.
31. See Christian Junge, "On Affect and Emotion."
32. Bayat, *Life as Politics*, 13.
33. Omayma Abdelatif, "Review of *Taxi*," *Foreign Policy* 162 (2007): 80–84, 81.
34. Alkhamissi, "Preface" to *Taksī*, 9–10. The preface is different in the English-language Kindle edition I refer to below, which was translated by Jonathan Wright.
35. There are many postrevolution caricatures that represent Mubarak as someone who speaks only *fuṣḥā* and is unable to understand or communicate in *ʿāmmiyya*. This is in reference to his last three political speeches especially, when he was refusing to step aside and thus ignoring the people's demand.
36. Alkhamissi, 19/155.
37. Mohammad Bouazizi immolated himself after he was slapped by a governmental municipality woman who prevented him from selling his goods in a marketplace in Sidi Bouzid, Tunisia.
38. See Fahmy, *Ordinary Egyptians*.
39. Massumi, *Parables for the Virtual*, 27.
40. Alkhamissi, *Taxi*, 22/182.
41. Downtown (*wusṭ al-balad*), the site of the Kefaya demonstration, became the epicenter of the demonstrations that overthrew the government in February 2011.
42. Alkhamissi, *Taxi*, 40/348.
43. This brings to mind Charles Hirschkind's reading of Muslim sermon tapes played in cabs to produce an architecture of sound and morality that counters the one sanctioned by the prevalent power structure. See Hirschkind, *Ethical Soundscape*.
44. Alkhamissi, *Taxi*, 182/1770.
45. Ibid.

CHAPTER 5

1. Http://arablit.wordpress.com/2013/10/21/karam-sabers-trial-set-to-resume-tomorrow-over-short-story-collection-where-is-god/. For a recent article and interview with the author, see http://www.almodon.com/Home/Main-Article/9267. On June 5, 2014, the appeals court upheld the ruling, condemning the author to five years in prison. The English version of the story contains the expression "context analysis" instead of "content analysis." Upon examining the Arabic sources, I determined that it must be a typo or mistranslation so I changed it to "content" in the quotation above.
2. See Emily Apter's reading of "translation zone" as something that emerges from the encounter with death, such as translation practices in Iraq during the American occupation, in *Translation Zone*.
3. Sinan Anton, "Mahmoud Darwish: My God, Why Have You Forsaken Me?," *Jadaliyya*, March 17, 2014, http://www.jadaliyya.com/pages/index/16941/mahmoud-dar

wish_my-god-why-have-you-forsaken-me. See video, https://www.youtube.com/watch?v=Py695v_gjLw. The booth of the Beirut-based press, Arab Network for Research and Publishing, was also ransacked in a night raid on the book fair.

4. I'm thinking here of the framework that the campaign to defend Ahmed Naji adopted, namely to contest "*muḥākamat al-khayāl*" ("the trial of fiction"). In this case, it's a fiction against fiction that is at stake and not so much an older model of defending the right to publish. It's a more complex model of persecution that I explore in this chapter.

5. *Jahiliyya* designates the pre-Islamic culture of Arabia. It is often imagined as a kind of Dark Ages associated with tribal warfare, excess, and cruelty. It was rehabilitated during the Abbasid era (8th–13th centuries CE) as the repository of Arab cultural and literary genius. See "Dj̲āhiliyya" in *Encyclopaedia of Islam.*

6. Jenkins, *Convergence Culture*, 208–9.

7. For a good summary of this model in the context of the "Occupy" movement, see Penney and Dadas, "(Re)Tweeting."

8. Michelle Goldberg, "Feminism's Toxic Twitter Wars," *Nation*, January 19, 2014, http://www.thenation.com/print/article/178140/feminisms-toxic-twitter-wars. This article was discussed in an NPR report; see http://www.npr.org/player/v2/mediaPlayer.html?action=1&t=1&islist=false&id=272455489&m=272455490&live=1.

9. Goldberg, "Feminism." Also see Quinnae Moongazer, "Words, Words, Words: On Toxicity and Abuse in Online Activism," January 3, 2014, http://quinnae.com/2014/01/03/words-words-words-on-toxicity-and-abuse-in-online-activism/.

10. Goldberg, "Feminism."

11. See *Badriah*, http://www.mbc.net/ar/programs/badriya.html.

12. For the #La_LiBadriah (No to Badriah) hashtag campaign, see https://twitter.com/hashtag/%D9%84%D8%A7_%D9%84%D8%A8%D8%AF%D8%B1%D9%8A%D8%A9?src=hash.

13. For an engagement with nation building and social transformations in the Gulf with a focus on Qatar, see cooke, *Tribal Modern.*

14. For a report on this campaign, see *Middle East Online*, May 22, 2011, http://www.middle-east-online.com/?id=110926.

15. See Neil MacFarquhar, "Saudis Arrest Woman Leading Right-to-Drive Campaign," *New York Times*, May 23, 2011, http://nyti.ms/2d4utZb. For the video of Manal al-Sharif driving in Khubar, Saudi Arabia, explaining why it's important for women to drive, engaging social and economic issues, and thanking among other people Badriah Albeshr for her support, see https://youtu.be/pPSFxKPC2GI.

16. For the #Na'am_LiBadriah (Yes to Badriah) hashtag campaign, see https://twitter.com/search?q=%23%D9%86%D8%B9%D9%85_%D9%84%D8%A8%D8%AF%D8%B1%D9%8A%D8%A9&src=typd&f=realtime.

17. Badriah Albeshr, "*Ghazwat al-Hāshtāg*," *Al-Hayat*, June 2, 2012, http://www.alhayat.com/OpinionsDetails/407387.

18. Sattam al-Ruwayli, "Ghazwat Hashtag Blinds Qatar University," *Elaph*, May 30, 2012, http://www.elaph.com/Web/news/2012/5/739041.html.

19. Ibid.

20. This attribute, which became popular in the 1990s, is loosely associated with public intellectuals and civil-society activists trying to enact democratic changes, support

women's rights, and critique religious absolutism in the Gulf region generally and in Saudi Arabia specifically. However, in a series of decrees meant to combat jihadist activities in Syria, the Saudi government declared atheism as a form of terrorism, thereby providing the judiciary more leeway to clamp down on various forms of dissent and criticism. See Adam Withnall, "Saudi Arabia Declares All Atheists are Terrorists," *Guardian*, April 1, 2014, http://www.independent.co.uk/news/world/middle-east/saudi-arabia-declares-all-atheists-are-terrorists-in-new-law-to-crack-down-on-political-dissidents-9228389.html.

21. The 2003 invasion of Iraq is commonly referred to in Arabic as *Ghazū al-ʿIrāq*.

22. "#La_LiBadriah," June 1, 2012.

23. Ibid., May 29, 2012.

24. Ibid.

25. Abel, "Dār al-Islām."

26. The "Land of War" also refers to the realm of the unbelievers or heathens. See Abel, "Dār al-Ḥarb."

27. "#La_LiBadriah," June 1, 2012.

28. El-Cheikh, *Women, Islam*, 26.

29. Ibid., 2.

30. Nadel, *Containment Culture*, 72.

31. "#La_LiBadriah," June 2, 2012.

32. *Nuṣra* is associated in contemporary discourse with the Salafi military group *Jabhat al-Nuṣra* ("The Nusra Front"), which fought in Syria and is tied to Al-Qaeda.

33. Kishk, *Al-Ghazū al-Fikrī*. I would like to thank Ellen McLarney for this reference.

34. Including Tarek Albeshri, for instance.

35. In fact, Kishk wrote another book in 1965 entitled, *Al-Mārksiyya wa-l-Ghazū al-Fikrī* ("Marxism and Ideological *Ghazū*").

36. Muhammad Saleh, "*Ghazwat Taṭhīr*," *Al-Hayat*, April 22, 2013, http://alhayat.com/OpinionsDetails/505655.

37. Ibn Manzur, *Lisān*, 11–12: 46–48.

38. Ibid.

39. Ibid.

40. Ibid.

41. In *Thaqāfat Twitter*, al-Ghadhdhami argues that the term *haghtaga* used in Arabic is to call people to attack and insult someone on Twitter (72).

42. I consider here *Jahiliyya* as a gothic literary genre that could be observed in a number of works, for instance, Amaqasim, *Sāq al-ghurāb* ("The Crow's Leg").

43. "#La_LiBadriah," May 31, 2012.

44. For an Islamic manifesto of new writing, see "*Addabanī Rabbī fa Aḥsana Taʾdībī: Manifesto al-Adab al-Thawrī al-Jadīd*" ("God Disciplined Me Well: Manifesto of the New Revolutionary Literature"), *Al-Adab al-Jadid* ("New Literature"), January 23, 2012, http://adabislam25.blogspot.com/2012/01/blog-post.html.

45. "#La_LiBadriah," June 2, 2012.

46. Albeshr, *Hend*, 13–14.

47. On could argue that comparing God to a woman (the mother) makes the infraction all the more serious. At another level one could read these circulating passages as titillating for the raiders, allowing them to vicariously read profanities like porn.

48. On the *maw'ūda* as a trope and a literary critical tool for reading contemporary Arab women's literature, see al-Samman, *Anxiety of Erasure*. Also see Leemhuis, "Wa'd al-Banāt."

49. "#La_LiBadriah," June 1, 2012.

50. Ibid., May 29, 2012.

51. Ibid., May 30, 2012.

52. Ibid.

53. Amina Ismail, "ISIS Celebrates Brussels Attacks in Chilling New Video," *World Post*, March 24, 2016, http://www.huffingtonpost.com/entry/isis-video-brussels_us_56f3f849e4b02c402f66921d?ncid=engmodushpmg00000004.

GLOSSARY

adab	subjectivity, docility, manners; also, literature
adīb/udabāʾ	intellectual author/s
ʿajab	bewilderment, marvel
akhbār	anecdotes, stories, eyewitness accounts, news
āliyya	mechanism, machinery
faḍḥ	exposing, scene-making
faḍīḥa/faḍāʾiḥ	scandal/s
fāḍiḥ/mafḍūḥ	exposer/exposed
ghazū	conquest
ghazwa	raid
ifshāʾ	revelation
ijtihād	Islamic jurisprudence
ʿilm	knowledge
iltizām	engagement, commitment
jahiliyya	"heathen times," or the period predating the advent of Islam in Arabia
kashf/makshūf	unveiling/unveiled
mawʾūda	the infant girl buried alive in pre-Islamic Arabia
mujtahid/d	exegete
mukāshafa	lifting of the veil
muthaqqaf/muthaqqafūn	intellectual/s
nuṣra	triumph, revenge
qaṣṣ	storytelling
qillat adab	lack of civility, manners, or *adab*
shatm	invective, cursing
taʾdīb	the process of rendering mannered, civil, polite; production of subjectivity
tafashshī	proliferation
ṭālib	student, seeker
tasrīb	leaking, leak
waʿī	consciousness, awareness

BIBLIOGRAPHY

Abbas, Wael. *Al-Hurūb min al-Ṭāṣa* ("Escape from the Pot"). Cairo: Al-Wa'i al-Masri Press, 2017.

———. *Al-Wa'ī al-Miṣrī* ("Egyptian Consciousness"). http://misrdigital.blogspirit.com/.

———. "*Min Awrāq Nāshiṭ Ḥukūkī*" ("From the Papers of a 'Scratchy Activist' "). *Huna Sotak* (June 23, 2014). https://hunasotak.com/article/8961?u.

———. "The Wael Abbas Daily." http://paper.li/waelabbas.

Abel, A. "Dār al-Ḥarb." In *Encyclopaedia of Islam*. 2d ed. Edited by P. Bearman, Th. Bianquis, C. E. Bosworth, E. van Donzel, W. P. Heinrichs. http://dx.doi.org.dartmouth.idm.oclc.org/10.1163/1573-3912_islam_SIM_1700. First published online, 2012.

———. "Dār al-Islām." In *Encyclopaedia of Islam*. 2d ed. Edited by P. Bearman, Th. Bianquis, C. E. Bosworth, E. van Donzel, W. P. Heinrichs. http://dx.doi.org.dartmouth.idm.oclc.org/10.1163/1573-3912_islam_SIM_1703. First published online, 2012.

Achcar, Gilbert. *Morbid Symptoms: Relapse in the Arab Uprising*. Stanford, CA: Stanford University Press, 2016.

Adonis. *Sufism and Surrealism*. London: Saqi, 2005.

Alaidy, Ahmed. *Being Abbas el Abd*. Translated by Humphrey Davies. Cairo: American University of Cairo Press, 2006.

al-Azmeh, Aziz, and Fawwaz Trabulsi, eds. *Introduction to Ahmad Faris al-Shidyaq: Silsilat al-A'mal al-Majhula* ("Ahmad Faris al-Shidyaq: Series of Unknown Works"). London: Riad el-Rayyes, 1995.

Albeshr, Badriah. *Hend and the Soldiers*. Translated by Sanna Dhahir. Austin: CMES/University of Texas Press, 2017.

Al-Ghadeer, Moneera. "Cannibalizing Iraq: Topos of a New Orientalism." In *Debating Orientalism*. Edited by Ziad Elmarsafy, Anna Bernard, and David Attwell, 117–33. New York: Palgrave Macmillan, 2013.

———. *Desert Voices: Bedouin Women's Poetry From Saudi Arabia*. London: I. B. Tauris, 2009.

———. "*Girls of Riyadh*: A New Technology Writing or Chick Lit Defiance." *Journal of Arabic Literature* 37, no. 2 (2006): 296–301.

al-Ghadhdhami, Abdallah. *Thaqāfat Twitter: Ḥurriyyat al-Ta'bīr aw Mas'ūliyyat al-Ta'bīr* ("Twitter Culture: Freedom of Expression or Responsibility of Expression"). Beirut: Al-Markaz al-Thaqafi al-'Arabi, 2016.

al-Hakim, Tawfiq. *'Awdat al-Wa'ī* (*The Return of Consciousness*). Cairo: Dar al-Shuruq, 1974. Translated by Bayly Winder. New York: NYU Press, 1985.

Alkhamissi, Khalid. *Taksī: Ḥawādīt al-Mashāwīr* (*Taxi*). Cairo: Dar al-Shuruq, 2006. Translated by Jonathan Wright. Doha: Bloomsbury/Qatar Foundation Publishing, 2011.

Allan, Michael. *In the Shadow of World Literature: Sites of Reading in Colonial Egypt*. Princeton: Princeton University Press, 2016.

Allen, Roger. "Fiction and Publics: The Emergence of the 'Arabic Best-Seller.' " *Middle East Institute Viewpoints: The State of the Arts in the Middle East*, June 29, 2009: 9–12.

al-Musawi, Muhsin. "Abbasid Popular Narrative: The Formation of Readership and Cultural Production." *Journal of Arabic Literature* 38, no. 3 (2007): 261–92.

———. *Arabic Poetry: Trajectories of Modernity and Tradition*. London: Routledge, 2006.
———. *The Medieval Islamic Republic of Letters: Arabic Knowledge Construction*. Notre Dame, IN: Notre Dame University Press, 2015.
———. *Mujtamaʿ Alf Layla wa Layla* ("The Society of the Thousand and One Nights"). Tunis: Markaz al-Nashr al-Jamiʿi, 2000.
———. *The Postcolonial Arabic Novel*. Leiden: Brill, 2003.
al-Qamhawi, Ezzat. *Kitāb al-Ghiwāya* ("Book of Seduction"). Cairo: Dar al-Ayn, 2010.
Al-Rasheed, Madawi. *A Most Masculine State: Gender, Politics, and Religion in Saudi Arabia*. New York: Cambridge University Press, 2013.
Al-Samman, Hanadi. *Anxiety of Erasure: Trauma, Authorship, and the Diaspora in Arab Women's Writings*. Syracuse, NY: Syracuse University Press, 2015.
Amaqasim, Yahya. *Sāq al-Ghurāb* ("The Crow's Leg"). Tunis: Dar al-Janub li-l-Nashr, 2010.
Amar, Paul. *The Security Archipelago: Human-Security States, Sexuality Politics, and the End of Neoliberalism*. Durham, NC: Duke University Press, 2013.
———. "Turning the Gender Politics of the Security State Inside Out?" *International Feminist Journal of Politics* 13, no. 3 (2011): 299–328.
Andén-Papadopoulos, Kari. "Citizen Camera-Witnessing: Embodied Political Dissent in the Age of 'Mediated Mass Self-Communication.'" *New Media & Society* 16, no. 5 (2014): 753–69.
Anderson, Benedict. *Imagined Communities*. New York: Verso, 1991.
Anton, Sinan. *The Corpse Washer* (2010). Translated by Sinan Anton. New Haven, CT: Yale University Press, 2013.
Apter, Emily. *Against World Literature: On the Politics of Untranslatability*. London: Verso, 2013.
———. "Fictions politiques/démarches impolitiques." *Raison Publique*. May 4, 2014. http://www.raison-publique.fr/article705.html.
———. *The Translation Zone: A New Comparative Literature*. Princeton, NJ: Princeton University Press, 2005.
Arendt, Hannah. *The Origins of Totalitarianism*. New York: Meridian Books, 1958.
Armstrong, Nancy. *How Novels Think: The Limits of Individualism from 1719–1900*. New York: Columbia University Press, 2005.
Arnold, Mathew. *Culture and Anarchy* (1869). New York: Oxford University Press, 2009.
Assange, Julian. *When WikiLeaks Met Google*. New York: OR Books, 2016.
Ayalon, David. "The Historian al-Jabartī and His Background." *Bulletin of the School of Oriental and African Studies* 23, no. 2 (1960): 217–49.
Azb, Rasha. https://twitter.com/RashaPress.
Badawi, M. M. "Commitment in Contemporary Arabic Literature." *Journal of World History* 14, no. 1 (1972): 54–61.
Balibar, Étienne. *Citoyen sujet et autres essais d'anthropologie philosophique*. Paris: Presse Universitaire de France, 2011.
Bamyeh, Mohammed. "Arab Revolutions and the Making of a New Patriotism." *Orient III* (2011): 6–10.
Bayat, Asef. *Life as Politics*. Stanford, CA: Stanford University Press, 2009.
———. *Revolution without Revolutionaries: Making Sense of the Arab Spring*. Stanford, CA: Stanford University Press, 2017.

Bearman, P., Th. Bianquis, C. E. Bosworth, E. van Donzel, W. P. Heinrichs. "Djāhiliyya." In *Encyclopaedia of Islam*. 2d ed. Edited by P. Bearman, Th. Bianquis, C. E. Bosworth, E. van Donzel, W. P. Heinrichs. Brill Online, 2014. http://referenceworks.brillonline.com/entries/encyclopaedia-of-islam- 2/djahiliyya-SIM_1933. First published online, 2012.

Beck, Kirsten. "Destabilizing Knowledge in Medieval Arabo-Islamic Society: Multiplicities and Wonder in Isfahani's *Kitāb al-Aghānī*." PhD diss., University of Texas at Austin, 2016.

Berry, David M. *Critical Theory in the Digital Age*. London: Bloomsbury, 2015.

Blasim, Hassan. *The Digital Hats Game*. 2016. http://www.teatteritelakka.fi/?page_id=4818&lang=en.

Booth, Marilyn. "The Muslim Woman as Celebrity Author and the Politics of Translating Arabic: *Girls of Riyadh* Go on the Road," *Journal of Middle Eastern Women's Studies* 6, no. 3 (2010): 149–82.

———. "Translator v. Author (2007): *Girls of Riyadh* Go to New York." *Translation Studies* 1, no. 2 (2008): 197–211.

Booth, Wayne. *The Rhetoric of Fiction*. Chicago: University of Chicago Press, 1961.

Brown, Wendy. *Walled States, Waning Sovereignty*. New York: Zone Books, 2014.

Burdick, A., J. Drucker, and P. Lunenfeld, eds. *Digital Humanities*. Cambridge, MA: MIT Press, 2012.

Burton, Richard Francis, trans. *The Book of the Thousand Nights and a Night*. Vol. 5. London: H. S. Nicols, 1894.

Butler, Judith. *Excitable Speech: A Politics of the Performative*. New York: Routledge, 1997.

———. *Precarious Life: The Powers of Mourning and Violence*. London: Verso, 2004.

Chun, Wendy, Hui Kyong, and Sarah Friedland. "Habits of Leaking: Of Sluts and Network Cards." *Differences* 26, no. 2 (2015): 1–28.

Chun, Wendy. *Updating to Remain the Same: Habitual New Media*. Cambridge: MIT Press, 2017.

Clough, Patricia, and Jasbir Puar. Introduction to *WSQ: Women's Studies Quarterly*, "Special Issue: Viral" 40, nos. 1–2 (2012): 13–26.

Coleman, E. Gabriella. *Coding Freedom: The Ethics and Aesthetics of Hacking*. Princeton, NJ: Princeton University Press, 2013.

———. *Hacker, Hoaxer, Whistleblower, Spy: The Many Faces of Anonymous*. London: Verso, 2014.

———. "Hacker Politics and Publics." *Public Culture* 23, no. 3 (2011): 511–16.

Colla, Elliot. "In Praise of Insult: Slogan Genres, Slogan Repertoires and Innovation." *Review of Middle East Studies* 47, no. 1 (2013): 37–48.

cooke, miriam. *Tribal Modern: Branding New Nations in the Arab Gulf*. Berkeley: University of California Press, 2014.

Dabashi, Hamid. *Can Non-Europeans Think?* London: Zed, 2015.

———. "La Vita Nuda: Baring Bodies, Bearing Witness." *Al-Jazeera English*, January 23, 2012. http://www.aljazeera.com/indepth/opinion/2012/01/201212111238688792.html.

De Blois, F. C., B. Van Dalen, R. S. Humphreys, Manuela Marin, Ann K. S. Lambton, Christine Woodhead, Ali M. Athar, J. O. Hunwick, G.S.P. Freeman-Grenville, I. Proudfoot et al. "Ta'rīkh." In *Encyclopaedia of Islam*. 2d ed. Edited by P. Bearman, Th. Bianquis, C. E. Bosworth, E. van Donzel, W. P. Heinrichs. Brill Online, 2014. http://dx.doi.org

.ezproxy.lib.utexas.edu/10.1163/1573-3912_islam_COM_1184. First published online, 2012.

De Lagasnerie, Geoffroy. *L'art de la révolte: Snowden, Assange, Manning*. Paris: Fayard, 2015.

Deleuze, Gilles. "Postscript on the Societies of Control." *October* 59 (1992): 3–7.

Deleuze, Gilles, and Félix Guattari. *Anti-Œdipe: capitalisme et schizophrénie*. Paris: Editions de Minuit, 1972.

———. *A Thousand Plateaus: Capitalism and Schizophrenia*. Translated by Brian Massumi. Minneapolis: University of Minnesota Press, 1987.

Derrida, Jacques. *Rogues: Two Essays on Reason*. Translated by Pascale-Anne Brault and Michael Naas. Stanford, CA: Stanford University Press, 2005.

Derrida, Jacques, and Maurizio Ferraris. *A Taste for the Secret*. Translated by Giacomo Donis. Malden, MA: Polity Press, 2001.

Di-Capua, Yoav. *No Exit: Arab Existentialism, Jean-Paul Sartre, and Decolonization*. Chicago: University of Chicago Press, 2018.

———. "The Traumatic Subjectivity of Ṣunʿallāh Ibrāhīm's *Dhāt*." *Journal of Arabic Literature* 43 (2012): 80–101.

Doueihi, Milad. *Digital Cultures*. Cambridge, MA: Harvard University Press, 2011.

———. *A Perverse History of the Human Heart*. Cambridge, MA: Harvard University Press, 1997.

Douglas, Mary. *Purity and Danger: An Analysis of Concepts of Pollution and Taboo*. London: Routledge, 1966.

Edwards, Brian. *After the American Century: The Ends of U.S. Culture in the Middle East*. New York: Columbia University Press, 2015.

———."*Tahrir*: Ends of Circulation," *Public Culture* 23, no. 3 (2011): 493–504.

El-Ariss, Tarek, ed. *The Arab Renaissance: A Bilingual Anthology of the* Nahda. New York: Modern Language Association, 2018.

———. "Future Fiction: In the Shadow of Nasser." *Ibraaz* 7 (June 26, 2014). http://www.ibraaz.org/essays/95.

———. *Trials of Arab Modernity: Literary Affects and the New Political*. New York: Fordham University Press, 2013.

El Cheikh, Nadia. *Women, Islam, and Abbasid Identities*. Cambridge, MA: Harvard University Press, 2015.

Elias, Norbert. *The Civilizing Process: Sociogenetic and Psychogenetic Investigations*. Edited by Eric Dunning, Johan Goudsblom, and Stephen Mennell. Translated by Edmund Jephcott. Oxford: Blackwell Publishers, 2000.

Elmahdy, Aliaa. *Mudhakkarāt Thāʾira* ("A Rebel's Diary"). http://arebelsdiary.blogspot.com/2011/10/nude-art_2515.html.

El Said, Maha, Lean Meari, and Nicola Pratt, eds. *Rethinking Gender in Revolutions and Resistance*. London: Zed, 2015.

Elshakry, Marwa. *Reading Darwin in Arabic, 1860–1950*. Chicago: University of Chicago Press, 2014.

Fahmy, Ziad. *Ordinary Egyptians: Creating the Modern Nation through Popular Culture*. Stanford, CA: Stanford University Press, 2011.

Farrin, Raymond. *Abundance from the Desert: Classical Arabic Poetry*. Syracuse, NY: Syracuse University Press, 2011.

Felman, Shoshana. *The Scandal of the Speaking Body*. Stanford, CA: Stanford University Press, 2002.

Fonrobert, Charlotte. *Menstrual Purity: Rabbinic and Christian Reconstructions of Biblical Gender*. Stanford, CA: Stanford University Press, 2001.

Foucault, Michel. *Discipline and Punish: The Birth of the Prison*. Translated by Alan Sheridan. New York: Vintage, 1995.

Fraser, Nancy. "Rethinking the Public Sphere: A Contribution to the Critique of Actually Existing Democracy." *Social Text* 25/26 (1990): 56–80.

Gardet, L. "Kashf." In *Encyclopaedia of Islam*. 2d edition. Edited by P. Bearman, Th. Bianquis, C. E. Bosworth, E. van Donzel, W. P. Heinrichs. http://dx.doi.org.dartmouth.idm.oclc.org/10.1163/1573- 3912_islam_COM_0458. First published online, 2012.

Gates, Henry Louis. *The Signifying Monkey: A Theory of Afro-American Criticism*. New York: Oxford University Press, 1988.

Ghonim, Wael. *Freedom 2.0: The Power of the People is Greater than the People in Power.* New York: Houghton Mifflin Harcourt, 2012.

Gold, Matthew K., ed. *Debates in Digital Humanities*. Minneapolis: University of Minnesota Press, 2012.

Greenwald, Glenn. "The Inhumane Conditions of Bradley Manning's Detention," *Salon* (December 15, 2010). http://www.salon.com/2010/12/15/manning_3/.

———. *No Place to Hide: Edward Snowden, the NSA, and the Surveillance State*. New York: Penguin, 2014.

Gregory, Derek. "Tahrir: Politics, Publics and Performances of Space." *Middle East Critique* 22, no. 3 (2013): 235–46.

Habermas, Jurgen. *The Structural Transformation of the Public Sphere: An Inquiry into the Category of Bourgeois Society*. Translated by Thomas Burger. Cambridge, MA: MIT Press, 1989.

Hafez, Sabry. "The New Egyptian Novel: Urban Transformation and Narrative Form." *New Left Review* 64 (2010): 47–62.

Halabi, Zeina G. *The Unmaking of the Arab Intellectual: Exile, Prophecy, and the Nation*. Edinburgh: Edinburgh University Press, 2017.

Halberstam, J. Jack. *Gaga Feminism: Sex, Gender, and the End of Normal*. Boston: Beacon Press, 2012.

Hammad, Hanan. *Industrial Sexuality: Gender, Urbanization, and Social Transformation in Egypt*. Austin: University of Texas Press, 2016.

Han, Byung-Chul. *The Transparency Society*. Translated by Erik Butler. Stanford, CA: Stanford University Press, 2015.

Harcourt, Bernard E. *Exposed: Desire and Disobedience in the Digital Age*. Cambridge, MA: Harvard University Press, 2015.

Hastings, Michael. "Julian Assange: The *Rolling Stone* Interview." *Rolling Stone* (January 18, 2012). http://www.rollingstone.com/politics/news/julian-assange-the-rolling-stone-interview-20120118#ixzz1jqjjK0dJ.

Hayani, Mohammed. "Arab Media, Political Stagnation, and Civil Engagement: Reflection on the Eve of the Arab Spring." In *Media Evolution on the Eve of the Arab Spring*, edited by L. Hudson, A. Iskandar, and M. Kirk, 15–28. New York: Palgrave Macmillan, 2014.

Hirschkind, Charles. *The Ethical Soundscape: Cassette Sermons and Islamic Counterpublics*. New York: Columbia University Press, 2009.

Hourani, Albert. *Arabic Thought in the Liberal Age (1798–1939)*. New York: Cambridge University Press, 1983.

Hui, Yuk. *On the Existence of Digital Objects*. Minneapolis: University of Minnesota Press, 2016.

Ibn Manzur, Muhammad ibn Mukarram. *Lisān al-ʿArab*. Vols. 11–12, 15–16. Edited by Ali Shirri. Beirut: Dar Sadir, 2008.

Ibrahim, Sonallah. *Tilk al-Rāʾiḥa wa-Qiṣaṣ Ukhra* (*That Smell*). Minya, Egypt: Dar al-Huda, 2003.

Irigaray, Luce. *Speculum of the Other Woman*. Translated by Gillian C. Gill. Ithaca, NY: Cornell University Press, 1985.

Jacquemond, Richard. *Conscience of the Nation: Writers, State, and Society in Modern Egypt*. Translated by David Tresilian. Cairo: American University of Cairo Press, 2008.

———. "Satiric Literature and Other 'Popular' Literary Genres in Egypt Today." *Journal of Arabic and Islamic Studies* 16 (2016): 349–67.

Jenkins, Henry. *Convergence Culture: Where Old and New Media Collide*. New York: NYU Press, 2006.

Jenkins, Henry, Sam Ford, and Joshua Green. *Spreadable Media: Creating Value and Meaning in a Networked Culture*. New York: NYU Press, 2013.

Juynboll, G.H.A. and D. W. Brown. "Sunna." In *Encyclopaedia of Islam*. 2d ed. Edited by P. Bearman, Th. Bianquis, C. E. Bosworth, E. van Donzel, W. P. Heinrichs. http://dx.doi.org.dartmouth.idm.oclc.org/10.1163/15733912_islam_COM_1123. First published online, 2012.

Katz, Marion. "Scholarly versus Women's Authority in the Islamic Law of Menstrual Purity." In *Gender in Judaism and Islam: Common Lives, Uncommon Heritage*. Edited by Beth S. Wenger and Firoozeh Kashani-Sabet. New York: NYU Press, 2014.

Kaur, Rupi. https://instagram.com/p/0ovWwJHA6f/.

Kendall Elizabeth. *Literature, Journalism and the Avant-Garde*. New York: Routledge, 2006.

Kennedy, Philip, ed. *On Fiction and* Adab *in Medieval Arabic Literature*. Wiesbaden, Germany: Harrassowitz Verlag, 2005.

Khal, Abdo. *Tarmī bi-Sharar* (*Throwing Sparks*). Beirut: Manshurat al-Jamal, 2009. Translated by Maïa Tabet and Michael K. Scott. Doha: Bloomsbury Qatar Foundation Publishing, 2014.

Khaldi, Boutheina. "Multiple Intellectual Engagements?" *Journal of Arabic Literature* 43 (2012): 197–226.

Khalil, Andrea. *Gender, Women and the Arab Spring*. New York: Routledge, 2014.

Kishk, Muhammad Jalal. *Al-Ghazū al-Fikrī* ("Ideological Conquest"). Cairo: Al-Dar al-Qawmiyya li-l-Tibaʿa wa-l-Nashr, 1964.

———. *Al-Mārksiyya wa-l-Ghazū al-Fikrī* ("Marxism and Ideological *Ghazū*"). Cairo: Al-Dar al-Qawmiyya li-l-Tibaʿa wa-l-Nashr, 1965.

Klemm, Verena. "Different Notions of Commitment (*Iltizam*) and Committed Literature (*al-Adab al-Multazim*) in the Literary Circles of the Mashriq." *Middle Eastern Literature* 3, no. 1 (2000): 51–62.

Koerber, Benjamin. *Conspiracy in Modern Egyptian Literature*. Edinburgh: Edinburgh University Press, 2018.

Kraidy, Marwan. *The Naked Blogger of Cairo: Creative Insurgency in the Arab World.* Cambridge, MA: Harvard University Press, 2016.

Kristeva, Julia. *Powers of Horror: An Essay on Abjection.* Translated by Leon S. Roudiez. New York: Columbia University Press, 1982.

Lacan, Jacques. *Le séminaire livre VII: L'éthique de la psychanalyse (1959–1960).* Paris: Seuil, 1986.

Le Bon, Gustave. *Psychologie des foules* (1895). Paris: Hachette-BNF, 2012.

Leder, Stefan, and Hilary Kilpatrick. "Classical Arabic Prose Literature: A Researchers' Sketch Map." *Journal of Arabic Literature* 23, no. 1 (1992): 2–26.

Leemhuis, F. "Waʾd al-Banāt." In *Encyclopaedia of Islam.* 2d ed. Edited by P. Bearman, Th. Bianquis, C. E. Bosworth, E. van Donzel, W. P. Heinrichs. Brill Online, 2014. http://referenceworks.brillonline.com.ezproxy.lib.utexas.edu/entries/encyclopaedia-of-islam-2/wad-al-banat-SIM_7795. First published online, 2012.

Lenze, Nele, Charlotte Schriwer, and Zubaidah Abdul Jalil, eds. *Media in the Middle East: Activism, Politics, and Culture.* New York: Palgrave Macmillan, 2018.

Le Renard, Amélie. *A Society of Young Women: Opportunities of Place, Power and Reform in Saudi Arabia.* Stanford, CA: Stanford University Press, 2014.

Lynch, Marc. "Young Brothers in Cyberspace." *Middle East Report* 245 (2007): 26–33.

Maggi, Wynne R. *Our Women Are Free: Gender and Ethnicity in the Hindukush.* Ann Arbor, MI: University of Michigan Press, 2001.

Mahdi, Muhsin, ed. *The Arabian Nights.* Translated by Husain Haddawy. New York: Norton, 1990.

———, ed. *The Thousand and One Nights (Alf Layla wa-Layla).* Vol. 1. Introduction by Aboubakr Chraibi. Leiden: Brill, 2014.

Mahfouz, Naguib. *Zuqāq al-Midaq* ("Midaq Alley"). In *Al-Muʾallafāt al-Kāmila* ("Complete Works"). *Vol. 1.* Beirut: Maktabat Lubnan, 1990.

Mahmood, Saba. *Politics of Piety: The Islamic Revival and the Feminist Subject.* Princeton, NJ: Princeton University Press, 2005.

Marks, Laura. *Hanan al-Cinema: Affections for the Moving Image.* Cambridge, MA: MIT Press, 2016.

McLarney, Ellen. "Freedom, Justice, and the Power of *Adab.*" *International Journal of Middle Eastern Studies* 48 (2016): 25–46.

McLuhan, Marshall. *Understanding Media: The Extensions of Man* (1964). Cambridge, MA: MIT Press, 2014.

McTeigue, James, director. *V for Vendetta.* USA, 2005.

Massumi, Brian. *Parables for the Virtual: Movement, Affect, Sensation.* Durham, NC: Duke University Press, 2002.

Mehrez, Samia. *Egypt's Culture Wars: Politics and Practice.* New York: Routledge, 2008.

Meyer, Stefan G. *The Experimental Arabic Novel.* Albany: State University of New York Press, 2000.

Mitchell, Juliet, and Jacqueline Rose, eds. *Feminine Sexuality: Jacques Lacan and the école freudienne.* Translated by Jacqueline Rose. New York: Norton, 1985.

Mitchell, Timothy. *Colonizing Egypt.* Berkeley: University of California Press, 1991.

Mohamed, Ali Sayed. "The Political Discourse of Egyptian Blogs: A Case Study of *Egyptian Awareness.*" *Seachange*, "Special Issue: Choice" (2011): 40–113.

Mourad, Sara. "The Naked Body of Alia: Gender, Citizenship, and the Egyptian Body Politic." *Journal of Communication Inquiry* 38, no. 1 (2014): 62–78.

Muhanna, Elias, ed. *Digital Humanities and Islamic and Middle East Studies.* Boston: De Gruyter, 2016.

Mujtahidd, *Al-Kitāb al-Muʿtamad fī Taghrīdāt Mujtahidd* ("The Reliable Book of Mujtahidd's Tweets"). https://docs.google.com/file/d/0ByFCK2y8C52aSklYRmg4dmRyajA/edit.

Munif, Abdul Rahman. *Cities of Salt.* Translated by Peter Theroux. New York: Vintage, 1989.

Nadel, Alan. *Containment Culture: American Narratives, Postmodernism, and the Atomic Age.* Durham, NC: Duke University Press, 1995.

Naji, Ahmed. *Al-Mudawannāt min al-Busṭ ilā al-Twīt* ("Blogs: From Post to Tweet"). Cairo: Arabic Network for Human Rights Information, 2010. http://anhri.net/?p=7052.

———. *Using Life.* Translated by Benjamin Koerber. Illustrated by Ayman Zorkani. Austin: CMES/University of Texas Press, 2017.

Negm, Nawara. https://twitter.com/nawaranegm.

Pasolini, Pier Paolo. "Interviewed by Philippe Bouvard" (October 31, 1975). http://flux-news.skyrock.com/2915445903-Derniere-interview-de-Pier-Paolo-Pasolini-realisee-par-Philippe.html.

Pannewick, Friederike, and Georges Khalil, eds., with Yvonne Albers. *Commitment and Beyond: Reflections on/of the Political in Arabic Literature since the 1940s.* Wiesbaden, Germany: Reichert Verlag, 2015.

Papacharissi, Zizi. *Affective Publics: Sentiments, Technologies, and Politics.* New York: Oxford University Press, 2015.

Penney, Joel, and Caroline Dadas. "(Re)Tweeting in the Service of Protest: Digital Composition and Circulation in the Occupy Wall Street Movement," *New Media Society (*March 15, 2013). http://nms.sagepub.com/content/early/2013/03/13/1461444813479593.

Pepe, Teresa. "When Writers Activate Readers: How the Autofictional Blog Transforms Arabic Literature." *Journal of Arabic and Islamic Studies* 15 (2015): 73–91.

Peters, John Durham. *Speaking into the Air: A History of the Idea of Communication.* Chicago: University of Chicago Press, 1999.

Piscatella, Joe, director. *#Chicago Girl: The Social Network Takes on a Dictator.* USA, 2013.

Poitras, Laura, director. *Risk.* USA, 2016.

Poorthuis, Marcel. "Hagar's Wanderings: Between Judaism and Islam." *Der Islam* 90, no. 2 (2013): 220–44.

Poster, Mark. *The Information Subject.* New York: Routledge, 2001.

Protevi, John. *Political Affect: Connecting the Social and the Somatic.* Minneapolis: University of Minnesota Press, 2009.

Rakha, Youssef. *Al-Tamāsīḥ* ("The Crocodiles"). Beirut: Dar al-Saqi, 2012.

———. "E-cards for Mohammed Rabie." *Al-Ahram Weekly Online*, Issue 1031 (January 13–19, 2011). http://weekly.ahram.org.eg/2011/1031/cu2.htm.

———. *Kitāb al-Ṭughra* ("Sultan's Seal"). Cairo: Dar al-Shuruq, 2011.

Raley, Rita. *Tactical Media.* Minneapolis: University of Minnesota Press, 2009.

Rancière, Jacques. *The Lost Thread: The Democracy of Modern Fiction.* Translated by Steven Corcoran. London: Bloomsbury, 2016.

Reinhardt, Kevin. "Impurity/No Danger." *History of Religions* 30, no. 1 (1990): 1–24.
ReMarks, Karl. www.karlremarks.com.
Saadawi, Ahmed. *Frankenstein in Baghdad*. Translated by Jonathan Wright. New York: Penguin, 2018.
Said, Edward. Introduction to *Days of Dust* by Halim Barakat, ix–xxxiv. Washington, D.C.: Three Continents Press, 1983.
———. *Representations of the Intellectual*. New York: Vintage, 1996.
Sakr, Laila Shereen (VJ Um Amel). "A Digital Humanities Approach: Text, the Internet, and the Egyptian Uprising." *Middle East Critique* 22, no. 3 (2013): 247–63.
———. "Tweet World: 3D Interactive Visualization of 500,000 Tweets on #Syria." https://vimeo.com/30667863.
Salaita, Steve. *Uncivil Rites: Palestine and the Limits of Academic Freedom*. Chicago: Haymarket Books, 2015.
Sedgwick, Eve. *Touching Feeling: Affect, Pedagogy, Performativity*. Durham, NC: Duke University Press, 2002.
Sedgwick, Eve, and Adam Frank, eds. *Shame and Its Sisters: A Silvan Tomkins Reader*. Durham, NC: Duke University Press, 1995.
Sévigné, Madame de. *Selected Letters*. Translated by Leonard Tancok. New York: Penguin, 1982.
Sheikh, Kamal, director. *Miramār*. Egypt, 1969.
Sherwood, Yvonne. "Hagar and Ishmael: The Reception of Expulsion." *Interpretation: A Journal of Bible and Theology* 68, no. 3 (2014): 286–304.
Shimon, Samuel, ed. *Beirut 39: New Writing from the Arab World*. New York: Bloomsbury, 2010.
Silverman, Kaja. *Flesh of My Flesh*. Stanford, CA: Stanford University Press, 2009.
Smolin, Jonathan. *Moroccan Noir: Police, Crime, and Politics in Popular Culture*. Bloomington: Indiana University Press, 2013.
Stewart, Devin J. "Popular Shiism in Medieval Egypt: Vestiges of Islamic Sectarian Polemics in Egyptian Arabic." *Studia Islamica* 84 (1996): 35–66.
Tageldin, Shaden. *Disarming Words: Empire and the Seductions of Translation in Egypt*. Berkeley: University of California Press, 2011.
Ta-Shma, Israel Moses, and Judith R. Baskin. "Niddah." In *Encyclopaedia Judaica*, edited by Michael Berenbaum and Fred Skolnik. 2d ed. Vol. 15. Detroit, MI: Macmillan Reference USA, 2007. 253–58. *Gale Virtual Reference Library*. July 26, 2015. http://go.galegroup.com/ps/i.do?id=GALE%7CCX2587514825&v=2.1&u=txshracd2598&it=r&p=GVRL&sw=w&asid=bca3adb62257e48f459c28697975113c.
Tawil-Souri, Helga. "Egypt's Uprising and the Shifting Spatialities of Politics." *Cinema Journal* 52, no. 1 (2012): 160–66.
Tiger, Rebecca. "Celebrity Gossip Blogs and the Interactive Construction of Addiction." *New Media & Society* 17, no. 3 (2015): 340–55.
Van Gelder, Geert Jan. *The Bad and the Ugly: Attitudes towards Invective Poetry (hijāʾ) in Classical Arabic Literature*. Leiden: Brill, 1988.
Warck, McKenzie. *A Hacker's Manifesto*. Cambridge, MA: Harvard University Press, 2004.
Warner, Michael. *Publics and Counterpublics*. New York: Zone Books, 2005.
Wehr, Hans. *A Dictionary of Modern Written Arabic: (Arabic-English)*. 4th ed. Edited by J. Cowan. Ithaca, NY: Spoken Language Services, 1994.

Wensinck, A. J., et al. *Concordance et indices de la tradition musulmane*. Vol. 3. Leiden: E. J. Brill, 1969.
Wilson, G. Willow. *Alif the Unseen*. New York: Grove Press, 2013.
Zayani, Mohamed, ed. *The Al-Jazeera Phenomenon: Critical Perspectives on New Arab Media*. London: Pluto Press, 2005.
Ziajka Stanton, Anna. "From a Labor of Love to Gulf Labor: The Ethics of Translating Arabic Literature in a Global Age." PhD diss., University of Texas at Austin, 2016.
Zizek, Slavoj. *Absolute Recoil: Towards a New Foundation of Dialectical Materialism*. London: Verso, 2014.
———. *Trouble in Paradise: From the End of History to the End of Capitalism*. New York: Penguin, 2014.

INDEX

Abbas, Wael, 22, 28, 54–55, 60–69, 71–88, 141, 169, 175–77; compared to Mujtahidd, 91, 96, 101–2, 113–14, 116–17, 120, 138; and embodiment, 21, 57, 98, 125; and ideas of "democracy," 54–55, 102, 169; and uploaded videos, 18, 58–59, 139, 141
Abu Ghraib, 8, 79, 184n4, 186n36
adab, 3–4, 7, 11, 28, 51, 54, 66–67, 71, 177; and civilizing process, 22, 62, 74, 82–84, 87–88; collapse of, 16, 68, 80, 98, 144; in the digital age, 16, 21, 24, 61, 148; and literature, 28, 62, 97, 133, 137, 148, 155, 170, 189n14; and Modern Standard Arabic, 140–41; as prohibitive category, 164, 168–70, 172, 200n44; *qillat adab*, 7, 61, 63–64, 74–76, 79, 81, 85, 141–42, 165, 175
akhbār, 7, 28, 91–97, 100, 104–5, 107–8, 110, 112–14, 120, 122, 124, 133, 138–39, 173, 178, 193n9
Alaidy, Ahmed, 22, 85–86, 129, 187n56, 196n51
Albeshr, Badriah, 28–29, 48, 148, 150–72, 176–77
al-Ghadhdhami, Abdallah. *See* Ghadhdhami, Abdallah al-
al-Hakim, Tawfiq. *See* Hakim, Tawfiq al-
Al-Jazeera, 32, 100, 160, 181n4
Alkhamissi, Khaled, 128, 138–44, 175–76
Alsanea, Rajaa, 107, 126, 128, 133–39
al-Sisi, Abdel Fattah. *See* Sisi, Abdel Fattah al-
Althusser, Louis, 11, 29, 69, 157
Anderson, Benedict, 4–5, 59, 85, 91, 175
Anonymous, 1, 17, 20
Apter, Emily, 7, 63, 183n59, 198n2
Arabian Gulf. *See* Gulf region
Arabian Nights, The, 27, 32, 34–38, 44, 47, 54–55, 57, 96, 100–101, 107, 119, 126
Arabic Booker, 6, 127, 129
Arab Spring. *See* Arab uprisings
Arab uprisings: art and artistic practices emerging from, 5, 14; "causes" of, 17–18, 59, 86, 140, 142, 174, 188n3; in Egypt, 3, 59–69, 75, 86, 139, 191n53; and gender, 186n32; and models of contestatory politics, 4–5, 7, 23, 85–86, 141, 143; Saudi involvement in, 123; and social media, 25–26, 59, 87, 148, 181n6; "success" of, 9, 69, 78, 84, 86, 168–69, 173
Assange, Julian, 17–21, 23, 27, 31, 44–49, 51–53, 55, 125, 164, 176–77; and the Arab uprisings, 86, 142, 173–74; compared to Mujtahidd, 91, 112, 119–20, 122; and the Saudi Cables, 89–90

Barthes, Roland, 128, 163–64, 167
bin Salman, Mohammed, 105, 108–9, 111, 118. *See also* Saudi Arabia
blogging: of Abbas, 60–61, 64–68, 71, 81; and activism, 3–5, 12–13, 41–42, 59, 82–83, 86, 94, 97, 100, 106, 149–50, 189n7; affective power of, 72–76, 78–79; after Arab uprisings, 14–15; as literary mode, 5, 128, 131–32, 145–46, 184n68; of Mujtahidd, 88, 92; and Naji, 62, 72, 99, 147. *See also* Abbas, Wael; Mujtahidd; Naji, Ahmed
Booth, Marilyn, 133–37, 151, 177, 197n17

canon formation (literary), 4, 16, 38, 62; in the Arab digital age, 3, 5–7, 13, 28, 88, 125, 129, 131–33, 137, 146, 170
Chun, Wendy, 19–20, 25, 50
classical Arabic literary tradition, 7–8, 23, 25–26, 28, 62, 91–97, 104, 107, 125, 130, 157, 163, 172, 177–78, 190n27. See also *akhbār*; *Arabian Nights, The*; canon formation (literary)

Deleuze, Gilles, 8, 15, 79, 179
Derrida, Jacques, vii, 14, 32, 48–49, 55, 173, 177–78, 187n58
digital humanities, 3, 25–26, 92, 95, 104, 157, 174, 178
drones, 49, 84, 130

Edwards, Brian, 12–13, 129–30
Egypt: and Arab uprisings, 3, 22–23, 25, 59, 61, 63, 75, 189n8, 191n53, 192n64; authors from, 3, 5, 62, 129, 131, 134; blogging in, 4, 14–15, 41, 72, 131, 191n48; as center of Arab culture and nationalism, 24, 71, 97, 129, 131, 182n27; after fall of Mubarak, 41; film industry of, 21, 63; during Mubarak regime, 80, 139; and Morsi, 160; and Nasser, 84, 139; security apparatus in, 17–18, 48, 58,62, 76, 80, 86, 88, 188n1; and al-Sisi,

Translation / Transnation

Series Editor Emily Apter

Writing Outside the Nation by Azade Seyhan

The Literary Channel: The Inter-National Invention of the Novel edited by Margaret Cohen and Carolyn Dever

Ambassadors of Culture: The Transamerican Origins of Latino Writing by Kirsten Silva Gruesz

Experimental Nations: Or, the Invention of the Maghreb by Réda Bensmaïa

What Is World Literature? by David Damrosch

The Portable Bunyan: A Transnational History of "The Pilgrim's Progress" by Isabel Hofmeyr

We, the People of Europe?: Reflections on Transnational Citizenship by Étienne Balibar

Nation, Language, and the Ethics of Translation edited by Sandra Bermann and Michael Wood

Utopian Generations: The Political Horizon of Twentieth-Century Literature by Nicholas Brown

Guru English: South Asian Religion in a Cosmopolitan Language by Srinivas Aravamudan

Poetry of the Revolution: Marx, Manifestos, and the Avant-Gardes by Martin Puchner

The Translation Zone: A New Comparative Literature by Emily Apter

In Spite of Partition: Jews, Arabs, and the Limits of Separatist Imagination by Gil Z. Hochberg

The Princeton Sourcebook in Comparative Literature: From the European Enlightenment to the Global Present edited by David Damrosch, Natalie Melas, and Mbongiseni Buthelezi

The Spread of Novels: Translation and Prose Fiction in the Eighteenth Century by Mary Helen McMurran

The Event of Postcolonial Shame by Timothy Bewes

The Novel and the Sea by Margaret Cohen

Hamlet's Arab Journey: Shakespeare's Prince and Nasser's Ghost by Margaret Litvin

Archives of Authority: Empire, Culture, and the Cold War by Andrew N. Rubin

Security: Politics, Humanity, and the Philology of Care by John T. Hamilton

Dictionary of Untranslatables: A Philosophical Lexicon edited by Barbara Cassin

Learning Zulu: A Secret History of Language in South Africa by Mark Sanders

In the Shadow of World Literature: Sites of Reading in Colonial Egypt by Michael Allan

City of Beginnings: Poetic Modernism in Beirut by Robyn Creswell

Leaks, Hacks, and Scandals: Arab Culture in the Digital Age by Tarek El-Ariss